Good vs. Good

Good vs. Good

Why the 8 Great Goods
are behind every good (and bad) decision

John C Beck

NORTH
STAR
BOOKS

For information:
North Star Books, PO Box 55870, Phoenix AZ 85078 USA.

Cover art by Elizabeth Beck (ellydraws.tumblr.com)

FIRST EDITION

Beck, John C.
Good vs Good: Why the 8 Great Goods are behind every good (and bad) decision/John C. Beck
ISBN-13: 978-0-9847491-4-0
ISBN-10: 0984749144

Acknowledgements

This book has been a long time in coming. Many close to me have suffered through theory after theory and draft after draft. To all of you, I apologize for absorbing your time and attention. Yet even as I ask for your forgiveness, I also admit that I revel in having friends and colleagues who are so supportive and wonderfully optimistic. And I am so lucky (blessed) to have so many around me who have adopted the thinking and terminology of the 8 Great Goods. It is frankly dumfounding to me that I can be away from some of these wonderful people for years and when we meet again, I observe them considering life from this particular vantage point; amazing and humbling. And, I hope against hope that this is a sign that the thinking in these pages will be useful to many more than just me and those who have helped me labor through this fitfully creative process.

So to all of you listed below; and to the many who I am certain I have inadvertently (and unforgivably) left off this tribute page: thank you, thank you, thank you.

Mona Al-Mukhaizeen, Gabi Barragan, Elizabeth Beck, Roger Beck, Meredith Brenalvirez, Adam Carstens, Andrei Cherny, Nancy Clark, Fabian Cuntze , Ramakrishna Devarakonda, Scott Frankum, Mark Fuller, John Harlow, Jon Huggett, Roy Jespersen, Paul Kayoboke, John Kotter, Ashish Lall, Paul Lawrence, Shaun Martin, John Mathis, Christopher McDowell, Yoshi Mitsui, Masakatsu Mori, Allen Morrison, Caroline Mulliez, Jacqueline Murphy, Yohsuke Nishitani, Nitin Nohria, KK Ong, Justinas Pagirys, Bev Postma, Oscar Postma, Phillie Runfei, Kumar Saket, Tami Sant, Tony Selway, Liz Simpson, Philip Sugai, Astrid Tuminez, Mitchell Wade, Sally Wade, John Warford, Shigeki Yamamoto

Table of Contents

Section IV: Goods in Practice: Leading Good Organizations

Bibliography

Index

JOY

EQUALITY

INDIVIDUALITY

GROWTH

BELIEF

STABILITY

LIFE

RELATIONSHIPS

Introduction

Good people disagree often—and sometimes violently.

This fact bothers me ... and not just because of the "violently" part. At a very deep level, it seems irrational that people who are trying to be good would be disagreeing in the first place.

In the middle of a disagreement—where I firmly and fundamentally believe that only one option is clearly "correct"—it's a lot easier to believe that the opposing views are either inherently "bad" or they are at least a "bad" choice in this instance. If that were so, I could paint almost every debate in pure whites and blacks without all those annoying grays.

Along the way, however, I've come to think that people—generally—are trying to be good. They are—generally—trying to do good things and make good decisions. Anywhere in the world, when people disagree, they are usually doing it from the goodness of their hearts.

If the top line equation in any decision algorithm is "Because ____ is Good, I will do ____", then there must be a way to categorize the Goods we are deciding amongst. This book is an effort to do just that.

Through interviews and surveys with over 3000 people in more than 20 cultures, I've come to understand that there are 8 Great Goods. All of our decisions in life can be sorted pretty easily into these categories. In one experiment, I found that a simple prioritization of these 8 Great Goods could predict a subject's stance on issues ranging from the burqa ban in France to health care reform in the US to Liu Xiaobo receiving the Nobel Prize. Once you understand the Goods—and accept that they are all "good"—you will have a different conversation with someone on the opposite side of that issue than you've ever had in the past. You will never again believe that a contrary viewpoint is evil.

In this book, I'll explore the topic from many vantage points: individual, organizational and national. I'll draw on disciplines as disparate as sociology, neuroscience, business management, philosophy, education, economics, psychology, and political science. I am proposing a fundamentally new way of looking at goal setting and decision-making in areas as far-ranging as consumer behavior, conflict management, and even nation building. Actually, since human existence is nothing more than a constant series of decisions, the 8 Great Goods offers a new model for thinking about life itself.

Abraham Maslow proposed a model of individual needs that has served the world well as a model for our individual lives for the last 70 years. I am suggesting a "Maslow's hierarchy" for our social life. The theory of The 8 Great Goods will help you and me to understand us.

I have set a few optimistic goals for the readers of this book and here's what I anticipate you'll get out of reading it:

A better understanding
- of how you and people around you are making decisions
- that there are eight big categories of trade-offs in our choices
- of why our brains naturally care about these eight categories
- that having a different decision-making algorithm does not make someone evil
- of why Growth is not the only Good that can or should drive your organization or your country

The ability to improve
- relationships both intimate and professional
- decision-making in organizations and in nations
- the way individuals see the big issues behind any complicated decision
- national consensus building around any issue

The opportunity to create
- discussions from a perspective of Good vs. Good
- cultures that agree more than they disagree
- organizations that understand where their priorities lie and how to achieve their goals
- new ways of thinking about your place in organizations and nations

A really fun read that will entertain, inform and give you something new to think about on every single page. With that, shall we begin?

Section I

Goods in Me: What Really Matters

Chapter One: Good People and their Goods

Life:

One of Lynn's earliest memories is of a casket. Her brother Jimmy had been such an exciting playmate for the three older girls in the family. Then one day with no warning, there was a little tiny casket. Lynn can't remember Jimmy being sick, but he had been, and she and her sisters ended up all dressed in black. Their playmate was gone.

As she grew up, Lynn put that trauma behind her. She learned to laugh easily and make friends quickly. She married a tall, handsome Navy Pilot, Paul, who sang in the Navy choir and appeared on national television on a few occasions. By the tender age of 25, she and her 7-month-old son were living in Naval officer housing—headed to the top of the social heap in San Diego. Life was good. Until …

"I got a call first. There had been an incident with Paul's training flight off the California coast. The plane had to be abandoned and everyone had bailed out. Then another call brought the news that three of the crew members had been found quickly, but they were still looking for my husband's parachute. But not to worry, they told me, Paul had a life jacket as part of the parachute apparatus, so as soon as they spotted the parachute, they were sure he'd be just fine."

"The wives of the other crew members who had been on the plane arrived at my apartment next. They arrived empty handed, but they looked like they wished they'd brought a casserole or something. But it was too early for that. I suppose a casserole would have meant that something was seriously wrong. It had still only been several hours since the accident, so no need to get too worried about anything. The wives all repeated the same story. There had been a fire. Everyone abandoned the plane. The last guy to jump had looked back just before his parachute opened and had seen Paul at the door of the plane. One of the other crewmen reported that he had seen Paul's parachute open."

"After a few days of searching, they declared him dead. His body was never recovered."

"For forty years now, I've had a recurring dream of him walking into the house and announcing, just like he always did, in his best Ricky Ricardo accent, 'I'm home, Lucy.'"

Lynn gave birth to twins just 6 months after the accident. Five years later she married Ken who already had 4 teenage kids, then together they had four more children of their own. She and Ken and the kids lived on a large orchard. They also had a cow and lots of small animals. Lynn was the classic life mother, surrounded by children and animals—always philosophical about the cycle of life.

"I'm always glad to see Paul, in my dream. But then reality sets in. I realize that I need to figure out how to fit him into my current life—how do I explain him showing up to my husband and to the kids. I want to be back with him, I want to hear him calling out that he is home, but in my dream it always seems like I'm going to have to abandon Ken and all 11 kids to be with him."

But it wasn't Lynn who did the abandoning. Ken died less than a year after his retirement; it almost seemed like too much for Lynn. Ken had scrimped and saved and had such big plans for retirement. With the illness hitting and then the long slow death, his retirement was nothing but pain.

"Not many women these days have to deal with the loss of two husbands. I've seen more death than most of my friends or family, but I've also seen a lot more life. And these days, sometimes, I can't see at all because of the diabetes. I've lost all feeling in one of my feet. I know I won't be around much longer, but I know how precious life is. I'm lucky to be alive and I cherish every day I have. There is no greater gift than life."

Growth:

"Why do you keep saying the house is so big?" Chanthol asks with an air of exasperation. "There are much bigger houses in America. Yes, this is big in Cambodia, but nothing like the houses that you have in your country."

"When we have guests or family visiting it is nice to have so much room. But at night, my wife and I often sleep in our daughter's room. So we can all be close to each other. So that we can be a family."

"This is just the way that the world works. As you get older you have more and more things. When you go to the villages, you see that the older people have more things. They give them to their children. That is the way that the world is supposed to work." Chanthol is unapologetic as he continues.

"Most of my financial success in life has just happened to me. In fact, when I was younger—when I first went to the United States—material wealth meant nothing to me. I came from a poor family. My older brother was a hippie who went to the US in the 1970s and lived in a small, dirty studio apartment in the suburbs of Washington DC. My parents were afraid of what was happening in Cambodia, so they sent me to live with him as a teenager. When I arrived, his only furniture in the apartment was a guitar. But he still lived better than my family in Cambodia. Looking around at my new surroundings, I couldn't understand why Americans needed so much wealth."

"When the Khmer Rouge took over the country, I was still in Washington DC. My brother and I were granted refugee status. That meant I could work legally and I got a job in a seafood restaurant. That job paid for my college education. It didn't pay for much else, but it did pay for tuition."

"I shared my brother's hippie attitudes about capitalism and the need for money. Perhaps, my attitude about money would have remained throughout my life, but my family's situation changed my mind. My family was being held by the Khmer Rouge in Cambodia during the days of the Killing Fields. There was a growing refugee community in Virginia and sometimes I would hear reports that some of my family members had been seen alive. Then I heard stories that there were "guides" who could bring whole families out of Cambodia for a price. The price was generally more than a hundred thousand dollars—and it had to be delivered in gold."

"I was nearing graduation and I looked for the job that would give me as much money as quickly as possible. I went to work for the finance group in GE Capital. This was the high growth period of that organization. Soon, I was travelling around the world as an auditor for them. My salary was high, but my yearly bonuses were more than I had thought one person could earn in a whole lifetime. My official address was still that little apartment with my brother, but I was travelling constantly so my usual home was hotel rooms around the world. I had no living expenses, so it didn't take me long to earn the money needed to get my family out."

"On one of my trips to Thailand, I delivered a pouch full of gold bricks to a man in the refugee camps on the border of Cambodia. A friend of my family vouched for this man, but I could only hope that I would ever hear from him—or my family members—again."

"Six months later, my whole family was with me in Virginia. They all lived in the one room apartment with my brother for a while until I was able to find a three bedroom place. I was never there because I was travelling. They couldn't speak English so they couldn't find work. I supported the whole family financially for years."

"Without money, my family would have died an awful death in Cambodia. Without money, they would have suffered in terrible poverty in the US. My whole life has been in finance and in economic development in government; I've seen the importance of money in building companies, nations and personal lives. My family would not have the chances that they've had without the money I was able to earn."

Chanthol—tall, handsome, and impeccably dressed—glances over a family portrait with his strikingly beautiful wife and three daughters. His oldest two daughters have made it into Ivy League universities and his youngest is still only in elementary school. All have very bright futures.

"If I hadn't earned so much early in my career, I couldn't have turned my attention to government service—with an almost negligible salary. It is wrong to say out loud, but many people think it: Without money, life can be almost impossible. I probably do have more money than I really need now. But I'm glad to continue doing government work for little pay and giving to charities and villages in Cambodia. I can help a lot of people with the good fortune that I've been given."

Relationships:

"There is nothing in the world that is as important to me as my family. I believe that family will last forever and that kinship bonds that we create on this earth will last with us forever throughout the eternities."

"It would be wrong for me to say that my Heavenly Father isn't the most important being in my life... of course He is. But I don't know where I'd be without my husband and my family and friends that have become like family."

"Family has always been good to me. Better in fact than I was to it. As the oldest of 6 children, I was supposed to help with the smaller kids. And, usually I did, but not always. I was a little selfish when I was a girl. Then when I got into high school, I wanted to sing and dance and spend time with my friends. I loved all of those things. I probably spent too much time working on my dresses and doing my hair."

"Before I knew it I was pregnant with my own child."

Here Faye pauses. She never tears up. But just a hint of pink emerges around her eyelids.

"Of course, that baby didn't survive."

"That was one of the saddest moments of my life. But because of that little baby, one of the happiest things in my life happened—Jay and I got married. Jay was two years older; he was graduating and going off to summer jobs and college; I probably wouldn't have stayed in touch with him after high school. But because of that baby, Jay and I were married just a week after high school graduation."

"His family disowned him for a while. My family was busy caring for me and preparing a good home for the new child. It was the middle of the depression and Jay was lucky enough to have found a summer job in the mines in Nevada. When he returned, his parents barely talked to him. So he moved into our small home with all of my brothers and sisters. He immediately started commuting to college—the first person in his family to go to college. He was up before sunrise and home well after dark. I didn't see much of him, but I had plenty to do taking care of my brothers and sisters and helping with the family business. I took care of my family, but really we were helping each other."

"We had two beautiful little girls while Jay was in college and then our third came along right after he graduated. It was well into the Depression by then and jobs were impossible to find. He got a quarter-time high school teaching job. I was about as busy and as tired as I've ever been in my life. One summer, the girls and I survived mostly on vegetables that we grew in the backyard. We really didn't have any money to use at the market."

"At our lowest point that year, our neighbor—a widow who was no better off then we were– brought us a small box of canned meat. I knew those were probably her last cans of food, but she was sacrificing for us. Her kindness, allowed me to take care of my family. I never ate anything in those cans, and stretched one can over two days of meals for the girls."

"Then, out of the blue, through one of his professor's recommendations, Jay was offered a position as a research assistant in a lab at Berkeley. The job would pay enough to keep us alive. They sent some money to help us with the move. I took some of that, without telling Jay, and bought a carton of canned meat and left it on our neighbor's front porch the day we moved."

"Jay and I weathered all of those tough times. My kids grew up and moved away, and I found a new family in neighbors and friends who were there to help and encourage me. My community has become my family—people are the most important thing to me. When you get older, you realize that houses, and cars, and clothing matter very little. People you care for are the only things that really matter in the end."

Joy:

"Why would I go to work every day if I wasn't having fun on the job? Wouldn't I look for something else to do? I'm even busier now that I'm retired than I ever was when I was working, so I need to make sure what I'm doing is more fun than ever. Why wouldn't I do that?"

Sometimes Roy's questions sound like the careful rhetoric of a preacher. At other times, they come across slightly defensive. But there is never any question of Roy's resolve and unwavering belief in his philosophy toward life. He doesn't know any other way to live.

"Right out of college, I couldn't imagine doing a boring corporate job. My friends and I knew there was a lot of money in company jobs; we had a whole career of office work ahead of us. When we heard about the chance to build some miniature golf courses in Southern California, we asked ourselves what could be better than that? We started a company and spent our days outside in the California sun while playing golf—something we'd choose to do for fun anyway."

"But a good thing can't last forever, can it? We got tired of that. It started to feel like a real job. I knew that the next thing I wanted to do would be interesting and varied and exciting. So, I got into investments."

"What could be more fun than working in a new industry every few weeks? Meeting new people? Convincing myself, and them, about our really good ideas? It was the dream job for most of my life. I got involved when the company was young and we were all idealistic. We rode the big waves in the stock market rises through the 1980s and 1990s and made a lot of money in the process. Life was good, wouldn't you say?"

"But just in case there wasn't enough excitement in my work life, I started taking in study abroad students to live with my teenage kids. From morning until night, I was involved in constant, new exploration. I was always learning new things. We would cook foods from their countries at home. My kids learned so much and we all had more enriched, happy lives because of it. That's not what the average investment advisor does when he goes home at night, is it?"

Roy pauses, and then shifts the conversation back to that preacher rhetoric. However, his tone is anything but defensive now.

"Why should all the fun end with retirement? I'm on three or four Boards now. I invest in Central Asian high tech companies. I've travelled with the Uzbekistan Olympic Committee Officials. I do my best to help the development of villages in Africa, Asia, and Latin America. That is all just plain fun for me."

"But when the sun goes down and the work day is over for me now, I do get a little retirement. Nothing makes me happier than walking down the street from our apartment in Buenos Aires to have an early evening latte, or sitting on our balcony overlooking the Pacific Ocean in Baja sipping on a margarita, or being surrounded by my family—my wife, my kids, and my "adopted" exchange students, and all of my friends."

"How can you find more happiness in your life than doing all of that?"

Individuality:

"I fought against my mother my entire life. I did not want to be—could not be—who she wanted me to be. She was a stunning woman—Miss Kingston Jamaica—and was accustomed to getting her way. Almost any man would do her bidding. Any man, except me. She had two problems on that front with me. First, I was her son—thus, fairly resistant to her charms. Second, I was gay—thus, fairly resistant to all women's charms."

"My mother knew I was probably gay from a pretty young age—she did not want to accept it—but deep down, she knew it. She constantly pressured me to be 'more of a man.' To her, I was soft, and she worried that people would take advantage of me. She always pushed me very hard."

"So hard, in fact, she finally pushed me right out of the house. I was 17 years old—when I left my childhood home to move into my own apartment with my 19-year-old boyfriend."

"My mother was still very young when she died an agonizing death and my reason for being seemed to go with her. Who was I now?"

"Sure, I tried to be a good son. As I look back on it now, I did more than my fair share of tending the younger kids—being home after school to watch out for them while she was at work. But growing up, it felt like I was rebelling constantly. It seems I was constantly saying 'no' and trying to make my own space."

"I lived with that boyfriend for five years, but an old theme returned—I felt like I was losing too much of myself to him. Finally, I ended it and for the next 13 years, I dated constantly but, could never settle down for very long. I was afraid of letting an attachment define me. I was afraid of losing that part of me that makes me Roger."

"After my mother died, I quit my job in the fashion business. I needed a profession that was more meaningful and one that would allow me to help other people, but I wanted to be my own boss. I wanted to be able to help them in my own, unique way. I didn't want to be part of a big organization. I needed the freedom to grieve and to help others at the same time—in my own time."

Roger is 47, but most people would guess he is in his late 20s. Perhaps part of his need for autonomy is the fact that he has been treated much younger than his age for his entire life. He was well into his 30s before people assumed he had even graduated from college. In American society, most men aren't taken terribly seriously until they are at least out of college. Maybe this is why he was into his mid-30s before he was finally able to settle down in a long-term relationship again.

"I think I'm beginning to accept that I can make compromises finally. It took half my life to get here. But, then, I'm lucky. Living in Phoenix just accentuates my freedom: wide-open skies, a wild-west culture, and neighbors who never interfere. And I have a partner who gives me lots of space. I can be with him and not be controlled by him. I can finally be me."

Stability:

"Running a farm is a constant cycle of financial ups and downs—fertilizer, equipment and better bulls are very expensive—everything depends on weather and markets. Overlay that with my parents' natural emotional mood swings and you can understand how I never knew, when I woke up in the morning as a child, if it was going to be a good day or a bad day. It all culminated when my father and brother died within four months of each other bracketing my 21st birthday. That sent my mother into inpatient care. My boyfriend and I left college, moved into the family home and had to take over much of the responsibility for the farm."

"That boyfriend—now my husband—had been through a similarly disruptive childhood. His parents divorced when he was only 5. He was the oldest of five kids and really bore the brunt of keeping them together and focused. They'd spend summers with his dad wherever his dad happened to be (he moved a lot) and the rest of the year in the mid-West with his mom. It was less than desirable for instilling a sense of predictability and calm in his life."

"So I suppose we ended up dating and spending time together because we were both seeking some kind of stability. When my husband went off to one college and I went to another, both of our lives were even more chaotic. After my mother got out of the hospital, I finally transferred to his school and life calmed down considerably. A year after that we were married—but we didn't tell our families because we just didn't want the uproar that would ensue."

Sally is the definition of calm nestled between two dogs on the couch. You might think she has nothing more to do than sit and chat about her psychological past, but this is not a topic that comes easily to her. In the 30 years I've known her, I still know so little. She looks behind her, past the turn-of-the 20th-century original wood floors toward the magnificent hand-carved oak staircase that leads to the sturdily built kids' rooms upstairs.

"I hope that is what we've been able to give to the children. A sense that we are there for them and that life is now—and in the future still can be— predictable and safe and good. We can't do that if we don't feel that in our own lives. So we work hard to be different people than we were raised to be. It is better for the kids and it is better for us as well."

"I had to start my own consulting company. I was tired of the roller coaster of politics and lay offs. I knew I had a skill that was very important, but until I ran my own company, my job was dependent on someone else being able to sell my skills to clients. Now I do that myself and the income flow is more consistent and predictable—partly because I know what is going on. I feel like I'm in control."

"And when I feel like I have some control in my life, the kids, my husband and people around me are probably happier—because I'm happier."

Equality:

"My mother was never allowed to take the exams to go to college. She never got over that. I'm sure I bore the brunt of her disappointment. I would have never received a scholarship to Oxford without her. Many parents push their kids. But with her, there was a kind of desperation in the pressure. Everyday I felt that if I didn't study harder, life would never be fair to me. That if I didn't struggle against it, life was going to get me. "

"Oddly, by going to Oxford, I came to believe in the unfairness of life even more. Sure, I got into a great school and could, in some ways write my own ticket in life. But I was reminded everyday in Britain, in a thousand small ways that I was not as good as everyone else around me. When I was a student,

Britain was very class conscious—it probably still is today, but I haven't lived there for so long that I really can't comment on it. "

"In that British consciousness, my Chinese face translated immediately to 'less important,' 'unintelligent,' 'dismissible.' Even fellow students and professors—and almost anyone else who knew I was an Oxford student— treated me almost as if I was an interloper in the tight knit group. I was doomed to forever being an outsider inside my own university. If I'd stayed in Asia, I might have psychologically dealt with the inequality dealt to my mother. I might have come to believe in my own self. I might even have come to believe that one could overcome life's natural inequities. But my stay in Britain just confirmed my learned biases."

"It is probably not surprising that I took a job with MTV right out of college. It was an organization full of people obsessed with proving that they "as young people" could be every bit as successful as their older and more experienced counterparts. I had dealt with class, educational, racial, and then in my first job, age discrimination.

But I will say, that here in New York City for the first time in my life, I have come to believe that my race is not an obstacle to be overcome. I am a young, upwardly mobile Oxford grad in a good company and China is seen by many in New York as the future of all economic growth."

Boon Li glanced at the elegant wooden clock on the wall of his small but beautifully appointed apartment. He had made time to talk with me, but I knew he had to leave soon to attend a fund-raising event for his latest cause. His eyes swept around the room and then focused back on me.

"I guess, according to most people, I've made it in life. They would say that I have no reason to struggle any more. But the psychological patterns are so deeply ingrained that I will never lose them. I will probably spend a part of everyday of the rest of my life fighting against inequality and unfairness. It is a fundamental part of me now."

Belief:

"I suppose all of my priorities in life are actually based on my belief in God. I make my decisions based on what my religion teaches me. WWJD—"what would Jesus do?" is my guiding principle in life. It is the basis of everything."

"Sure, I was in the business world for 30 years and you can get sidetracked a lot during your career. I was a salesman, and a darn good one. In my line of work, it is easy to get drawn into some pretty unethical behavior. Most of my colleagues have done something stupid at one point or another. I can't say I was completely immune to it during my whole career. But I will say that I tried to be as ethical as I possibly could."

"I pride myself on doing the right things and the things that God would want me to do. I've tried to raise my kids that way. And my relationship with my wife has been made so much better because of the teachings I believe in."

Dave is 62 years old and has been able to take an early retirement. He's working with his oldest son on some business deals now. But mostly he can take it easy and just do the occasional consulting to bring in a little extra cash. His home and life appear relaxed and comfortable, but without a lot of showy extras. Pictures of his family adorn the walls of his living room, but the most prominent spaces are devoted to pictures of Christ.

"I was drafted into the Vietnam War. I think that is when I found Christ. I was afraid, and needed something to rely on. Most of my friends at the time were very anti-war, so I couldn't even talk to them. My parents didn't need to hear my fears, it just made them scared and unhappy. I needed someone to talk to, someone to confide in; someone who I could trust with my inner-most feelings. Turned out that someone was God. I prayed all the time. When some of my platoon-mates would see my lips moving, I know that they thought I was talking to myself, but I was just praying to get through the maneuver or through the exercise or through the day."

"So when I have a major decision to make, I pray first. I try not to have anything else in mind. I just pray. My only real priority is what God wants me to do."

"I know some people believe that I just use God as my excuse for doing what I want to do anyway. But I really try to listen when I'm praying and sometimes I make decisions and give advice that I wouldn't normally. For instance, a friend came to me to ask about his young teenage daughter who was pregnant. Now, I believe that abortion is an awful sin. I would never tell anyone it is right. But before I talked to my friend about the situation with his daughter, I prayed really hard. I got an answer that I didn't like. I prayed some more. Still I had the same feeling. So I prayed some more. It never changed. So I finally told my friend that maybe in his daughter's case an abortion was the right thing. I never thought those words would come out of my mouth. But I advised him and his wife and daughter to pray long and hard about it because it is their issue—not mine—and maybe my divine communication wires were crossed."

"My friend didn't talk to me for months. Finally, he told me that his daughter was going to have the baby. And a few weeks later, there was a blessed event. It seemed I had been wrong and everything was going to be fine. Baby and mother seemed happy and well. But then a terrible tragedy. Before the baby turned a year old, her very depressed young mother took the life of the baby and her own life."

"I didn't hear anything from my friend for almost a year. Then one night, he rings my doorbell. He tells me that I had it right all along and that he and his wife should have listened to their daughter and to their own prayers more. He told me that he really got the same answer that I had given him, but he couldn't believe it."

"If you put God first—before other people, before doctrine, and even before laws—I believe you'll always be blessed. And you'll make the right decisions."

* * *

These eight people are all admirable. They are all wonderful people. These are my mother, sister, partner and many of my closest friends. I get along with all of them—even if our priorities of what we believe is "the greatest good" are different. They have all done a tremendous amount with their lives. They have loved and they are loved. These are the kinds of people that you would want to have over for a dinner party—there would be great conversations.

If they told each other their stories, each one of them would be moved by the others' stories. They would see the importance of the different priorities that each individual has developed over the years. If you asked them their values, they would all give a similar list.

But if you put them on a business or government committee to work together, there would be inevitable conflict. They would see the world with different—and sometimes competing—priorities.

At first, they would not know why they were not agreeing. They might decide that the problem was too complex. They might decide that they needed more data. They might try to convince each other based on the issues that they value most in the world.

But, when all the data collection, analysis, and debate came to an end, these eight people would still probably disagree with each other. And during the contentious process, they may have come to hate each other—an unnecessary outcome if there had just been a little more understanding.

This whole book is about our understanding individual rankings of the 8 Great Goods and our ability to still cooperate with others who may have completely different priorities. But it all starts in our individual heads.

Chapter Two: Attention and Mental Models

Our brains are limited; the world is vast; yet, we as humans have done a pretty good job of using our small brains to do some pretty amazing things. We, surprisingly, don't get completely overwhelmed by all the information available. And we've managed to make correct—or at least sufficing—decisions with a fair amount of regularity on our way to greatness.

We can't pay attention to much. Despite what teenagers tell you, no one can really multitask very well. Our brains like to focus on one thing at a time—in fact, it is not just a preference. Our brains can ONLY focus on one thing at a time. And we can only hold about seven or eight pieces of data in our mind at a time. The reason AT&T made phone numbers 7 digits is because that is what psychologists in the 1940s said was the maximum number of items that could be held in the brain simultaneously. And even with all the new informational requirements placed on our brains in the last century, that number doesn't seem to have increased much. Basically, we are significantly limited by our small, slow brains.

One Thing at a Time

One study that illustrates this is impressive not only in that it demonstrates how restricted our processing power really is, but also because it was conducted in the first place—sometimes you really do have to wonder how much free time psychologists have on their hands! Baba Shiv at Stanford University gave one group of students a two-digit number to remember and another group was given a seven-digit number to memorize. Both groups were offered the choice of a piece of chocolate cake or a fruit bowl as they walked down a hall. Oddly, members of the seven-digit group were two times more likely than the two-digit subjects to choose the cake. Shiv's explanation is that those having to memorize five extra numbers were overtaxing their prefrontal cortex—which is in charge of short-term memory, focus, abstract problem solving AND willpower—making it much harder to resist chocolatey goodness. (Shiv & Fedorikhin, 1999)

Basically, if our brains are busy trying to remember numbers, they lose the ability to exert any willpower. That experiment illustrates what one-trick ponies our brains really are. (Actually, that is not fair...our brains can do many tricks, but only one at a time.) No amount of practice seems to make us better at it. So we've learned to cope instead. And we cope by making mental models. Since we can only make one calculation at a time, our brains throw as much detail into that calculation as they possibly can.

Better Coping through Categories

If you are a native English speaker, you are not reading all of the letters in this sentence. You have learned to group words as shapes and read them as a whole instead of letter by letter. In fact, we learn to read whole sentences as we expect them to to flow. Which is why about 40% of you probably didn't realize that there was an unnecessary "to" in the previous sentence. You read the sentence as a whole without focusing on the individual letters—or even the individual words.

We cope by categorizing and creating mental models. And our brain is busy making these connections—simplifying the world around us all the time. In fact, that is what our brain does really well—it connects. At computation, it is a horse cart; at connection, it is a Ferrari. We can't even begin to understand how complex the connections in the brain are. When we try to imagine, about the most complex image you and I can hold in our head is ten or twenty neurons all connecting with each other. We cannot fathom one hundred billion neurons all intertwined, firing and making sense out of our complex world.

The first time we happen upon some new fact, or landscape, or idea, or process, our brains don't really know how to deal with it. And the process is slowed a bit. We try to equate it to something we've done before, for which there IS a clear model. But if previously learned models don't work, our brains have to slow considerably as we try to make sense of the unfamiliar. Most of us don't like doing this at all. And we as humans are not alone in this dislike.

Safer if You're Different

Zoologist and biologists observing wild animals have found that some predators will avoid prey that looks different from the norm. Sometimes it doesn't take anything more than slightly different coloration to make a predator think twice about attacking what would otherwise serve as a tasty morsel. The only explanation is that it is unfamiliar. And in the heat of the chase when a predator's brain is working overtime, something unfamiliar is simply rejected because it would take too much effort to figure out how to classify this "prey substitute." (Fitzpatrick, 2009) A lounging leopard might pay extra special attention to a gazelle with a longer than normal neck—trying to sort out what kind of animal it is—trying to categorize it. But when hungry, and in the heat of the chase, the leopard will typically go after the usual type of prey.

If you've ever travelled abroad, you know the feeling. You may be starving, but figuring out the local cuisine is problematic (foreign language, unknown ingredients, etc.). You see a McDonald's and voila, you are downing a Big Mac before you can say "viva la revolución!" You have a mental model of a Big Mac being food; you don't need to know any nifty French dining customs; and you're sure how to pay the bill. Easy.

So, you may be asking yourself ... actually, you're probably not asking this question, but you should be; why is Lady Gaga (or fill in your own generation-appropriate pop-star: Elvis, Beatles, Kiss, Boy George, Nirvana, or—perhaps Madonna) so popular? Every several years some new music act comes along that is really different from the rest of that generation and they become run-away stars. If we don't like different things, they don't fit into natural patterns for us, then how could anything new become popular? The fact is that new and different does get attention—naturally.

The Rare Gaga

So like the abnormal gazelle, Lady Gaga commands a lot of attention. At first, you may not know what to do with her, but after a while you (and your society of friends and acquaintances around you) develop a new category to put the strange music and looks into. And once you've done that, a pop musician moves out of the "strange and unknown" category into a new, acceptable (and sometimes, WILDLY successful) category; thus, a star is born. This move from unknown to familiar is only accomplished through a series of unusual tactics that reinforce "newness" even while the frequency of exposure to the new act or idea accustoms the brain to it. There is no small amount of luck involved in it either.

But the Lady Gaga success stories are rare. Most completely new and different music you hear will get rejected immediately. Usually "different" IS rejected. During the dot-com boom, I got to sit in on a number of business plan pitch meetings. In these meetings, a team of 20-somethings would come in and try to get venture capitalists interested in their new business. Surprisingly, there were few really good new ideas, but the most novel ideas were almost always rejected. The funders wanted a good story that tied into a venture with a success story already in place. The fundable ideas tended to be expressed as something like "This is an Amazon-meets-Yahoo-meets-MapQuest kind of business." The venture capitalists' brains say to them, "Those are all successful companies, so this proposed venture has a possibility of being successful as well." Then they'd give them money.

I can't tell you the number of times I've heard from publishers "Well, that is just so different, we're not sure it will sell." I hate it when they tell me that, but I understand it. First they need something that can be described in a sentence or two—a complicated logical argument just won't be marketable. Then, publishers don't have the mental model to accept something new if it doesn't fit into a clearly established category. But even if publishers were willing to suspend their disbelief and try to understand it, they are afraid that book buyers wouldn't know how to classify a particular book. And if book buyers can't imagine a familiar taxonomy for the book, chances are they will never buy. So there is logic in a publisher's need to have simple descriptions that fit into a top-selling category.

Reverting Attention

When our attentional resources are overtaxed, we will default to the "known" every time. Recently, a bunch of famous Twitter users (and academics who study them) attended a conference in an auditorium where organizers tried to make the proceedings more relevant by erecting large screens next to the podium. Everyone in the audience was able to join the tweet conversation. And join they did. "Could this speech be any more boring?" "Red Sox up by 2" "I like her power point color scheme"... you get the idea. Finally, when speakers were interrupted regularly by laughter from the whole audience that had nothing to do with their messages, the sponsoring organization turned off the screen. The audience couldn't multitask; and as a room full of avowed tweeters, they naturally paid attention to their most common form of communication (hint: it was not listening to lectures).

Our first reaction to anything new is to try to find something familiar in it. We naturally pay attention to something completely unfamiliar because we don't know what to do with it. We may be intrigued, and as long as we can just observe the new thing from afar, it will keep our attention. But as soon as we realize we have to interact with the new thing, we are likely to want to flee. We haven't developed any models for coping with the new thing and, at some time, we probably know it is going to take a lot of work to figure out what to do with this new something.

Psychologists tell us that there are three basic ways that we deal with a new problem that we need to solve—we have to rely on knowledge that we've acquired in some other circumstance to solve a new problem that we've never seen before. So we have to "transfer" that knowledge from one situation to another. We do this through a three-step process.

1) Analogy
2) Knowledge compilation
3) Constraint violation

Okay, that's the academic-speak. Let's simplify. Our first thought is: "This problem is like another problem that I've solved before, I bet I can solve it the same way." This first step is completely experiential—it is based on some action that we've taken before that we are going to try to replicate. Over time we begin to build up a mental model of ways to solve problems that are similar.

If we can't find a good analogy, we move on to knowledge compilation. This means that we search for a learned knowledge base or set of rules that may help us solve the problem. "I remember learning about Archimedes' principle in school," you may think to yourself, "I bet that is the reason that the steel ship floats."

If we have no learned rules to apply to the problem at hand, then we revert to "constraint violation." This is basically trial and error. We try something until it violates the constraints of the problem (i.e. doesn't work), and then we try something else.

The first time many American drivers are faced with a roundabout (a traffic circle or circus), they are confused. Most of the Western US was not built with traffic circles. So the first time you come upon one, you will first try an analogy. "This is just like an intersection," you may think. The rule of traffic in the US (knowledge compilation) is that the car to the right at an unmarked intersection has the right of way. So, in the traffic circle, every time a car comes in from the right, your natural response might be to yield to let that car into the circle. About the second time you yield in a busy roundabout, you will probably experience "constraint violation": the cars behind you will involuntarily play bumper cars with you.

Trial and error will have taught you a single lesson, but you'll probably ask a friend (or a lawyer) when you get a chance, "So what are the rules of traffic circles?" The answer to that question will help you compile more knowledge. And that first roundabout will serve as an analogy for you for the rest of your life—I yield to get into the circle; once in, I have the right of way.

You have just created a new mental model.

The next few times you see a traffic circle, you'll have to pay a lot of front-of-mind attention to the process—you probably won't be able to carry on a conversation while you maneuver. Once you've been in dozens of them in your life, you will be able to give it back-of-mind attention. You'll speed through the roundabout while carrying on even highly emotional conversations.

Now, anything that looks like a traffic circus—for the rest of your life—will have to be judged by that model.

More than Meets the Eye

According to scientists who study brain functions, it doesn't even have to look like a traffic circus to be interpreted by the brain as a traffic circus. In an interesting study published in *Neuron* in May 2009, researchers found that whether a category is formed by actual physical similarity or assigned to that category, it is all processed in the part of the brain used for analyzing visual signals. So if you naturally see all squares and rectangles as part of one category, but you are told to assign equilateral triangles to the "square" category, after a period of using these rules, your brain will begin to naturally process (and actually "see") equilateral triangles the same way it processes ("sees") squares. And once the brain is trained to do that, your decision-making systems will react to squares and triangles the same way in making decisions. (Li, Mayhew, & Kourtzi, 2009)

To cut through all of the complexity in our world, we have to recognize and create patterns. Those patterns take on meaning for us. Once we have categorized data, then we are ready to use those categories as the basis for our mental models.

We have developed an uncanny ability to create relatively simple models of the world around us. And it is these models that form the basis for every decision we will ever make.

John C Beck

Chapter Three: The 8 Great Goods

"For there is nothing either good or bad, but thinking makes it so"—
Shakespeare's Hamlet

Somehow along my life's path, I've come to think that people, generally, are trying to be good. They are, generally, trying to do good things and to make good decisions. And I've found this pattern anywhere I've been in the world.

But in the middle of a disagreement, where I firmly and fundamentally believe that one option is clearly "correct," it would be a lot easier to believe that the people supporting the other cause are either inherently "bad" or they are at least making a "bad" choice in this instance. If that were so, I could paint almost every debate in pure whites and blacks without all those annoying grays.

Truly Bad … Usually

Okay, there are some decisions that are truly bad. Killing and stealing are two good examples. Most of us don't waste much energy debating the wholesomeness of these felonies. Yet, there are instances when even the badness of killing and stealing takes a backseat to more important "goods." Killing in the name of God, or stealing so your family can eat are both gray areas for most of us.

Usually, when we disagree, we do it from the goodness of our hearts. We differ because we believe our way is the right way or the best way. We are just trying to do the right thing, to be good—in the way that we personally define "good." But the way that I define "good" and the way you define "good" may be completely different, and it creates some of the most important drama in life.

A Good First Step

We all, initially at least, run our judgments through a series of filters to determine if something is good for us. In its simplest form, the first step in the algorithm is really an analogy that looks something like this: "SINCE _____ is good, THEN I SHOULD do _____."

That first phrase "Since _____ is good," however, has led to some of the biggest dilemmas, clashes, and philosophical arguments of human existence. Because it is the very first step in many of our decision-making algorithms, our individual definition of the most important "Good" tends to define us in particular ways, influence the people we like to be around, and determine how we conduct our entire existence.

Explicitly deciding (or at least uncovering) what our prioritization of "Goods" is, can make our lives (individually and in groups) much easier and much more understandable.

The 8 Great Goods

Over the course of five years of studying, interviewing, and surveying over 3000 people, I arrived at these 8 Great Goods. My list had to start somewhere … and I've come to call the top priority Good "the Greatest Good." I'm going to go out on a limb here (actually, it is not very far out on the limb because this is all backed up with research), and say the first "good" that we assess in any decision is the issue of life or death. And generally because most of us believe that life is good, we decide in favor of life. So Life is the Greatest Good in most of our minds. (In fact, 38% of Americans and 47% of Japanese in my initial 2009 surveys ranked it as the Greatest Good; interestingly, a few years later with a relabeled Good of "Relationships" in the mix, only 26% of Americans ranked Life as number one—but I will get to that later.)

I was surprised, and I bet you are too, to find that less than half of these survey populations ranked Life as number one. (Granted, if a suicide bomber had been standing in the doorway as they filled out the survey, they might have chosen differently—but we'll come to that in Chapter 8) But even in the abstract, people were more likely to opt for one of the other greatest Goods as often as they did Life itself. And it is exactly because these other Goods substitute for Life as often as they do that I included them in the top eight. If we can't think of multiple instances when people risk or take a life in support of one of the other Goods, that Good hardly qualifies as one of the Greatest.

For each of these 8 Great Goods, I've tried to make them as "value positive" as I can. I don't want any bias in talking about them, so I've endeavored to find labels that most of us would find truly "good." Most of the time I have spent researching this book, I have also been engrossed in finding the right labels for these goods—labels that really describe the priority in question. Goods that were originally labeled Society and Fairness are now called Relationships and Equality. This label alteration changed the rank ordering of these concepts; a point I will revisit when I come to a more in-depth discussion of each of these.

The possible choices to fill in the blank in the first step of the Goodness Algorithm are limited—my thinking and research on the topic has led me to eight broad categories of Goods that appear atop most people's lists. I call them the 8 Great:

Life is good. Life is the basis of all the other Goods on this list. It is, for most people, the Greatest Good. If we didn't believe that life is good, we probably wouldn't be alive to read this paragraph (nor would anyone have been alive to write it!). The first step most of us take in any decision is to assess whether it is a "life or death" decision. If it is, the first choice is usually to stay alive— and to keep significant others alive as well. A decision here could be about birth or murder. But it is more commonly about things that contribute to life: health, nutrition, sex, etc.

Relationships are good. We, as humans, like being around other humans and community is an important part of what we find to be good about the world. Our desire to be around others may have started when ancient man had to depend on other humans for hunting, shelter, and safety and as a result, we became really social beings along the way. Most of us love to be around other people. We depend on people for the first part of our lives, expect to be depended upon for much of our lives, and then have to depend on others again as we reach old age. And while our basic food and sex needs ("life is good") could be accomplished without much sociability (people could just loot and rape to meet their individual Life goals), even anti-socials such as pirates tend to like to band together into gangs of criminals. Most of us see family, schools, corporations, communities and nations (or if we happen to be a pirate, pirate gangs) as very good things. We accept (and some even exploit) the natural trappings of social relationships (hierarchy, power, etc.).

Stability is good. Without a sense that tomorrow will be pretty much the same as today, we can't do much else besides cope. Humans are surprisingly good at coping with change (it is why we have survived—even thrived—in every climate on earth). But we don't like constant and unpredictable change. That stability brings with it a set of rules, laws, or customs that govern our individual and social worlds is seen as a good thing. With a sense of security and predictability, we can begin to focus more on the other Great Goods.

Growth is good. Bigger is better. Sure, in the natural world, being bigger helps you to stay alive, but if we think of this category as separate from survival, we can see how important Growth has become as a good unto itself. Economic well-being (above subsistence level) and material gain are parts of growth. Our capitalist system is based on growth … and most of our modern lives are designed around this Good. (Isn't it interesting that the term is "gainful" employment—not "needful" employment?)

Individuality is good. The flip side of Relationships being important is the ability to retain a sense of individuality. This tension between relationships and individuality is at the heart of many of our most valued laws and rights. We depend on others for nourishment and safety and companionship, but we still fight for our "place" in that set of human bonds. We want to establish a unique personality, preserve our dignity, and make an individual mark on the world around us.

Joy is good. Having fun is damn important. The Roman poet Juvenal, in 100 AD, said that all the populace cared about was bread and games. Putting his analysis into the 8 Great vernacular, the people of Rome cared most about Life and Joy. Juvenal may have said this as a criticism of the shallowness of his countrymen, but he was right not only about ancient Romans but also about people even in our time.

Belief is good. There is a basic need in many (if not all) of us to want to believe in something more powerful and more perfect. We want a bigger reason for this life. In this book, I have defined Belief relatively narrowly as a set of ethical or religious beliefs. It could even be a "cause" but not a cause that would fall into any of the other categories. For instance, my friend, Masa Kogure, helped found and runs an organization called Table for Two to help alleviate world hunger. In terms of the Great Goods, his cause would not be classified as Belief, but rather as Life—feeding people who might die if they did not get food is clearly a Life priority. A patriot may have a "cause" of the nation, but I would classify that as the Good of Relationships rather than Belief. At its most basic definition, Belief, for the purposes of this book really only means religion or honesty.

Equality is good. Somewhere between the goods of relationships and individuality is this notion of equality. We want to be in relationships (which are naturally hierarchical), but we don't want to be treated that differently from the rest of those in similar relationships (we hate hierarchy and inequity). So we hope for equal rights or at least rights that we perceive as fair even if they are not exactly the same. Equality is not Individuality. An individualist will want to do things that no one else will be allowed to do. But if Equality is your Good, you'll believe if you're allowed to do something, everyone else should be allowed the same right.

There was point in my conceptualization of these eight when I had included Learning as one of the goods. It is a very good thing and something we humans are constantly doing. But the more I interviewed, discussed and surveyed, I came to the conclusion that Learning is not a separate Good. Learning is a part of all of the other Goods. Throughout life, we continually learn how to preserve Life, enhance Stability, be more efficient at Growth, effect Equality, improve Individuality, protect the bonds of our Relationships, hone our Belief system, and have more Joy. The way people usually make tradeoffs among Goods makes Learning look more like Joy than anything else. And as sad as it made this lifelong educator to admit that Learning is not a tradeoff for Life itself, I finally had to conclude that Learning is part of each of the 8, not a Good unto itself.

Maslow's hierarchy for the social being

For those of you familiar with Maslow's hierarchy of needs, some of the 8 Great Goods may feel familiar. And there is good reason for that. In 1943 Abraham Maslow, a psychology professor at Brooklyn College, developed a theory of human needs with a predetermined level of importance: physiological needs, safety needs, social needs, esteem and self-actualization. (Maslow, 1943) The first of the 8 Great in the list above: Life, Relationships, and Stability are very similar to Maslow's first three needs. But there is a difference between "needs" and "Goods" and once we get past the pure need stage, there are myriad nuanced decisions we make which don't obviously fit into "needs" categories. If Maslow were around to argue about this today (naturally, a good-hearted argument), he would say that many of the 8 Goods can be found in his self-actualization category. But I would argue (again, nicely) that there are many of his basic needs like food, sexual activity, or security that we humans relinquish because we are focused on a Good that is not technically a "need"—things like Joy, Belief or Equality. Furthermore, Maslow's theory was about individual needs. The goods that I'm describing here are both individual and social—which is why they are the source of so much disagreement and discontent. I like to think of the 8 Great as a sort of Maslow's hierarchy for the social being.

The First Step is a Doozy

Once the first decision in the algorithm has been completed there might be a cascade of IF-THEN statements before there is a decision to act. But in a surprising number of the big decisions we make in life, it is that first step in the algorithm that makes the decision for us. The decisiveness of a great leader, the unambiguous strategic direction of an excellent company or a country can be attributed in many cases to the precision of the highest level decision in an algorithm tree. If a choice to act or not can be made at the top level of the algorithm, there is no need to gather more data, to debate, to dither, or to delve deeper. A decision can be made with crystal clarity. Consequently, developing these priorities is not a task to be taken lightly. Your whole life (and if you run a company or a country, the lives of others) can take a whole new direction based on these top-line Great Good decisions.

Why Eight?

Sometimes you get so wrapped up in a project that you forget to say the most important things. That is what happened with this question. It was not until a third or fourth draft of this manuscript that I visited the Dean of the Harvard Business School, Nitin Nohria. He kindly gave me a healthy chunk of his time and agreed to read the whole manuscript before publication. But it was the above question that really got me thinking.

Now, Dean Nohria has an obvious reason to ask the question, "Why Eight?" He and a former professor of mine, Paul Lawrence, wrote a book about the *four* great drives that underlie all of our behavior. (I will talk about more about their research in the next chapter.) I have to admit that I am a bit jealous that they got it down to four. I wanted to get the number as low as possible myself.

Because of my work on the topic of attention, I started with the belief that the number *must* be seven or less; that is the magic maximum that we are all able to hold easily in our heads. At one point, I reduced it to six by grouping Relationships, Individuality and Equality together—these Goods are all part of the natural tension found in our interactions with other people. But I felt like I was losing too much important detail about our big decisions in life when I artificially agglomerated these three.

After months of tossing around various top-level Goods, I found that I was developing my own simple algorithm for making this decision. To be a Good:

1) it must take priority over Life—the Greatest Good—on a fairly frequent basis in people's lives throughout history

2) there must be at least one nation that bases its policies and laws on the principle as the national greatest good (Section III is all about these nations)

Based on that two-step algorithm, *8* Great Goods emerged.

I Don't Understand You …

What is important about the Goods is not the number eight or seven or four, but the use of these Goods in decision-making in social situations. What matters—and the point of this whole book—is that if someone places these Goods in a different order than you do, the two of you will come to different conclusions about some question—using the same data! And when that happens, you will find it next to impossible to understand how they could have arrived at that particular decision. You probably won't sympathize and you will never empathize. If your Goods priorities are different, you see the world through very different decision-making lenses.

Somehow, the way that your brain and their brain are seeing the issue is being interpreted very differently. And the difference in interpretation means that we should probably step back for a moment and look at how the brain does interpret things. Where in our heads do we make these decisions and why is it that these 8 Great Goods are so important to us as human beings— but first, I need to put the issue of "values" to rest.

John C Beck

Chapter Four: Values versus Goods

I have a friend, Jon Huggett, who is very supportive of the 8 Great Goods ideas, but insists on calling them the eight "values." I suppose this chapter is written to him. But I also suppose that he is not alone in wondering what the difference between Goods and values might be. After all, as my friend could argue, the discussion and research about values is well established. To avoid the proliferation of terms that basically describe the same phenomena, we should just stick with the term "values."

I see his point and even switched the terminology to "values" in one early chapter. But I have a problem with that word. Actually I have a handful of problems with the word "values."

Aren't Goods and Values the Same Thing?

The fundamental issue I have with "values" is that you can have *good* values or *bad* values. Since I am proposing, as the core of my argument, here that almost all people make their decisions based on things they believe are "good things," the term "Goods" seems—at the very least—to be an easy shorthand for "good values."

In actuality, I have more issues with the term "values" than just having to append the word "good." Part of the problem is in the past.

For as long as there have been philosophers, they have been talking about values. Modern academics have taken up the cause as well, but with a more data-driven—and therefore, more publishable—approach to the topic. This has usually resulted in long lists of values, running into the hundreds, which are tested against some other variable to see which values matter in a particular context: values and economic prosperity, values and academic achievement, values and stable family lives, etc. Just about any pairing you can think of has probably been tested.

But often the values—at least the exact wording and definition—that are tested vary widely from study to study. One study may use the words "brotherly love" another the word "charity" another "humanism." It is a complicated lot and hard to find much consistency.

Shortcomings

So, values can come close to what I'm describing as Goods, but there are some serious shortcomings. The term "values" has simply been overused: it is used often; and it is used to mean many things.

Use It or Lose It

In its simplest definition, a "value" is just an intangible characteristic that we find precious or valuable; which does beg the question how the oxymoronic term "bad values" came into common parlance. But even if we stay focused on "good values," the term can be applied—however erroneously—to an attribute that may or may not have anything to do with our own behavior. For instance: I may value honesty, while being mostly dishonest. If you value something but don't act on it, then it seems the study of values becomes rather useless.

Perhaps, a value is not evident in your behavior because you are weighing many different values on the journey to your ultimate destination ("I value honesty, but I also value human life; if there is a trade-off, I'll lie to save a life"). Because we all walk around valuing hundreds of things, according to the people who seriously study these things, how can we know which are really most important in deciding a particular behavior? There are so many values, that each one becomes relatively unimportant in our actions.

By contrast, I think of Goods as important decision-making tools that lead to action. These Goods are not just a way of operating on the path to a particular goal. These Goods become the ultimate goal.

Hostage to a Cause

Another good reason not to use the term "values" for American readers is that the word has become a staple of political conservatives in the United States. Dan Quayle, Vice President of the United States in the early 1990s, gave the term "family values" household-name status in his infamous Murphy Brown speech in which he castigated the lead character—a single, successful career woman who didn't want children or a long-term relationship—in the eponymous television comedy series as lacking the values that he thought should characterize American life and thinking. He wanted Americans to hearken back to the good old days of television when popular sitcoms were about families not about middle-aged single women.

One of my personal reasons for not using the term "values" came from an experience in the fall of 1990 when a neighbor of mine, Karl Snow, was running for US Congress in Utah's Third Congressional District. I had known the Snow family for 20 years and they were good people. Snow was seen as rather "old school" in an election year that was about bringing new ideas to Washington. The Democratic candidate, Bill Orton, was much younger and perceived to be more idealistic; and, in that year, Orton was actually running a very tight race with Snow. This is an oddity in Utah—especially in the Third District, which was one of the most Republican districts in the nation.

It just so happened that a relative of mine—let's call him Bob—who had worked in Washington DC for a number of years was called into the campaign at the last minute to see if he could advise a path toward a big win for Snow and the Grand Old Party.

Bob had plans for an advertisement that he was sure would cement a win for Snow. The morning the advertisement was set to run, I met Bob and he described it to me. "It's all about values," he said. "Snow has a big family, which is a Mormon value. Orton is a single man in his thirties, which is not very Mormon. It may even mean that Orton is gay." So we'll show the Snow family and the Orton "family" side by side in the ad and let voters decide who has the right values.

On the next page, you can see the ad that ran just a few days before the election. There was an outcry in the press and among all but the most conservative in the state. What was a very close campaign turned into an election rout. To the credit of Utah voters, Bill Orton, the Democrat, won the election by a 21% margin.

Too Aligned With Just One Good - Belief

In the Snow-Orton campaign ad, values was not only a political statement, it was clearly a statement on religious belief and pious behavior as well. When religion hijacks the word "values", it is hard to see all "values" in any other context. In the 8 Great Goods framework, the single good Belief can contain all those religious values while leaving the rest of the Goods independent of religious connotations.

Money for Values

More secular values also exist. To many who work in corporations, the term has come to be closely associated with corporate values statements. A common complaint among those involved in writing these statements is that they are a colossal waste of time. It can be a grueling process as the key decision-makers in a firm sit in a room and try to agree on the exact wording of a statement to express what they value. But if you took the values statement of most corporations and laid them out next to each other, you'd have a devil of a time figuring out which statement belongs to which corporation. Many corporations value all the same things and yet they spend a lot of time churning through minute meaning in words that may be important to the people creating the statement but the fine-tuning is lost on most of the employees.

A Baby in That Bathwater

In this book, I've chosen to avoid the word "values" (and a few other worthy candidates that I'll mention below). But there has been some really good research and thinking done on these subjects. Let me introduce a couple of those ideas just to show the good and rigorous work that precedes the 8 Great Goods.

Schwartz (Values)

There are a number of standardized schemas about values that have emerged in the academic literature. The one that I find the most useful is Shalom Schwartz' theory of basic values. (Schwartz, 2006) In surveys of 25,000 people in 44 countries, Schwartz found that there are 56 different values that can be grouped into 10 categories—these categories certainly encompass many of the Goods that I am describing. His 10 categories are:

- Power (authority, leadership, dominance)
- Achievement (success, influence, intelligence, self-respect)
- Hedonism (pleasure, enjoying life)
- Stimulation (daring, varied, exciting life)
- Self-direction (creativity, freedom, curiosity, independence, choosing own goals)
- Universalism (broad-mindedness, wisdom, equality, peace, beauty, nature, inner harmony)
- Benevolence (helpfulness, honesty, loyalty, responsibility, friendship)
- Tradition (accepting place in life, humility, devoutness, moderation
- Conformity (self-discipline, obedience)
- Security (cleanliness, national security, social order, sense of belonging)

An eleventh category of "spirituality" was proposed, but it was found not to exist in certain societies.

As I said, I like this grouping of values. It is a small enough number that it is actually useful. Yet, the problem that I see is that these categories are still rather academic, not geared toward actual decision-making, and some of the labels can be rather off-putting.

McClelland (Needs)

In many ways, Schwartz' theory of values springs from individual psychological needs—the higher levels of Maslow's hierarchy. And while it is a good and fairly comprehensive model, it is not as elegant as David McClelland's theory of needs. (McClelland, 1987) His is one of the most useful theories I've ever seen—and I've used it regularly as a way to conceptualize my world. McClelland's argument is that people build their behaviors around one or more of three needs: power, affiliation, and achievement. If you know which is motivating the people around you—and yourself—you can better structure your world to satisfy those needs. What I like is that the three categories are simple enough that I could easily remember them and describe them to people. But I've always been troubled by the behaviors and thinking that couldn't quite fit to this model. What about God and religion? What about the adventure junkie or the person who likes nothing more than to sit quietly alone and read a book? In other words, McClelland's theory does not account for all "needs"; and, even as a psychological theory, it is quite inward looking and does not necessarily take into account decision-making in a social context.

Lawrence and Nohria (Drives)

In 2002, Professors Paul Lawrence (one of my mentors and a founder of the modern field of organizational behavior) and Nitin Nohria (the current Dean of the Harvard Business School) wrote *Driven*. (Lawrence & Nohria, 2002) In it, they described the four basic drives of human behavior: the drive to bond (Relationships in Goods terminology), the drive to defend (Stability), the drive to acquire (Growth), and the drive to learn. This last one, as I mentioned earlier, was one of the Goods in my early thinking on this subject. But I found it hard to distinguish Learning from the other Goods. It was arguable—and some of my early test subjects indeed argued—that learning was a part of Belief and Life and Relationships and all the rest. Although, when there was a real trade off involved in prioritization, people seem to be considering Learning as a pastime or a hobby—a part of Joy. ("I want to learn about volcanoes, so I risk my Life climbing down into a caldera.") I think that Lawrence and Nohria actually ran into the same quandary to some extent. When they describe the emotions most closely related to the drive to learn, they are things like: awe, joy, wonder and curiosity. However, while I might label one drive differently from Lawrence and Nohria, their arguments are sound and the trade-offs amongst the drives are clear. What I like about these is that they are distinct potential bases of decision-making.

And, in fact, I believe that Lawrence and Nohria might even suggest that Drives and Goods are at different places in the decision-making equation. These Drives are very much subconscious actors that need to be examined more closely. Meanwhile, the Goods that I describe are deliberately considered trade-offs—requiring choice. My inclination may be to have Joy all day, but is that the way I really want to be making decisions in my life or for the lives of employees in my organization? The answer may be "yes"; but a prioritization system for consistent, clear, and candid decision-making is the whole point of the 8 Great Goods.

End Goals

Here's the way I see the difference between Goods and values: values are—in most of our minds—about the journey; Goods are really about the destination. One way to look at my viewpoint can be described in the diagram below.

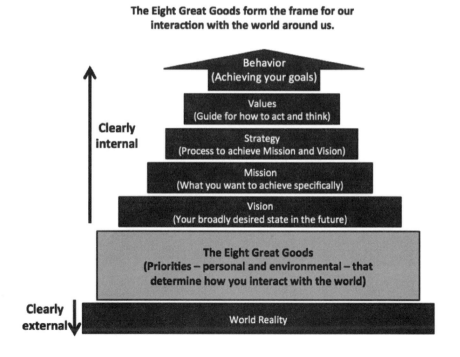

The Eight Great Goods form the frame for our interaction with the world around us.

Goods are the connective materials that bring together an external world reality and how individuals, organizations, or communities try to prosper in that world. Values are still very important in this construct as the higher-level guidelines for behaviors to help you achieve your vision. But even your idealized vision of the future of the world around you will ultimately be determined by what you believe is good.

Ends Demand the Means

Some of the evaluative criteria that any good public policy textbook will describe are things like: economic efficiency, equity, accountability, ethical behavior, or even adaptability. As I look at this list, only one of them is a reasonable end goal—equity. I can actually make policy to achieve "equity" or "equality." Now doing something equitably can also be a process, but there is at least a potential for it to be an end goal. The rest of these are really adverbs—they are processes or methods to reach the end goal.

Efficiency, while a noble aspiration, is not a goal in and of itself. There was an interesting debate twenty years ago in business strategy literature about whether or not efficiency was a strategy. Michael Porter, the Harvard Business School strategy guru, took the reasonable position that efficiency may be a necessary behavior (means) if you are trying to have a low cost strategy (ends); efficiency—or as he calls it, "organizational effectiveness"—itself is not a competitive strategic goal. (Porter, 1996) For one thing, efficiency is too easy to copy. Now, decades of business data show *process* advantages to be replicable and non-sustainable. In a world where many countries are placing an emphasis on national competitiveness, efficiency is a means to an appropriate end goal. By this reasoning, US congressional debates over cutting costs versus raising taxes are really just "process" arguments that obscure the fact that the end goal of what the Federal Government is trying to achieve has really been lost. A clear definition and agreement about that end-goal might help clarify how we need to get there.

No one value alone

In 2003, British Telecom and the Forum for the Future engaged in a joint research project on defining a sustainable company. One of the findings was that "univalence is untenable." (BT, 2003, p. 15) In other words, you cannot reduce a company that will have any kind of lasting power down to one essential, simple goal—like profitability, for instance. Any company that can renew and sustain itself and its people must have multiple end goals that are seen as important to the future of the organization.

If you have tried to prioritize your individual Goods, you may have seen how difficult it can be. Now imagine trying to run your life according to only one of the Goods—many problems would simply not have a clear answer.

While I believe that getting the Greatest Good right is very important and delineates patterns of behaviors for individuals, organizations and communities, the usefulness of the 8 Great concept is really in the careful ranking of most (if not all) of the Goods.

Computerized methods of prioritizing

London School of Economics professor Carlos Bana e Costa (probably the best known among a group of academics working on the subject) has spent a career trying to understand how prioritization of goals does and should take place in organizations. (Bana e Costa, 2001) He's developed a rather complex mathematical model to help multi-actor organizations decide what is most important in a world where everything seems important.

And there will be times when military organizations and even corporations may want to engage in a prioritization process using this kind of a computerized system. But if you've ever been in a corporate boardroom or a parliamentary debate, you know that the conversation doesn't stop while someone runs off and plugs the numbers into a program.

I am, in theory, all for this kind of modeling, but to be truly practical—a model that affects behavior (particularly group behavior)—must be simple, attention-keeping, and emotionally engaging. I believe the simplicity of the 8 Great Goods does all of those things.

The new generation and priorities

One of the most interesting insights that my coauthor, Mitchell Wade, and I gained about inter-generational work attitudes and behaviors in our book *Got Game*, was that the generation of people who grew up playing video games actually make decisions differently from those who didn't. (Beck & Wade, 2004) Since that book was published in 2004, we've consulted in dozens of organizations and learned even more about the importance of priorities. If you want young people to perform well, as a manager you need to let them know very clearly how they should prioritize their tasks. They will ask for constant feedback and want to know how they are doing minute by minute. A clear prioritization of end goals will help them to decide where to put their attention—even at those times that you are not around to personally guide them. You'd think this would be intuitive in any organization, but it is not. And it becomes more important with the generation who was raised playing video games because they easily slip into multitasking behaviors.

I remember in my early jobs, I was usually given one task and told to do it well. I was expected to concentrate. If you've grown up playing video games, you've learned to flit in and out of assigned tasks. When Gamers encounter an obstacle in a game and they can't figure out how to deal with it, they will turn to some other less difficult—or lower priority—tasks and then return to the more complex task later. I constantly emphasize to managers who oversee the work of this generation that these Gamers need a list of things to do, not just one … because when they run into a brick wall they'll still do something else, but it is unlikely to be work related (perhaps Facebook or Twitter?). So, give them multiple tasks, *but* prioritize those tasks.

While this is the advice I give about Gamers—and in developed nations just about anyone under 40 grew up with some form of video games—it is probably good advice for anyone; particularly if you want people to make decisions by themselves without a lot of hand- holding.

Complexity and decision-making

The more complexity there is, the harder it is to make a decision. Generally people focus in on a small set of variables and make their choices based on those elements.

What if we as organizations and societies could articulate: "this is who we want to be, and this is how we will make the decisions to get there." If we could state that simply and clearly, we would have a basic template of how to make decisions—and a lot of the infighting, debate and anger might actually go away.

I propose a way of decision-making that doesn't rely on the varying priorities in each of our minds; or on priorities that shift much based on context. A set of priorities that is generally acceptable to people can be developed and then governing can be carried out based on that. Later in the book, I'll spill a fair amount of ink about creating priorities among these Goods so that we can govern ourselves and others with more clarity and consistency.

First, however, I want to show how our brains are prepared—maybe even over-prepared—to embrace these 8 Goods as the basis of our most important decisions.

John C Beck

Chapter 5: The Brain and its Goods

A lot of the "brain science" experiments that are taking place in labs around the world right now are of the "where does it happen" ilk. Subjects are asked to do things or think things and then the brain is monitored for blood flow and electrical activity to see where the brain "lights up" on the tracking video screens. From these studies, scientists are learning what parts of the brain process what information and how all the parts of the brain are connected to each other.

Just a quick caveat on this: One of the important findings of the last decade is that—it turns out—the brain is a lot more plastic (or malleable) than anyone ever thought. So even though there is a "normal" visual cortex that is in about the same place in most people, if someone loses their sight, other parts of the brain can compensate and even take over some of that function. It is not as hardwired into "place" as scientists first thought.

Where Does What?

My favorite experiment along these lines was one conducted by Paul Bach-y-Rita, a neuroscientist at the University of Wisconsin. After his father suffered a serious stroke, he started trying to figure out how you can give "sight" to someone through an input pathway not attached to the eyes. He ended up fashioning a disc to be held on the tongue—he tried fixing it to other body parts but the tongue worked best—which was connected to a small camera worn on the forehead. The electrical signals from the video camera translate into pressure patterns on the tongue plate. Interestingly, the brain pretty quickly learned to interpret these tongue patterns as images. In his fascinating study, congenitally blind people were able to assemble and inspect miniature diodes on an assembly line, catch balls rolling across a table, and identify faces. (Bach-y-Rita, 2001)

My long-winded point here is that location studies can be useful in helping us understand a lot more about the brain than we used to, but it is still pretty limited because the location of brain processing can change. The logical ultimate outcome of understanding what happens where and which neurons are connected where will be to construct a map of a brain. But that is really complicated given the billions of connections in the average human noggin. However, the first brain mapping project is already under way with a much smaller subject. Scientists at Ecole Polytechnique Federale de Lausanne are trying to construct a map of a single neocortical column of a two-week old rat. This part of the rat's brain is only half a millimeter in diameter and one and a half millimeters high, yet it contains about 30 million synapses. It is painstaking work that has been underway for the last ten years. Lab technicians have to test thousands of neurons and synapses to understand what connects to what. That should give some indication as to how far we have come in understanding how brains work, but how far away we truly still are.

Until this kind of map is done for the human brain, we really won't know completely which parts of the brain are involved in all of our decisions and moral choices. But even though a complete brain map hasn't been accomplished and even though brain research is still in its infancy, there are some things we have learned that show pretty clearly that the 8 Great Goods are hardwired into our brains.

Soulless Brains?

In his 1994 book, *Descartes' Error*, Antonio Damasio takes on the well known quote "I think, therefore I am" and tries to understand what makes us human. (Damasio, 1994) Is it the soul or the brain? Not unsurprisingly, Damasio—the David Dornsife Chair in Neuroscience; Professor of Psychology and Neurology; and Director of the Brain and Creativity Institute at the USC College of Letters, Arts & Sciences—believes that our brains are what allow us to feel emotions and make decisions. Unlike other mammals, we have three major regions in our prefrontal cortex. These three parts work together to generate emotions and thinking necessary for good, consistent decision-making.

George Streidter, in *Principles of Brain Evolution*, found another important function of this part of the brain is the ability to inhibit automatic responses to stimuli. (Streidter, 2005) We couldn't come up with creative, novel responses if we always just reacted in a preset, automatic manner.

In his book, *Human*, Michael Gazzaniga from UC Santa Barbara spends almost an entire chapter (titled: "Is Anybody There?") talking about the role of the left-brain interpreter in figuring out all of the signals in the brain and making sense of them. He explains that the parts of the brain are a little like different officers in a court of law. The right side of the brain is mostly responsible for just recording events exactly like they happened; it is the court recorder who is just writing things down as they happen. Then the left side of the brain tries to figure out what it all means; it is the judge and jury. And, according to Gazzaniga, this left-brain interpreter is uniquely human and perhaps is why we are able to create a self-conscious self. (Gazzaniga, 2008)

According to all of these brain scientists, there are significant portions of the brain—the areas that make us most human—that are singly devoted to making decisions about how we can be "Good."

Our Old Brain's Memories

The prefrontal cortex and left-brain interpreter are not the only parts of the brain that makes us human, in fact according to people who study this issue, bits and pieces are distributed all over the place. But there is only one "new part of the brain" that is unique to later-evolving primates, meanwhile the other two major parts of the brain have been around for a long time in less sophisticated animals. Those old parts of the brain are mostly about memory. An emerging theory of brain science suggests that, contrary to popular opinion, the brain really doesn't compute at all—it only retrieves answers from memory. When you get into your car on a stormy day, the brain doesn't calculate "it is raining so I'd better not roll down the windows," rather it dredges up a memory of a time when the rain got in through the windows and made the upholstery soggy. Our sophisticated "calculators," according to this theory, are no more than photo albums.

This is why we focus so intently on something that is out of the ordinary—an exception. If something happens that memory doesn't predict will happen, we *have* to pay attention to it. Some of the earliest memories that most of us retain are of events that were out of the ordinary—things that should not have happened according to our experience to that time but that happened anyway. One of mine is of when my mother tripped and fell down in a city street. Strangers gathered around her and picked her up and made quite a fuss. That was not supposed to be my mom. Nothing in my memories to that time led me to believe that she could fall or could ever be vulnerable. With attention focused on the moment, a new and very strong memory was burnt into my brain, and from that moment on, I am sure that my memories predicted the potential fallibility of my mother in a way that they never had before.

And I don't have to see my mother on an uneven sidewalk to recall that memory. I can pull it up as evidence of any number of issues: mother, vulnerability, strangers, kindness, sidewalks or 'early memories'. My brain has filed it under all of those headings and probably a dozen more. The fact that I can recall this memory whenever I want to is important to my ability to turn memories into decisions. And it explains a lot of the complexity of our decision-making processes. We can remember hundreds of situations as we are trying to make a difficult decision. In fact, this ability to recall on cue is called "autocueing" and it is unique to humans. In a 1993 article, Merlin Donald points out that one of the more important things that you as a human can do is this: you can pause for a moment right now and say, I want to pull up a random memory from when I was 7 years old ... and *voila*, you have your memory. Your dog can't do that. (Donald, 1993)

These memories are exactly what we draw on in determining how to make decisions. Our different memories of different experiences are what make a unifying theory of Good so difficult. But there are some patterns.

Your Brain Wants to be Good

The new part of the human brain is mostly about emotion—this part of the brain is unique to some primates and all humans. It is exactly this non-predictability in an individual brain that causes problems within group settings. And it is in social contexts where we strive to be most consistent. Here is where algorithms and the 8 Great Goods become imperative.

Professor Damasio has pointed out that the prefrontal cortex, where we handle all conscious thought, has a direct and reciprocal connection to the amygdala—which is all about emotions. We may think that we are making rational, emotion-free decisions. But we never are. The amygdala is involved in all of our decisions—they cannot be objective. (Damasio, 1994)

Damasio used a card game experiment to show that emotions are naturally tied to memory and therefore influence decisions. His test subjects started with a pile of play money and then drew from one of four decks of cards in front of them. Cards from decks A and B allowed them to win up to $100 but also lose as much at $1250. Decks C and D had a more conservative maximum payout of $50 but losses were also capped at $100. Players all started the game by sampling from each deck, but over time normal players shifted their draws almost exclusively to decks C and D. The large losses scared them away from A and B. But non-normal test subjects—those who have lesions in their ventromedial area of their prefrontal cortex—never developed an aversion to the A and B decks and continued to draw from them until they went bankrupt.

Damasio explains that the ventromedial area of the brain is connected to the amygdala. So those with no damage found themselves experiencing negative feelings associated with big losses due to drawing cards from decks A and B. Even if they couldn't express the issue in words, their memories of card draws from those two decks were tagged with "badness" and when it came time to make a decision, they avoided those decks. All of our memories are encoded with emotion. This is how we decide good and bad. And an unimpaired brain will almost always choose Good.

The Future Remembered

Even animals associate emotions with particular memories. This is why scolding or feeding a dog or a cat works when training them. But we have something that our house pets don't; something that makes our decisions much more complex. We have big prefrontal lobes in our brains. Apes have foreheads that slope back, as did our early ancestors. Our foreheads are almost vertical. And what got stuffed into all the extra headspace were our prefrontal lobes. They are important because they help us think about the future. Without them, we couldn't envision a future at all.

In the 1940s and 1950s a revolutionary new procedure was invented to help people overcome debilitating anxiety. It was called a frontal lobotomy. Scientists found that if you cut the connections between the frontal lobe and the rest of the brain, patients became much more calm about everything—no worries. This procedure was considered so revolutionary that the 1949 Nobel Prize for Medicine was awarded to Antonio Egas Moniz for discovering the therapeutic value of this simple operation. Over 40,000 people received this treatment in the US alone before anyone really understood the reason for its effectiveness and its terrible side effects.

One of the more chilling descriptions of what it would be like to be a human without a functional front lobe comes from an article in *Canadian Psychology* in 1985. (Tulving, 1985) University of Toronto Professor Endel Tulving described an interview with a patient who suffered extensive frontal lobe damage in an automobile accident. In the interview, a doctor asked the patient what he'd be doing tomorrow. After a 15 second pause the patient smiled faintly and said, "I don't know." And when the psychologist probed further into what is going on in the patient's mind when he heard the question, the brain-injured man replied that his mind was blank. When pushed to describe, using analogies, what he was thinking when he heard "tomorrow" he says: "It's like being asleep" or "like being in a room with nothing there and having a guy tell you to go find a chair, and there's nothing there" or "like swimming in the middle of a lake" with nothing to hold onto.

Our ability to decide what to do is so much more complex than animals because we can imagine the future based on our past experiences. In fact, our ability to do so much with our relatively small brains is predicated on the brain's ability to project past experiences into the present *and* the future. It doesn't have to reprocess the elements in your living room every time you are in it. It uses an old picture of your living room and simply adjusts for any changes. Our brain uses a lot less energy this way than if it had to process everything all the time. As a University of Glasgow researcher says, "It's almost like remembering the future." (University of Glasgow, 2010)

We imagine what will be Good for us in the future based on our past experiences. From that image of the future remembered, we make trade-offs and take action.

The 8 Great Goods Supersystem

The brain is not just stingy with its energy in imagining the past and future, it is also careful not to entertain every possible option available at any time. Rather, it configures our ideas hierarchically—as decision-trees. In *Descartes' Error* (1994), Damasio calls these a "supersystem of systems." The brain presents a limited number of high-level ideas to us in any moment of decision. Once a decision is made and a higher-level neuron network is cued up, lower-level charges and chemical reactions kick in. In other words, a bunch of actions and decisions flow naturally from making a higher-level decision. So, many of our decisions—even about relatively minor day-to-day behaviors—are driven at the supersystem level. This is why Goods and basic belief systems are so important to us as human beings. These are the decisions that are the starting point of an almost infinite number of behaviors and ideas. But our choices—at the highest level—remain few so that we can actually compare and contrast them without spending too much energy on the myriad possibilities.

Another reason for us to withdraw to higher-level decision-making is when we are faced with the unknown or the unfamiliar. Anything new triggers our prefrontal cortex where our reflective consciousness resides. In other words, in the face of novelty we naturally pull back to the big picture. If our brains can figure out a quick fix, they'll move on pretty quickly. (Goldberg, 2001) But if our old saws won't work any more—if something is truly counterintuitive—then that is when we question our normal paradigms and may begin to reprioritize our 8 Great Goods.

Moral modules

Once our emotions get involved in sorting out our memories to make decisions, we are in the realm of what anthropologists and philosophers call morality. This where we decide certain things are right and wrong. We would like to ascribe the ability to determine right and wrong to animals, but there is no evidence to show that saying "bad dog" to Sport a million times will trigger any moral regret in his small brain. What will happen is just that the memory of a torn up shoe may get associated with bad consequences (disapproval from the Alpha) and therefore decisions will be made in a particular way.

In humans we go beyond mere memory in certain areas to making moral decisions about things. Psychologists Jonathan Haidt of the University of Virginia and Craig Joseph at Northwestern University have done an interesting study of human universals across cultures and even comparing the "precursors" of moral behavior in chimpanzees. (Haidt & Joseph, 2004) What they found was that there are five moral modules. These are not individual pockets of activity in the brain and we don't know where these activities take place, but we do know that every human being has them. They are: social boundaries (coalitions), hierarchy, reciprocity, suffering and purity.

Haidt and Joseph's moral modules map easily to the 8 Great Goods. Social boundaries and hierarchy are purely about what I refer to as Relationships in my schema. In fact, all five have something important to say about Relationships. But reciprocity is the moral module that governs Equality for us. Suffering is an important moderator of how we think about Life—particularly the non-mechanical part of Life. If a life is one of nothing but suffering, is it worth being alive at all? If a rancher sees a horse with a broken leg that can't be set, the moral response is to kill the horse. In humans, this question is also asked but—in this context—it is harder to make the decision to end a life of suffering. The last moral module is purity. Again this is about Relationships—cleanliness in living in close human quarters—but there is also a Life and a Belief component to this module. Many ancient religions or belief systems had components of their moral codes that were simply about good hygiene. But the purity symbolism in most religions runs deep—virgin sacrifice, white clothing, baptism, bathing in The Ganges, Japanese temple *tsukubai* (hand cleaning), mores about women's periods and men's foreskins and so on.

Anthropologist Richard Shweder and his colleagues propose just three areas of moral concerns: the "ethics of autonomy" (Individuality), the "ethics of community" (Relationships), and the "ethics of divinity" (Belief). (Shweder, Much, Park, & Mahapatra, 1997) These ethics and moral modules are the portions of the 8 Great Goods that are most difficult to explain in terms of pure survival—the Goods that we are least likely to see in animals and the Goods that are hardest to find in brain scans—perhaps because their activity cannot be tracked to any one event in the brain because it is more of a "module" (a bit of programming—or an algorithm—for enabling fast, automatic responses to particular triggers).

Let's look briefly at each of the 8 Great Goods in the brain.

John C Beck

Chapter 6: The 8 Goods in your Head

In this chapter, I will describe the ways our human brains encourage us to pay attention to the 8 Great Goods. Each of these Goods is universal and has not only a neural component but also evolutionary reasons for being. Because I want you to be able to get to the application of The 8 Great, this chapter touches only briefly on each Good. If you want to read about, what I believe is, some really fascinating research and thinking on each of these Goods, which is available on the book website.

Life

"To live is so startling it leaves little time for anything else."
- Emily Dickinson

Our brains really want us to stay alive. The conscious brain is even willing to turn itself off to keep other parts of the body alive. Some scientists believe that comas represent the brain's willingness to sacrifice its own function in order to preserve or strengthen other parts of the body. While there is some debate about this issue, there are some indications that the body is better able to heal from infection when the brain is put into an induced coma. The first person to ever survive late stage rabies was a 15-year-old girl who, in 2004, was put into a coma to protect her brain from a viral attack and help her body concentrate on fighting the infection. It worked. Four years after her bout with rabies, her speech was slower than usual, but Jeanne Giese, the victim, had learned to drive and was attending college.

Usually the brain remains "on" to protect us though. We have an inordinate number of neural pathways that are just meant to keep us from harm. Every decision we make has to run through a "like or dislike" component of the brain. If the brain doesn't like it—it sends signals that this may be dangerous in some way—it is really hard for us to override something that the brain thinks may hurt us.

In December 2010 a study published in *Current Biology* discussed the strange case of an unusual woman, SM, who completely lacks an amygdala and therefore, never shows any signs of fear. When walking through a park alone at night—something most women wouldn't do—a man accosted her and held a knife to her throat. She calmly said to him, "If you're going to kill me, you're gonna have to go through my God's angels first." The man freaked out and he let her go. She thought the situation with the man had been "strange," but didn't report it to the police, and the next night, she walked through the park again! (Sohn , 2010)

So why, if our amygdala is still intact, would we ever decide to do things that might put our lives at risk? And yet, we do it all the time. If we hadn't been able at some point to take some risks, we would never have become such a dominant species. It isn't hard to imagine an early form of almost-man that felt safe on a particular island and never ventured off. From a genetic perspective, that tribe would have never had the same rigor of a group of nomads constantly moving through new environments and picking up new coping mechanisms in each new ecosystem.

A tribe that stayed safely on their island would never have been prepared to deal with climate change or a tidal wave or a drought on that island. Without the ability to put life at risk, there are many other important risks that people would also never take.

We are willing to make life-for-life decisions pretty easily and regularly. We kill an armed man to protect the life of a kidnapped child. We go to war and kill hundreds of people to protect the safety of our family and community. But some famous experiments show how fickle the brain can be about certain life trade-offs. If interested, you can read more about these on the book website.

Stability

> *"No civilization would ever have been possible without a framework of Stability, to provide the wherein for the flux of change."*
> *- Hannah Arendt*

Stability is naturally, closely related to Life. Physical safety is pretty important to us staying alive. But there is an additional characteristic of the brain that makes stability important to us in and of itself. While it is a myth that we are born with all the brain cells we will ever have and that we can't alter the neural pathways of the brain after we are adults, we are still surprisingly "hard-wired." Despite this, old dogs *can* learn new tricks, but not easily.

Remember, our memories and behaviors are all based on actual structures in the brain—synapses. Until information or action is "attached" in our brain in some way, it means nothing. And that attaching involves a physical structure being built. Once those structures are in place, they don't want to "unbuild" themselves very easily. Can you still remember your home phone number from when you were a kid? I can, but I have troubles remembering one that I had five years ago. Those early structures that are put in place LOVE to stay in place—you have troubles forcing them to go away. They are stable.

There is an interesting logic to this. We want to remember things clearly in our normal environment. We want to remember them exactly. Then, if something is out of place, if there has been some disruption to the norm, we will know it. Our attention is drawn to the out of ordinary because it may be a threat to our lives. So we naturally seek out environments that are familiar because we have to do a lot less processing than we do in places we don't know as well.

If we still lived in tribes in villages, the equivalent of our childhood phone number would never go away through our whole lives—the village at the end of our lives would be a heck of a lot like the village where we were born. So we remember important things from our youth forever. We were designed to be highly stable. Modern life is something that our brains have had to learn to put up with. Fortunately, even our old brains can form new synapses, if they didn't, we as humans wouldn't have survived as long as we have. But that does not mean that our brain makes it easy for us to change.

War or peace

From studies of the brain, we do know why we get feelings of anxiety, fear and uncertainty. When the brain senses threats and instability, the amygdala releases neurotransmitters: norepinephrine, serotonin, cortisol and CRF (corticotropin-releasing factor). Throughout history, we've done amazing things—like building the Great Wall in China and creating massive arsenals—to keep the amygdala from releasing those neurotransmitters.

And this need for stability is not just on a large-scale level, every time you put money into the bank, more of your anxiety goes away. It is a double bonus, you not only achieve a level of Stability through your bank deposit, but you know that you can use that money in the future to achieve some of your other Goods; win-win.

But our definitions of stability may change over time or with circumstance. A study in Scotland showed that women in countries with higher mortality rates, lower life expectancies, and higher rates of communicable diseases are more likely to find more masculine faces—stronger jaw lines, broader faces, stronger eyebrows—as handsome. Women in more developed, "safer" countries preferred the look of men with "softer" features. The researchers posit that the link here is testosterone. Women find more masculine features more attractive when the need is for their personal protection and the survival of their offspring. In a safer environment with fewer threats to life and health, a more feminine looking man is associated with less philandering, less aggressiveness and higher long-term loyalty. Stability in one context just means "staying alive"; in another context, stability is all about long-term, peaceful coexistence. (Face Research Laboratory at the University of Aberdeen in Scotland)

Growth

> *"It is the dream of every cell to become two cells."*
> *- François Jacob*

Growing is the job of every organism at some point in its lifecycle. As a result, for most of natural history—literally, a dog-eat-dog world—big has always meant more powerful and more likely to survive. The dinosaurs and mammoths offer obvious cautionary tales about being too big for your own ecosystem; however, growth and the drive to bigness are natural tendencies. But, I don't really want to talk about physiological growth here. Most of you reading this have grown about as physically big as you are going to—and I mean that in a positive way. The word "growth" can mean learning or wisdom as well, but that is not the point here either. The point here is that we humans all want more—it is built into us and like all of the other 8 Great Goods, this Good only becomes a Bad when it is not used in moderation.

On the book website, you will find my diatribe on the Five Mores of Growth—that is "more" as in "greater" not "mores" as in "manners." Here are just two things our brains like to do: acquire territory and money.

Territory

Lions and chimps and all manner of other organisms are territorial: they claim a certain amount of space and then defend that space and even work to expand it.

A study published in the July 22, 2010 issue of *Current Biology* provided the first clear evidence that intergroup violence between chimpanzee groups is often about territory. Over a ten-year period, 18 bloody attacks were observed as one group of 150 chimpanzees encroached on another group's land and eventually expanded their own territory by 22%. With new land, the conquerors acquired new sources of food, water and shelter. (Mitani, Watts, & Amsler, 2010)

With man's move into a predominantly agricultural economy, territory became important and valuable. The most lush, convenient holdings were the most popular. Others required work. But not much more than a century ago in the Americas, land—in distant and less desirable locations—was freely available to anyone willing to do the work to live there.

Now, the only way to get more space in our very finite world is to buy it or take it from someone else. That involves either money or aggression, and we *love* money.

Money

In an interview with the Bloomberg press in 2006, Stanford brain researcher Brian Knutson, said of the results of his experiments: "We very quickly found out that nothing had an effect on people like money—not naked bodies, not corpses.... It got people riled up. Like food provides motivation for dogs, money provides it for people." (Levy, 2006)

Other brain studies have shown that the neural activity of someone who is making money on their investments is exactly the same as someone who experiences a drug-induced "high." We love getting more stuff! Meanwhile financial losses are processed in the same part of the brain where we respond to physical danger or the fear of losing our lives. While "growth" is a Joy-filled high, the flip side, "loss", drags us almost as low as a death in the family. Lots of studies by psychologists have been done on the behaviors and brain functions of people who are making and losing money. Increasingly, there is even big money in the study of how people make financial decisions.

The findings show that we are unsurprisingly rational in our money Growth decisions. Marian Gomez-Beldarrain of the Hospital de Galdakao in Spain and her colleagues studied how we decide to trust where to put our money. (Gomez-Beldarrain, 2004) Four "investment advisors" were shown on a screen giving advice and the test subjects were able to compare the predictive ability of each of these advisors to actual growth outcomes. Not surprisingly, the subjects always favored the advisor with the best outcomes. But here's the interesting part of this that is germane to our understanding of how Growth works in the brain: a set of subjects who had brain damage to their prefrontal lobes were unable to make choices of the best advisors. These brain-damaged subjects could still make good, rational decisions on many issues in life, but when it came to the money issue, they didn't base their investments on the track records of the advisors; instead they chose to put their money at risk based on things like the color of the background in the video.

Relationships

> *"Humans are in some ways like bees. We evolved to live in intensely social groups and we don't do as well when we're freed from hives."*
> *- John Haidt, The Happiness Hypothesis*

In the shift from *Homo habilis* to *Homo erectus* about 2 million years ago, brain size increased. At about the same time, our teeth became smaller. (Boaz & Ciochon, 2004) This may be a hugely important indicator of how we became social. You may ask: what do teeth have to do with socializing if you're not a vampire?

Small teeth, warm hearts

In 2009, Richard Wrangham a professor of anthropology at Harvard wrote a fascinating book, *Catching Fire: How Cooking Made Us Human*. (Wrangham, 2009) In it, he describes his observations of chimp dining behavior. He observed that a chimp's diet consisted of raw fruits, leaves, tubers and monkey meat. He sampled some of this himself and realized that chimps chew for half of every day because the food is really tough and fibrous. They need big teeth for all that hard work.

Somewhere along the way, the precursors of *Homo erectus* realized that meat and vegetables that had been in a fire were a lot easier to eat—ever tried to eat a raw potato? The smoldering ashes of a forest fire were probably a feast for these pre-humans. And at some point, they learned to control fire for cooking. According to Wrangham, cooking helped us in so many ways:

- Our stomachs didn't have to process as much so all the metabolic energy going to digestion could go to the brain instead. Brains got bigger and smarter and figured out even more and better ways to hunt, fish and forage.
- Time previously allocated to chewing could be used for other activities like making tools, hunting and figuring out how to get more food and better protection.
- Cooked food could be preserved and carried, allowing humans to go on longer and longer hunting expeditions across terrain that was not replete with easily accessible vegetation or meat.
- The fire that they learned to control for cooking was also great for protection at night, allowing them to sleep for longer periods and to remain on the ground or in caves throughout the night with a fire at the mouth of the cave, instead of retreating into the trees to avoid being eaten by large animals.
- The fire provided warmth and allowed us to lose our body hair, which allowed for more activity without overheating; *Homo erectus* could move into territories that were colder than where *Homo habilis* could have survived.
- Finally and most important to this discussion, rather than each individual starting their own fires and doing their own cooking, our ancestors started doing the cooking together. This allowed for socializing and the beginnings of divisions of labor that didn't exist before. Women who were less mobile than men just before and after childbirth became the keepers of the fire, and cooks. Men spent more time out gathering and hunting food.
- In the process of cooking, men and women found the need to coordinate in ways they had never done before. And they had the time to talk and eat and take much longer rests between feedings. They became social beings.

Size matters

This socializing started in pretty small groups at first. We can be pretty sure of this because there is a fascinating correlation between the average size of social groups and the size of the brain's neocortex of any mammal. Robin Dunbar explored this correlation by looking at bats, carnivores, insectivores, and especially primates. (Dunbar, 1998)

Our human ancestors needed a bigger brain not just because they were venturing into increasingly complex physical environments but because of the complexity of dealing with other people in closer and larger groups. They had to learn to interpret visual signals, remember relationships between people, keep track of faces and names, and analyze the emotional states of those around them. All of this takes a lot of processing power. And while the average person can attach names to up to 2000 faces, we can only cognitively *manage* about 150 people at a time. (This magic number of 150 is the focus of a lot of research described on the book website.) But the ability to manage that many complex human interactions is truly an amazing feat. Our brains were made for socializing.

Individuality

> *"Remember always that you not only have the right to be an*
> *individual, you have an obligation to be one."*
> *- Eleanor Roosevelt*

Mother nature has really outdone herself when it comes to making us different. From finger whorls to facial structures to voice prints, we are all distinct. Scientists have long puzzled over why this variation was built into us in the first place. And the answer is probably "rigor." Simple cell division creates organisms that are exactly the same—predictable and uninteresting. For survival, that predictability is also a liability. Viruses and parasites that want to attack an organism know exactly how to do it if every organism is the same. Sexual reproduction—using parts of two organisms to produce a third—has the advantage of creating a potentially incompatible host for a parasite even though one or both parents were compatible. Individuality is a highly desired Good in most of our natural world.

John C Beck

Each brain is really different

We know that the basic genetic code for each of us is unique—except for identical twins. Yet, even with the same fundamental genetics, twins think different thoughts and do different things. So, how different are the brain functions of identical twins? In 2009, the first brain imaging study using twin and non-twin siblings was published in the journal *Science*. Jan Koten led a team that studied ten sets of siblings. Each set contained two identical twins and one non-twin sibling. They found that twins actually do think quite a lot alike. The findings noted that twins had a much higher overlap in the location of brain activity—not exactly the same but really close—than did non-twin siblings when completing the same tasks. They estimated that heritability explained 60% to 90% of the variability in brain activity. Our brains are all different in function, but twins are a lot closer than non-twins. (Koten, et al., 2009)

At a deeper genetic level, even twins who have the same DNA in most of the cells of their body, have different DNA in their brains. In fact, all of us have different DNA code in our brains than the DNA in the rest of our bodies. "Whaaaaat?" you say—well maybe you didn't, but you should have. A team led by Fred Gage at the Salk Laboratory found that brain cells and immune system cells have "mobile elements." (Attwooll, 2009) To fight off constantly new and emerging threats, the immune system needs to change more rapidly than the generation-to-generation evolution would facilitate. Mobile elements allow for slightly different genetic codes to occur each time a cell divides—known as "jumping events." This same jumping also takes place in brain cells. There, Gage's study found up to 100 extra copies of DNA per brain cell. These mobile elements allow each neuron in the brain to be different from the one that generated it—adding to our uniqueness and individual variability.

Equality

"I believe in equality for everyone, except reporters and photographers."
- Mohandas Gandhi

Just like our individuality is in-born, so is our need for equality. Studies across cultures have shown for years that we humans have a general and shared sense of what is fair in dealing with others. But better scientific tools are allowing us to understand how we accomplish that shared understanding—it is not just social norms. We try to be fair because our brains tell us to.

Getting to equal

Rutgers' psychology professor Elizabeth Tricomi and her colleagues' study "Neural evidence for inequality-averse social preferences" recently reported the extent to which our brains really care about Equality. (Tricomi, Rangel, Camerer, & O'Doherty, 2010) In Tricomi's study, 40 participants were presented with money transfer scenarios while lying in a functional MRI (fMRI) machine—a type of specialized Magnetic Resonance Imaging scanner that measures the change in blood flow related to neural activity in the brain. One subject, for instance, might be told he was being given $50 while another subject was being given $20. In another scenario, one would be offered $5 while another is offered $50. But before any of this money transfer began, one participant was made "rich" with an endowment of $50 while the other participant started "poor" with no money. The scientists were trying to understand where and how the brain was reacting to these inequalities. The results were quite remarkable.

The differences in the way the ventromedial prefrontal cortex and the ventral striatum—the rewards centers of the brain—reacted to the money transfers had more to do with the subject's starting positions of "rich" or "poor" than it did to the amounts of money being transferred in each transaction. A couple of interesting findings:

- People who started "poor" had strong reactions to gaining money themselves and almost no brain activity for money being given to their "rich" colleagues.
- Those who started rich and witnessed a poor person getting money had more activity in the rewards portion of their brain than they did if they personally were given money.

Tricomi and her colleagues point out that the motivation for this brain activity could be self-interested: when poor people get money, the social discomfort and "guilt" feelings of the rich are alleviated. Maybe this is one reason why the Danes, who pay more than half their income in progressive taxes to help even out income disparities, were also named the happiest people on earth in 2008.

Whatever the motivation, we now know that the rewards portions of the brain are highly involved in our making decisions based on Equality. Generally, our brains prefer a fairly high level of equanimity.

Belief

"I've fallen into Belief *like I fell into love."*
– Graham Greene

While Goods like Life and Stability—and even Joy—can be seen as decision-making bases for other species in the animal kingdom, our current methods of understanding the natural world around us has not yielded any correlates in the animal kingdom for Belief.

Is Belief really just Individuality?

Interestingly, some recent studies posit that belief in God and belief in one's self (Individuality) are highly related. This arises partly when functional MRI scans show that the same parts of the brain light up when subjects are instructed to think about what God wants them to believe and then asked to consider what they personally want. Additionally, Nicholas Epley of the University of Chicago and his colleagues found that survey respondents reported their personal views on various topics closely aligned to what they said God's attitudes would be on those same topics. Then the team conducted a more clinical study on the beliefs, asking some test subjects to read a strong argument "for" a particular issue and a weak argument "against" that same issue; for other subjects the strength of the argument was reversed—a weak "pro" position paper and a strong "anti" piece. After this "priming" through logical arguments, the test subjects were more likely to report that not only did they believe in the strong argument's side of the issue, but they believed that God was on that side as well. This was the result no matter which side of the issue was presented as the stronger argument. If an individual later changed his or her mind on the issue, apparently so did God. (Epley, 2009)

Dean Hamer's book, *The God Gene: How Faith is Hardwired into our Genes*, made quite a splash when it was published in 2004. (Hamer, 2004) Hamer described the VMAT2 gene as one present to a higher degree in people who report spiritual or mystical experiences. And because there was some evidence that spirituality seems to run in family lines, he proposed that the different mutations of this gene could explain why about 15% of the human population are highly susceptible to hypnotism and others aren't. But in the case of spirituality, the percentage of the susceptible population is much higher than 15%: according to the Gallup organization, 85% of Americans claim a religious identity. In Europe about the same percentage believe either in God or some spiritual life force, says Eurobarometer. And those facts argue for some good evolutionary reasons why our processes of natural selection would favor a willingness to believe in God and religion almost universally. For more on this research and thinking, there is a long section on this on the book website.

Joy

> *"Men are that they might have Joy"*
> *– The Book of Mormon*
> *(the original one, not the Broadway musical)*

In the 1950s, researchers were trying to understand if lab rats were made uncomfortable by electric currents to certain parts of the brain. They rigged their cages so that electrical stimulation was administered only when the rats were in one corner of the cage. They theorized that rats that were made uncomfortable by the electrical stimulation would avoid that corner. What they found was that rats with the electrodes in their nucleus accumbens would return to that corner over and over again—they really, really, really liked electrical shocks to that part of their brains. (Olds & Milner, 1954)

The pleasure organ

With that finding in the forefront of their own minds, scientists fashioned a new test where rats that pushed a lever would administer an electrical impulse to their own nucleus accumbens. They lined up for the opportunity. The lab rats would do it almost non-stop; often dying of thirst or hunger because they were so happily shocking their brains.

Although the nucleus accumbens was dubbed the pleasure center of the brain, it is actually more complex than that. While dopamine and serotonin are regulated by the accumbens, it also works closely with the ventral tegmental area (VTA), which is one of the most primitive parts of the brain—the area targeted by heroin and morphine.

Other parts of the brain involved in our feelings of happiness and pleasure are *the prefrontal cortex*—a part of the brain that is usually pretty logically involved in planning, but also gives us motivation for future activities; *the locus coeruleus*—full of norepinephrine and the driver of addictions; *the amygdala* which creates our immediate, initial impressions of good and bad; *the hippocampus* which stores memories of pleasurable experiences; and *the insular cortex*—which seems to store information about the relationship between our bodies and our emotional experiences. These are the parts of the brain that keep us happy.

Without having to shock our brains, we produce happy emotions in a variety of ways. And each individual seems to have a Joy producer of choice: winning, succeeding, thrill-seeking, exercise, eating, drinking, romance, music, laughter, videogames, or drug use. We seek these out in an almost single-minded fashion.

Stuck in our Heads

The point of this chapter is to show that the 8 Great Goods are important elements of natural brain functions. We are designed to care about these Goods. I would even go so far as to argue that these eight represent the basic functions of the brain. In all my study of current topics in brain science, I did not come across any research that did not fall quite neatly into one of these Goods.

But sometimes, even though our brains want all of these Goods for us, two or more of them come into conflict. We come upon situations where we could have Growth, for instance, but it means a potential sacrifice of Life or Joy. We consciously have to make the trade off decision. The rest of the book is about those trade offs and the priorities that we consciously impose upon these natural functions of our minds.

John C Beck

Section II

Goods in Decisions:
Making a Conscious Choice

John C Beck

Chapter Seven: Definitions and Labels

If we plan to rule our lives or the lives of others based on the 8 Great Goods, then we need to make sure that the definitions of these Goods in the context of our lives, our organizations or communities are very clear. Our brains really like these Goods, but the way that your brain defines a particular Good and the way my brain sees the same Good may be very different. To live together in some semblance of harmony, we had better make the definitions explicit and exact.

Difficult Definitions

The ongoing debate about abortion is a case in point. We may all be able to agree that Life should be a top priority in any community, but the problem that arises with a controversial subject like abortion can be found in the definition of Life—is a fetus its own self or is it still part of the mother? If it is part of the mother, then the Good of Individuality (the rights of the mother) is the basis for decision-making on this issue. If the fetus is a person, then Life should be the rule. The debate over this kind of definition can (and has been proven to) rage for decades. Some of the biggest social debates in the history of mankind are exactly of this ilk. And they are debates worth having.

During the first three years I worked with the concepts in this book, I had called Equality "fairness." But I found that while being a word and a concept that sounds very high minded, fairness ends up as a rallying cry on both sides of many debates. Too often the word is used as "that is not fair to me," rather than that is not "equal" for both of us.

Let me use the Civil Rights and Gay Rights movements in the United States as an example. In the 2008 General Social Survey, 58% of Black respondents (compared with 46% of Whites) opposed same-sex marriage rights. (General Social Survey, 2008) If the Civil Rights movement was all about Equality for all, then you might expect Black people in America who have benefited from that movement would be more supportive of gay marriage. But they are not. This seems like an inconsistency viewed from a Equality point of view.

But if Civil Rights was a Relationships issue for most blacks (looking out for their own community) or even an Individuality issue (I should be able to do what I want to do), then while they wanted "fairness" for themselves and Equality with whites, Equality may not really be the Good that drives African-Americans.

I still prefer the sound of the word fairness, but since this good was really supposed to be about us all treating each other the same, I finally relented and changed the name to the more appropriate Equality.

Boundaries

Even though we have a pretty clear definition of the Goods, there will be times when those decisions will need to be bounded for practical or philosophical reasons. For instance, I may place my parents (Relationships) as one of the top priorities. But when the air ticket to visit them for Christmas is too expensive, I decide not to go even though I know it will hurt their feelings.

On the issue of Black attitudes toward gay marriage, even if Equality was a real basis for many black people's advocacy of the civil rights movement, that Equality may be bounded by Belief. Black churches are notoriously conservative on the issue of gay marriage. The teaching is often that "gayness" is a choice, not innate. And the conviction that God condemns this choice makes it hard for believers to condone this behavior by legalizing gay unions. In a believer's mind, God's Will is likely to become a boundary for all the other Goods no matter how high they are in the ranking.

Exceptions

The potential problem with prioritization is that the first priority may only be the first priority only to a certain extent and in certain circumstances.

For instance, even though one's first priority may really be Life in most instances, there will be economic, safety, or any other number of limits on how far you will go to protect a life. Colorado, for instance, enacted a law (which has been come to be known as the "make my day" law) decriminalizing killing an intruder on one's property if the property owner feels his or her life

Percentage of responses to the statement:
"I would kill an intruder who was trying to take my property"

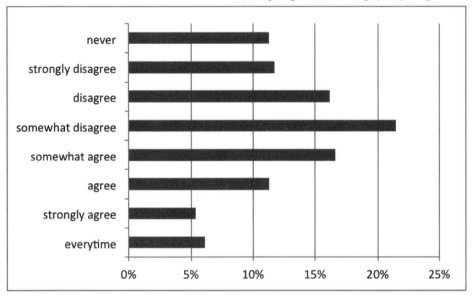

may be in danger. With this exception, the law becomes: Thou shalt not kill *unless* someone enters your property without an invitation. And a lot of my survey respondents buy into this definition. Only about 12% of Americans in my survey said they would always protect life (see the chart above). For all the rest, there were varying degrees of willingness to take a life for a good reason.

I grew up at the base of a mountain where every year a hiker or two would find themselves caught on a ledge without an obvious way down. Emergency workers and helicopters were always dispatched to save these inexperienced climbers. But there was an ongoing community debate about when exceptions should be made to the policy of saving the climbers. Since most areas were clearly marked with "do not climb" signs, there was some sentiment that dispatching rescue workers might be sending a signal that the law prohibiting climbing is not very serious. There, of course, was a cost reason for refusing help, but the strongest argument was that to preserve the rule of law ("do not climb" means *do not* climb), sometimes a life would need to be lost.

Now, if you're finding yourself making a lot of exceptions to your prioritization rules, perhaps you need to reassess the order. If there is always a monetary limit to how much you will spend to save a life, then Growth may be a more important Good for you.

But if there are just limited instances of exception, then you need to examine the rules for exceptions. Governments and organizational leaders should spend all the time necessary to define these exceptions. I would argue that once prioritizations are set, all boardroom, legal, and legislative debates should really only be about exceptions and definitions.

Label Conscious

While I am a huge advocate of making 8 Goods priorities clear and explicit, I do understand that in real life, many of us like to hold our cards a little closer to our vest. In an elected government, for instance, there is freedom to be gained by appealing to a variety of constituencies. In fact, in a study of the Greater London Authority, the authors found that the city government—and particularly the mayor—was chameleon-like in order to gain the support of as many of the diverse stakeholder groups as possible. (Rydin, Thornley, Scanlon, & West, 2004) This may appear to be disingenuous—or even dishonest—but the authors of the case study argue that the mayor would have been unable to accomplish anything (or to become mayor in the first place) without the support of these disparate groups.

So for a moment, let's move away from "espoused" goals (what you say to the public to keep them happy) to "in practice" goals (the goals that actually drive you as you conduct business). As discussed in previous chapters, there are mental models behind all of our individual and collective decision-making. And particularly in organizations—where there are many people involved in getting to the ultimate goal—it is important for everyone to understand the priorities that will be guiding them.

High-end Labels

As was the case for the mayor of London, many politicians hate to be categorized—so do many business leaders. They don't want to be too closely tied to a particular stance on any issue because it may make them vulnerable to their enemies—they're a bit afraid of being labeled.

There are some downsides to being labeled, as anyone who has had a rough junior high school experience can attest. My experience was being called a "narc" for an entire school year. I hadn't exposed anyone's narcotics use or anything else; I had too many secrets of my own to run around telling other's. But someone called me "narc" one day and the label stuck. To this day, my pulse still quickens a bit when I even write the word.

And it is not just the way others label us that can be hard to change; we end up believing a lot of labels that have been reinforced since we were young. Research suggests that a conservative or liberal mindset is instilled during childhood and is not easily changeable—a point poignantly illustrated to me by a staunch Republican friend who cast her first presidential Democratic vote for Barack Obama in 2008. She talked to everyone about her decision and justified it many ways; it was not easy for her to move from her childhood preferences. She never fully articulated why she always voted for Republicans, although self-labeling was part of it: "I am a Republican," and yet she was liberal on many issues. The label alone, though, was perhaps enough to keep her voting a particular way. By 2012, she was back to voting the Republican ticket.

But the way our surprisingly small minds work is that if we are going to pay attention to anything at all, we are going to want to put it into a category. So if a particular schema or set of labels help us to mentally grasp an object more easily, our minds are ready and willing to attach a moniker. Horoscope signs, professions, home states, age (generation), religion are all common categories that we find ourselves using to label people. The Japanese use blood type as a method of understanding people's personalities and compatibility with others. Type As are earnest and sensible; Type Bs are wild and active; ABs are rational and controlled; Os are social and optimistic. Who knew?

We do the same kinds of labeling in our organizational lives. Many companies swear by Myers-Briggs categories as a way to understand who will be a good manager and who will be good at being managed by others. And corporations too end up being "typecast" into various roles: innovative, quick follower, low-cost, nimble, bureaucratic, acquirer, etc. Nations and nationalities also get labeled: imperious, reclusive, aggressive, snobbish, prudent, or corrupt. Once a person, company or nation has been typecast, it is hard to move out of that niche easily. The ecosystem begins to expect—

even demand—that it will always behave that way.

So labels can be wrong; they can be hard to change (even when you want to); and they can end up being used by detractors (those with different priorities) to make your life miserable. All of these are good reasons to avoid labels—and arguments for why you may not want to prioritize your greatest Goods.

Better Living through Labels

Still, it is not an entirely bad thing to be labeled. In fact, until a person, organization or nation is labeled, it is hard to achieve at least four attributes that are essential for success:

Consistency. It is hard for a group of people to move in the same direction if the destination has never been defined. Without that definition—or label—there is likely to be a lot of milling around. And even an individual will find it difficult to be consistent over time without a defining Good for himself or herself.

Efficiency. It's hard to do things in the best possible manner if we don't know what we're trying to achieve. If I'm a candle maker who has been told to make as many candles as possible, my behaviors will be completely different than if I've been told to make a product with the highest possible quality.

Cultural cohesion. We all get along better if we're after the same goal. We all think of the Japanese as being very group oriented and similar in their thinking. What if this is more about them sharing a common Good than anything "cultural?

There is some evidence that, in fact, the Japanese are not terribly conformist. Do you remember the classic Ashe experiment? You know, the one you heard about in social studies class where people were shown lines of obviously different length—as a "vision test"—and then asked to say which was longer. If a confederate (a "plant" working with the experimenter) insisted that the short one was really the long one, then 32% of the test subjects actually went along with the incorrect answer. Robert Frager replicated this in Japan in 1970 and the result was that the Japanese actually showed less conformity to others in the group—in fact, they showed a high degree of anti-conformity.

The Japanese subjects were actually highly likely to oppose another view *just* because the majority was choosing something else. (Frager, 1970) A study by Klauss and Bass supported this experimental finding which showed similar non-conformity behavior among Japanese managers. (Klauss & Bass, 1974)

So how did we come to think of the Japanese as so conformist? Part of the answer, I believe, lies in the almost universally shared goal of Japanese to catch up to the West after WWII. The problem came when Japan actually did catch up in the early 1990s. Suddenly there was no goal—no label other than 'Japaneseness'—to drive cultural cohesion. The anti-conformity mindsets and behaviors can be seen in Japanese politics and even in large Japanese organizations—like Sony—that have seen progress thwarted by a natural tendency toward disagreement.

Distinctive positioning. Marketers have told us that if you don't call out the distinctive qualities of your product to potential buyers, they may not understand the reason for buying yours versus another's. If you don't label yourself, your organization or your polity, everyone may be running around with different labels, or different (possibly divergent) views of the world. That makes it hard to attract and engage like-minded people to work toward a common goal. And it will cause confusion down the road.

As you go through the 8 Great Goods decision process, you'll find yourself saying: "This is who I am." You'll be labeled, and remember that's not always a bad thing. If the label sticks it could define you for much of the rest of your life. And sure, the label can be changed in the future, but let's not get ahead of ourselves.

John C Beck

Chapter Eight: Trade-offs

My experience tells me that whatever you list as your prioritization of the 8 Great may be quite aspirational the first time you do the exercise. Your priorities may not be showing up in your behaviors yet (which is not to say that they never will.) Generally, if you ask your closest friends and family what they think your order is, it will be slightly different from your own self-rating.

Checking It Twice

As I was writing this book, prioritizing the 8 Great Goods became a bit of a parlor game whenever I met with friends or loved ones. Often the most fun was asking others to predict others' or my own priorities. In assessing me, my friends often told me that they thought Individuality should be very high, if not my Greatest Good. And yet in my own list, Individuality is actually third after Joy and Relationships. I understand how my friends came to this perception; I have eschewed traditional jobs and career paths and usually go at problems in a fairly non-traditional manner. When I would finally reveal my priorities, as I perceived them, I found that friends never had trouble with the idea that I put Joy above Individuality. They just could not believe that I really thought Relationships were more important than Individuality. I must admit that their feedback did give me pause.

I finally figured out that "the disconnect" came in my definition of Relationships. I was not thinking of community or organizations, but of my immediate family. And only my really closest friends had ever been privy to how family considerations impacted my choices. Four examples came to mind about how I put family Relationships over most other considerations:

1) For a number of years I was in a job in which I was, frankly, miserable. But I stuck with the job because my family needed the income. That was not necessarily a personal Joy or Individuality decision. I did it for the happiness of my kids and for my family Relationships. (I will admit that as soon as a severance package was being offered to employees, I was more than happy to take it!)

2) Early in my career, I remember quitting the local Rotary Club because

they wouldn't allow my then-wife to join me at their luncheons (there was a fairly strong anti-woman bias in the Club then). I chose the Relationships of my family over the Relationships of my business colleagues.

3) When my current partner and I were being wooed by the same employer for a couple of posts in their organization, I cut off my set of discussions after they treated him in an unethical manner.

4) This is the first non-fiction book that I have ever written solo. On every other book, I have had a coauthor. When I started working on this I did cast around for a potential co-author because "that is what I always do." But it was clear to every friend I approached that this was so much my book that to *foist* it on someone else would not be fair. And the working together with someone on a book is really hard to get out of my system. In revision after revision of this book, I continually find the word "we" creeping into the manuscript. And there is a "we" in some ways. I figure that everyone who has talked to me about this or proposed an interesting angle on this idea is really a "we" in some ways. I am sure that even the draft you are reading now has a the occasional "we" in the text. I am sorry for that, but this old habit of collaborating really is dying very hard.

The proof of our prioritization is really found in the pudding of trade-offs that we make on a daily basis. Some of these trade-offs will be obvious to those around us. Some will not be. In fact, we may become quite enigmatic to those around us when we are making decisions on a different priority basis than their own. But if close friends are questioning your priorities, it is always good to go back and really check to see if you are being consistent.

These trade-offs take place every day: every time you get in the car to go to work (Growth), the movies (Joy), or church (Belief) you are risking your Life. But I'm not going to put a whole lot of emphasis on these small trade-offs—or trade-offs that involve a small chance that something might happen in the future. But, there are some major trade-offs that all of us have either experienced or heard about. These are the important ones.

We Love and Hate Trade-offs

Let me make a sweeping statement here that many of you will scoff at—but I believe it is true: All great literature (and associated movies, plays, etc.) is about the trade-offs among the 8 Great Goods.

A cursory analysis of IMDB's top 30 films of all time, shows that all of these films feature a major theme involving each one of these 8 Great. We are naturally fascinated by all of these Goods in general. But the stuff of legends is the trade-off amongst them. The difference in the way that I define "good" and you define "good" creates some of the most important drama in life. We can't take our eyes off the screen when Andy (Tim Robbins) chooses his dignity (Individuality) over Life by fighting off "the Sisters" in The Shawshank Redemption. Don Corleone (Marlon Brando) seeks to preserve his place in mafia Relationships and values his Belief system over economic Growth when he turns down the chance to get into the narcotics trade (making us wonder what the Godfather's ethics code really was). We all watch on the edge of our seats as Lisa (Grace Kelly) in *The Rear Window* climbs through a neighbor's open casement to look for a dead body: risking her Life to put right the inequity (Equality) of an unrequited murder and potentially to preserve justice (Stability) in her community.

Trade-offs as the Basis for All the 8 Great Goods

When I was originally thinking through the 8 Great Goods, one of the rules that I used to determine if a particular Good was a candidate for the Greatest Goods was that there had to be good examples in history or in everyday human existence of each Good taking a higher priority over every other Good.

On the next page is a chart that I put together at the time. (The way to read this is that the Goods along the top row "win" in competition with the Goods along the left side of the chart.)

I admit that some of these are kind of silly examples. Some are from my personal life. But I bet—if you took the time—you could fill in every one of these boxes with stories from your own experiences.

The biggest stuff

The most dramatic trade-offs are the unambiguous life-for-life trade-offs. At some point we've all played the "survivors in a life boat without enough food" game. Remember, the one where you have to throw someone overboard

Eight Great Goods

	wins:	Life	Belief	Growth	Equality	Relationships	Individuality	Joy	Stability
loses:									
Life	eating reproduction health care	sacrifce to save another life	Crusades Martyrs Jihad	Overwork / Territorial War	Revolutions	Dying for Country / Family	Mountain men / Intruders	Thrill-seekers	Death Penalty
Belief	religion God spirtuality	Renunciation	religious debates	Marriotts and Alcohol	Humanism	Changing religion for marriage	Leaving the Fold	Bill Clinton / Preacher Scandals	Mormon give up Polygamy
Growth	gain / power acquisitivenes	Feudalism	Ascetics	investment decisions	Socialism	Stay at home parents	small business/indeppendence	Spending on fun / luxury goods	Anti WalMart protests
Equality	rights everyone treated equally	Iraq War Slavery	The Annointed	Capitalism	fairness for many means less equality for some	Democratic Rule	Hierarchy Aristocracy Meritocracy	Gladiator Games	Tienanmen Massacre
Relationships	family /group community nation / hierarchy?	Political Refugees	Monks	Gold Rush family abandoners	Activist Courts / American Revolution	choosing nation over family	Pioneers / Mountain Men	Football widows	Military Draft
Individuality	ownership privacy space voice fame	Villages Community	Congregation / Man is Evil	Division of Labor / Large Corporations	Redistribution (wealth/ property) zoning laws	All kinds of non-mortal Sacrifice	neighbor property disputes	Hazing / Bullying	Tax Enforcement
Joy	entertainment sports fun	Hard Work	Strictures	Protestant Ethic	Taking Turns	Order / Seriousness	Closing a party down early for neighbors?	how to spend excess	Anti-Drug Enforcement
Stability	laws prdictability	Harboring fugitives	Missionaries to unsafe places	Singapore allowing casinos	Communist revolutions	Imperialistic wars	Moving from your home town	Gambling / Drug use / Adventure	which law or custom is more important

so others have a chance of living longer? This is a pretty clear-cut Life for a Life trade-off—and the game naturally absorbs our attention.

As long as Life is in the equation, it will be a really tough decision and a rough process. For instance, the governmental cost of enforcing the death penalty is much greater than enforcing a lifetime of incarceration. That is not a logical conclusion. You would think that the cost of feeding and guarding a prisoner for a lifetime would far outweigh the cost of killing someone. But the highest expenses are not in the act of killing, it is in the decision-making process that allows that final act. Because killing someone is so final (there is no way really to apologize if you get it wrong), the appeals process is particularly robust. Court time and legal pay is what drives the cost of a death penalty well above a life sentence. In 2007, New Jersey became the first state to ban the death penalty in decades. The reason was not a moral argument; it was pure finances. They figured that it cost the state $4.2 million to prosecute each death penalty case. It is just much cheaper to imprison than try to kill society's worst criminals.

What's Life got to do with it?

Human beings generally don't like to kill others, themselves or make the trade off of one life for another. This may be why so many of us are so fascinated by those rare occasions when life is at stake. It is the stuff of high drama. In my surveys, I expected Life to have quite a high priority over everything else given how infrequently we exchange a human existence for almost anything else. But I was wrong. Life, surprisingly, took a lower priority for many Americans.

This fact calls into question all of the Good priorities. And after reviewing these survey data, I had to sit down and give all of the research I've been doing for the previous four years a good rethink.

I have come to the conclusion that when respondents first are confronted with a simple prioritization or a set of "story problems"—trade-offs among priorities that they imagine themselves having to make—they are likely to make their decisions more based on their aspirations than on actual behavior. This doesn't make the Good priorities any less real, it just means that there may be a gap between what we'd like our priorities to be and our actual behavior.

Your responsibility as a human is to stay alive

Because "life" is such a dramatic example, let's focus on the role this Good plays in the surveys I conducted in 2012. Self-preservation is built into us; we reflexively want to survive. It is tough to commit suicide because all of our systems are designed to keep us "naturally" from doing something that endangers our own life. As Dr. House of the eponymous US television show screamed as he was strangling a suicidal patient in one of his last episodes: "You're resisting because it's our human responsibility to STAY ALIVE."

Yet, Life does not far outpace the other priorities in the minds of survey respondents. In my 2012 survey of 1100 Americans, 25.9% put it as their top priority, slightly behind Relationships (26.2%) Belief is not far behind these other two (22.8%) while all the other Goods are much lower priorities for Americans. What could explain Life's statistical dead heat with Relationships and Belief?

For one thing, most of us have been taught from a very early age that it is righteous to give up one's life for loved ones and for religious freedom. If I'm right in my theory that priorities are more about ambitions than reality, then there is nothing more noble than giving up one's life for a good cause. But how do we understand what "real" behaviors of survey respondents might be?

Do your friends smoke pot?

When I was first learning about questionnaire methodologies—particularly survey design—as a graduate student, one of my professors explained that on some sensitive questions, we would get a better understanding of "truth" if we phrased the question to ask about other people. He cited a study of drug use where less than 10% of the teenagers surveyed admitted to currently using drugs, but if the question was rephrased as "Out of your ten best friends how many have used drugs in the last two months," it turned out that about 40% of the school was currently using.

There may be a similar phenomenon underway here. In the chart below, you can see that Relationships lose a little ground when asking about others'

How survey respondents rank the Great Goods for themselves and people and institutions around them.

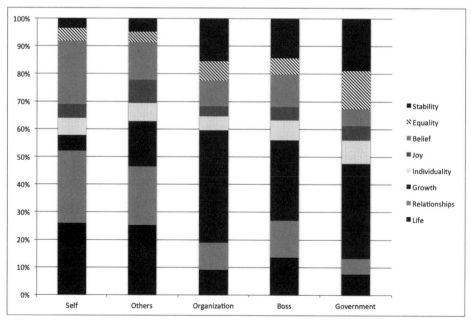

John C Beck

priorities versus one's own. But the bigger loser is Belief, which gives up almost half of its number one priorities to Growth. This could just be because many people keep their personal beliefs personal. On the other hand, a neighbor's Growth priority is pretty obvious when a new car or a new boat shows up in the driveway.

Equally interesting to me, is that the percentage of respondents claiming that their own top priority is Life (25.9%) is almost exactly the same as the percentage believing that those around them value Life as the number one priority (25.3%).

That suggests to me that either in aspiration or in observable behavior, about 25% of Americans really do value Life as their top priority. Still a much smaller percentage than I would have ever predicted given how low suicide and death rates are among people under 70 (the upper age limit of survey respondents).

War? Sure! ... Hunger? No way!

When you compare the simple prioritization of the 8 Great Goods with a set of questions I asked about decisions between priorities (see the box below), the story becomes even more complicated. We are more willing to risk Life for Joy than any other reason. Going to war for religious reasons is the next highest rationale for taking or giving up a life (several percentage points higher than going to war for the cause of liberty). But we are highly unlikely to share our rations equally if it means that we might die. Maybe the fact that we've all been a little hungry at one point in our lives is

---

Questions to assess some trade-offs between Life and the other Goods

1. I would risk my own life for the fun of something like learning how to fly small planes or skydive or scuba dive or climb Mt. Everest
2. I would go to war to fight for my religion or for my way of believing
3. I would share rations equally even if that meant I might starve to death
4. I would volunteer to go to war to protect rights of liberty and freedom
5. I would lay off an employee -- even one with no prospect of finding another job -- to keep my company profitable
6. I would allow two strangers to die to keep one similar (same age, race, gender) loved-one from dying
7. I would kill an intruder who was trying to take my property

---

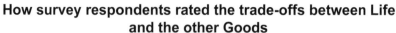

How survey respondents rated the trade-offs between Life and the other Goods

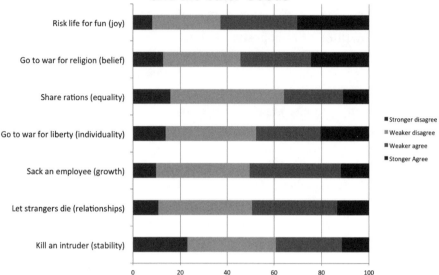

the closest brush with death that most of us have ever experienced—and we don't want to go through *that* again!

But what is probably more striking about this chart is that no matter the reason for taking a life, about half of us gladly admit on a survey we would do it under certain circumstances. In this set of questions, I never asked the "sacrificing one life for another one life" question; in every case, there was a Life being put at risk for another one the Goods.

There are a number of interpretations of these data:

1) We really don't care as much about Life as you would think we would: Maslow's hierarchy may even been wrong in putting survival as the top priority.

2) We watch so much TV and so many movies that Life has become a fictional commodity. Unless we go out of our way to avoid popular culture or modern society, we are inundated and inured.

3) Until we are really faced with the choice—in real life—we think other things are more important than Life. But, that doesn't change the fact, that many of us do life-threateningly risky things with some abandon.

4) The fact that almost half of the time, we trade off all the other competing priorities for Life, suggests that we believe life is pretty damn important to us; but not all-important.

Choose the one you prefer or come up with your own explanation. But I, for one, was pretty surprised by how little we admit on a survey that we value "life".

The small stuff

However, once we have thought through the biggest decisions involving Life in some detail, the trade-offs among the lesser Goods seem much easier to make. "This isn't a life-death decision" is a reassuring statement—one that usually is used to motivate us to come to a conclusion without perseverating too much or too long.

One of the reasons that we are fascinated by these trade-offs—even the non-Life stuff—in movies and literature is probably because we all know we may be forced to choose some day (or we've had to choose in the past) and we really wonder if we will get (or did get) the priorities right.

Making Trade-offs Less Painful: The Case of the Big Dig

These trade-offs are unbelievably important in our personal lives and in our societal lives. Particularly when we have to live in a society with other people and get along with them, there is a certain amount of real understanding and real compromise that will be necessary.

The key in social living is to structure our lives and activities so that, without forgoing our Greatest Goods, we can give other people at least a part of their Greatest Goods as well. It is a compromise.

One of my favorite examples of individuals and organizations finding a way around significant trade-offs while making a really significant change is the story of the Big Dig in Boston.

To ease traffic worries in the early 1950s an overhead six-lane highway was built through the center of Boston. By the 1980s it was obvious that this highway was seriously outmoded. It was too small, it was an eyesore, and it was a cause of noise and air pollution right in the center of the city. A replacement was needed. But, how? The old highway carried millions of cars a day and you just couldn't shut it down and relocate. Besides that, there was really nowhere to relocate to: there was no land left for more highway construction downtown. When it was originally built in the 1950s, homes were razed in the name of progress without much owner recourse. By the 1980s, in a much more conservative environment, it was going to be hard to displace even one family to build a new highway.

The first time I became aware of the Central Artery was as a college freshman in Boston. I remember going to the North End of Boston for Italian food a few times that year. Every time we took the subway to the North End and then back to the center of the city near City Hall. They seemed like two completely different worlds. Only much later did I realize that the North End and the center of the city were only a few blocks away from each other. But one of the "blocks" contained the overhead highway known as the Central Artery. This was a no-man's land. Sure there were some homeless people who lived under it and the area provided some parking for office workers during the day. But at night, we students never just walked those few blocks to the North—it seemed noisy, ugly, and unsafe.

A new plan for solving the problems of the Central Artery was developed in the 1980s. It called for putting the highway underground and expanding the number of lanes and its connectedness between downtown Boston and suburbs to the west and to the north. Because of the enormity of the project it was dubbed the Big Dig. It is the largest single municipal building project in United States history.

But to find political acceptance, it had to appeal to just about everyone. Even a small portion of the electorate opposing it could have scuttled the idea completely. While those who designed the Big Dig did not have the 8 Great Goods to guide them, they brilliantly had strong arguments for the Big Dig that appealed to all of the Greatest Goods.

Growth: Downtown merchants and business had been losing business for years because it was so difficult to get into and out of the city. The municipal area of Boston had identified the clogged highway system as one of the impediments to new businesses choosing to locate in the Boston area. A newer, bigger, better-connected highway system could create new opportunities for growth. By running the new highway through downtown Boston rather than circling the outskirts of the city, downtown business could actually attract new customers. The plans for the construction of the new highway called for the old overhead highway to remain in operation until the day the new underground system opened—local merchants were not required to close their shops for a single day while the project was implemented.

Relationships: The severed North End and central Boston would be reconnected as the eyesore Central Artery was buried. And the planners developed a highway and construction route that promised not to uproot even a single family from their current abode.

Belief: Religious organizations had been some of those most vocally opposed to the destruction of neighborhoods and family homes when the Central Artery was built in the 1950s. There was no opposition to this plan. The powerful Catholic Church was a proponent of the Big Dig as it would restore neighborhoods and make the city– their strongest traditional neighborhoods—more livable. From an ethical point of view, the city and state strove to make all contracting processes as transparent as possible.

Joy: There had been little joy in the long commute times or the ugly nature of the green-painted overhead highway. The plans for the Big Dig called for burying the highway and then after tearing down the elevated highway structure, the ground that had for years been the shadows of the highway was designated as park land.

Individuality: One commonly heard alternative to the Big Dig had been to abandon the highway system completely and allow only public transportation into the city. In an individualistic American economy that is built around the use of the car, this alternative was generally less desirable than finding a way for individual automotive transportation.

Stability: While those most enamored with Stability are not happy to see any change, here was a change that would rehabilitate the area surrounding the Central Artery—one of the more lawless areas of Boston. The police were convinced that this change would lead to lower crime rates and easier enforcement of the law.

Equality: There was a promise with this construction that no homes would be lost; businesses would remain open; and in the end those in the North End would finally be able to participate in the economic benefits of being in downtown Boston again.

Life: Of course, all of this construction and upheaval had to be conducted with a strict eye toward safety and security of the citizens and workers. The Big Dig construction project lasted for sixteen years. During that time four construction workers were killed—and one early user of the new underground highway died when her car was struck by a loose overhead panel. This was an unnecessary loss. But contrast these five lives to the number of lives lost in other engineering projects of this type: ten people lost their lives in the construction of the Chunnel between Britain and France; 34 Japanese construction workers died building the tunnel connecting Hokkaido to the main island of Honshu.

The point here is that if you can find a way to propose an idea or project that taps positively into all 8 Goods, you have a much higher chance of success.

A major premise of this book is that we live in a world where the people around us have different priorities from our own. Any attempts to live with or work with others will be chock-full of trade-offs. Sometimes we will have to sacrifice our own Greatest Good for the harmony and peace. But if we can come up with compromises that allow others to get to their Greatest Good without having to give up our own, all the better.

Chapter Nine: Getting to consistency

It may seem odd that I would follow up a chapter on compromise and trade-offs with one about consistency. But this is one more example of the complexity of this 8 Great Goods world we live in. We are going to have to give in to make things work with other people. But the more clear and consistent we personally can be—and our organizations and communities can be, the easier it will be to fit in and even easier to work with others.

In trying to live harmoniously with others, it would seem a perfect chameleon would be the perfect strategy. Just accept what everyone around you wants/likes and you'll always fit in. But we love literature and movies partly because we love the puzzle of trying to figure out who someone really is at their core. We have these big brains that are mostly designed to understand and work with people around us. So if we only see a mirror when we look at another person, only the most narcissistic of us would *not* be bored by the interaction. We like things that challenge and push our horizons. We like solving the dilemmas of trying to get along with someone different than us. Compromise and trade-offs allow us to be socially innovative and find solutions to problems that are truly creative. We wouldn't be human if we couldn't make these trade-offs. Nature has designed us that way.

Context

So it should not be a surprise that we've developed a broad range of coping mechanisms for various social situations. And it turns out that we give ourselves a lot of leeway in prioritizing our Goods from one situation to the next.

In a 2009 of the surveys of 1000 Americans that I conducted, I asked respondents to list their Goods priorities in the abstract and then in five different contexts. Here were the five different scenarios.

1) You just lost your job
2) You are voting for the next leader of your community or country
3) You have just been arrested for a crime you did not commit
4) You just got home after a long hard day at work
5) Your child was diagnosed with a potentially fatal disease

Not surprisingly, when our respondents considered that they had just lost a job, Growth and Life become more important Goods for them than they had been before. When imagining themselves voting for a community leader, Relationships and Stability were more important. If they had just been arrested, Equality became key. And if a child had a serious health problem, understandably Life rose to the fore.

I Probably Won't Change into You

None of these are big surprises; our priorities will vary rather significantly based on the context in which we are placed. But, to me, a more interesting finding of the survey was that individual variations based on context turned out to be less than the priority differences from person to person.

In addition to asking survey respondents to rank their own priorities ideally and contextually, we also asked them to list priorities that they attributed to the people around them. (In a follow-up to the survey, we asked some of the respondents to define "people around me." They reported that they were thinking of family, neighbors, and people in their town when they answered the survey.) There was a quite a large gap between personal priorities and the respondent's perceived priorities of others—on average an 18 point difference (or delta).

To get to that number, I calculated that if a respondent said that Belief was their top priority, but they responded that it was the 7th priority for those around them, that would be a 6 point difference. If Individuality was #2 for them and #3 for those around them, there would be a 1 point difference. Then, I added up the difference in rankings between self-reported priorities and the perceived rankings of others. And that averaged to an 18 point difference for all the respondents to the survey.

What is interesting here is the average difference (delta) between personal "ideal" prioritizations and the prioritizations in contexts is only 12 points versus the 18 point difference between self evaluation and ranking of others. In other words, no matter how much context changes our way of thinking about the Greatest Goods, it usually doesn't change us into another person. We do not become like Jekyll and Hyde when we are placed in different situations in our lives.

Those who were likely to have an 18 point or more swing between their ideal to their contextual priorities (as big a difference as they saw between themselves and others) also were statistically different from those with lower point spreads in the following ways:

- Younger
- Less energetic
- Less sense of humor
- Less loving
- Less independent
- More critical
- Less self-aware
- More financially successful
- Less likely to report themselves as "always happy"
- More comfortable with life's ups and downs
- Not as likely to consider themselves "part of a revolution" at work
- Much more willing to steal something of value from their workplace

Generally those who think of themselves as more in touch with themselves and others changed their priorities less based on context; while those more comfortable with change and more focused on financial success were more likely to reassign their priorities in different life situations.

While there are some natural prioritization shifts that we all make in different life scenarios, for the most part we are more consistent than not. That is a good thing.

If you are a Joy person, I am not suggesting here that you should keep Joy at the top of your list even though you just learned that your daughter has a serious illness. It is normal that Life would shoot to the top. But don't forget your base-line priorities.

In fact, if you are changing your prioritizations too often, my guess is that you are making someone around you pretty crazy. You can imagine the frustrations of being an employee or leader in an organization where the policy was: "we'll decide everything at that moment based on the mood we happen to be in."

The fact is that our stability-seeking selves like to have a clear set of rules.

We like to know that when A is happening, B will also occur. Most of us are a lot more comfortable when the A and B link is somewhat predictable. And when a lot of people have to make decisions and buy in to carry out those decisions, that consistency becomes more important than ever.

Big Issues

I designed a web application to test a theory of mine about how we apply the 8 Great Goods to our political decisions. You can find it at www.great8it. com. Users of the site were asked to fill out their own personal 8 Great rankings. Based on those rankings, the program predicts a user's position on five topical issues at the time I built the site. Let me give you an example.

One user (drawn at random) prioritized their 8 Goods as follows:

1) Joy
2) Relationships
3) Life
4) Individuality
5) Growth
6) Equality
7) Belief
8) Stability

Based on that ranking of the 8 Great Goods, our application predicted that this person would take the following stands on these five public debates:

AGAINST the Arizona Immigration Law
FOR allowing a Muslim Community Center near Ground Zero
FOR Health Care Reform in the US
AGAINST a Burqa ban in France
FOR giving the Nobel Prize to Liu Xiaobo

In a follow-up, this respondent reported that all five were actually her positions on those policy issues!

I know from feedback on this site that not all respondents felt that the program predicted their policy stances with 100% accuracy. But of those who reported back to me (about 30% of the total), only one respondent reported that three or *less* of their policy stances were predicted by the program. For all the rest, the program predicted correctly at least four out of their five policy stances.

In a few cases, the program seemed to have become a moment of enlightenment for them. One person, for example, reported that he was opposed to the Muslim Community Center near Ground Zero but the program predicted he should be FOR it. The website lists the arguments for and against a particular issue broken down by each of the 8 Goods. He had ranked Belief and Individuality as very high in his priorities and both of those Goods should be rather supportive of a Muslim Center. Belief suggests that there should be a place where someone can go to worship and be with other believers. Individuality says that each person should be able to make his or her own decisions and government should really stay out of the issue. In his personal rankings, Relationships and Stability were below Belief and Individuality. A Relationships priority might oppose the Center on the basis of loyalty or solidarity with the families of the victims of the 9/11. A Stability argument might be that building the center could provoke a violent reaction.

As this respondent looked at these arguments in light of his 8 Great Goods prioritization, he reported that he actually changed his position on this issue. Mostly because of Belief and Individuality. He felt that he if were to expect the right to worship where and how he pleases, others should have that right too. It was a bit of a eureka-moment for him. And it helped him to keep his 8 Goods priorities consistent.

In the first chapter of this book, I told the stories of eight people who have pretty predictable decision-making patterns—all along the lines of the 8 Great Goods. These are all real people...friends and family of mine. And it is reassuring to know that: they'll basically be the same people no matter what their mood or mine; that they still can be a lot of fun; and, that they will all (although to varying degrees) try new experiences and challenge themselves with new ways of thinking. But, in the end, I know they will basically be who they are all the time.

And that makes my life richer.

John C Beck

Chapter Ten: Deciding to Prioritize

By this point in the book, some of you have probably thought pretty carefully about your personal priorities. But if you haven't done it yet, now is the time to write down a list of your Greatest Goods. Don't just do it in your mind, literally write them down. You can even go to www.great8it.com and see what your prioritization might mean to your position on various current issues. But as you've already guessed, this will take you a little bit of time ... and that fact alone will probably stop you in your tracks.

It's About Time

At the beginning of the book I talked about the importance or attention in decision-making but that is even further exacerbated by the pressures of time facing all of us. Even sitting down to prioritize your 8 Goods may seem like a waste of time. Whether it is about personal, business or policy choices, all the rational decision-making models in the world fall apart really quickly as soon as the pressure of time is introduced.

Time and attention constraints are not new—for any organism. You see a similar pattern in the animal kingdom; a lion charging a herd of gazelles can't pay attention to all of them. The lion that tries to chase them all will starve. So, instead, the big cat will quickly prioritize the potential prey according to its most useful algorithm: the young or infirm animals become the immediate focus of the attacking animal. Likewise, our ancestors learned to make split-second decisions to capture game and to save their own lives. Patterns, mental models and prioritization were the keys to those quick decisions—and they still are today.

Common wisdom holds that a complex problem must be solved with a complex method. However, according to Gerd Gigerenzer, of the Max Planck Institute for Human Development, this does not have to be the case. Gigerenzer examined the incredibly complex decision trees that physicians in a coronary care unit use to determine whether to admit a patient or not. He found that the same physicians were able to make better decisions about admitting patients when using a much simpler decision tree. More information is not always better, and sometimes a quick and easy heuristic method is a more effective approach. As Gigerenzer put it: "In order for an animal or human to make a good prediction, some information must be ignored." (Gloss, 2008)

How We Like to Decide

Like doctors and lions, anyone living in a complex, fast-paced world probably seeks to limit the range and number of alternatives to which they give attention. There are just too many alternatives to consider in almost any given moment. We humans are at least as good as lions at coming up with time-saving decision heuristics. We use them all the time. The most common are: choose what has always been done in the past, opt for something different but most familiar, or use a rule to make the decision.

The easiest time/attention saving method in a complex decision is simply to keep doing the same thing you've been doing. Rather than having to analyze a new situation to understand the good and the bad, we cling to the old. It worked well enough in the past, so it seems easier and safer than having to expend the energy to understand the implications of a change. In an organization or in politics, this is usually safer too. You'll rarely be criticized for not changing fast enough, but if you change something and it fails, guess who gets all the blame.

Looks familiar

When we really can't "stay the course" any more—when we are REALLY can't keep doing what we used to be doing—when we really have to make a new decision in a complex environment, we end up relying on frameworks, categorizations, and priorities. If there is an alternative that looks more familiar—more like what has been done successfully in the past—we'll likely choose that. The best way to get a new book published is to write one that looks a lot like another bestseller. The best way to get venture capital money is to propose a business that looks a lot like another successful one. In interpersonal terms, we will decide to work with people most like ourselves because we think they'll behave most like we would. In a multicultural/ multiracial world, this ends up looking a lot like discrimination, but it is a pretty natural decision heuristic. We have to actively work at overcoming our natural bias toward what looks and seems familiar.

The rule

Even on decisions that have very little to do with future success, life or death, we develop formulas. A few years back, I remember being on the wrong side of one of these formulas. I had a new security system put into my house and it was badly installed. Within the first two weeks there were two electrical system problems that resulted in false alarms. Both times the police arrived. A few weeks later the dog set off the alarm by mistake and the police arrived again; soon after the city issued a fine for the city services of the police's visits due to three false alarms. Since the first two were really the alarm company's fault, I appealed the penalty; I argued that the alarm company should be fined, not me.

I appeared before the appeals committee. I explained my story. They had one question: "So you admit that the third alarm was your fault?" I couldn't deny that it was. Their decision: "You need to pay the fine. The rule is that you can appeal the third alarm only—we don't care about the cause of the first two. Since you admit that the third was your fault, you must pay the fine."

Goals First, then Data

The alarm appeals committee had developed a clear goal and a very smart process that eliminated the need for huge amounts of data. With the goal clear (eliminate false alarms through fines)—and the rule well established (only consider the third false alarm)—they only needed one piece of information to make a final decision.

Unfortunately, applying this theory in most personal or organizational lives suggests that we need to find more data to make a case for change. Waffling and indecision are rarely about lack of data—even though we as decision-makers often claim that is the problem. When we have troubles making a decision it is more often because we lack well-formed goals. If the goals are really clear, decisions can often be made immediately based on the current information on hand.

This is one of the reasons that the 8 Great Goods can be such a powerful tool. It will take you a little time and attention to do your prioritization of the 8 Great. But once you are comfortable with your choices, you will be well on your way to making decisions with more clarity and more speed than ever before in your life.

Makes Me Emotional

Even with a clear set of priorities and goals there are still some natural obstacles on the road to a final decision. For one thing, it is tough to stay focused on them when emotions are involved. Partly, this is just the way that the brain works.

Those who study the activity of the brain during decision-making have found that there seems to be a signal coming from outside of the parietal lobes (the seat of rational decision-making) that would appear to "short circuit or delay" the decision slightly. Researchers theorize that this might be an emotional interjection into the decision-making process. (Wang, Coble, & Bello, 2006)

It is not just that the brain seems to let emotions interfere with rational decisions, our social selves are designed to connect and decide based on emotions. J.M. Barbalet put it better than I ever could:

> "Emotion is central to social processes not only in being central to identity and affiliation, in which its role is frequently acknowledged, but also in being the necessary basis of social action and in being responsible for the form action takes." (Barbalet, 2001, p. 65)

None of this is new news. Leaders have always known that if they can heighten emotion in their followers they can accomplish amazing things with very little resistance. Even when a decision flies directly in the face of the most important priorities of a nation or a culture, if the emotional level is high enough, there is a chance to flout all the current rules and conventions. For instance, there is no way that the Patriot Act, which passed after 9-11, would have flown through Congress on September 10, 2001. It might not even have passed a year after the tragedy. But in the heat of the moment, when the US felt under attack, to all but one Senator (Russ Feingold), it felt downright unpatriotic to vote against the bill—even though it took away rights to individual privacy that had been protected in the US for two centuries.

The use of emotion in decisions is not just limited to changing long-held mores; it is a powerful tool for political confrontation, as well as the breakdown of a system of priorities that holds a society in peaceful equilibrium, but that can be weakened by confrontation. The more emotional the issue, the more likely a confrontational policy will be adopted. Nikolas Zahariadis, in his 2005 book used the example of Greek opposition to the name Macedonia in the early 1990s to show how confrontation can be born of emotion. (Zahariadis, 2005) More recently, the brewing tensions between Japan and China may be rationally based, in part, on Japan's displacement as Asia's supreme economic power. But the relationship doesn't really become confrontational until the Chinese evoke images of past Japanese atrocities.

In terms of the 8 Great Goods, there are two important points on emotion: 1) if you want to keep yourself or others focused on rational priorities, be on guard for emotional arguments that will naturally sway the debate; 2) if you want to change the prioritization of Goods, emotional issues will be important in dislodging an entrenched set of priorities.

Simple, Stupid

While simplicity is important even in individual priority setting, when you get more than one person involved in the process, the rules have to be even simpler, and sometimes that means they may seem almost stupid. In the case of the false alarm appeals committee, I, as a complete outsider, may have disagreed with the very simple policy—I even thought it *was* stupid—but I cannot say that I did not comprehend it.

When the decision-making prioritizations are less rule-based and more cultural, it may be even more difficult for outsiders to comprehend. And if you are not steeped in a local culture, they may seem more stupid than ever. Anyone who has ever tried to work with someone from another culture probably knows the feeling. Not only is language not conveying everything, you get the feeling that there is something going on in the room that is understood by everyone else, but that you're just not getting. Sure, we all know there are shared behaviors in every culture, but the issue here is more than behavior, it is how the decision-making process takes place. If you don't know the code … the algorithm … the mindset, you can't possibly comprehend how the outcomes are like they are.

In my very first non-US job, I was the beneficiary of this misunderstanding, but it still shows how a different prioritization of Goods can lead to a rather hard to understand outcome.

The mistake

One summer when I was in college, I got a summer internship as the Assistant Systems Manager at the American Embassy in Tokyo. They had a Systems Manager, Mr. Itoh, who only spoke Japanese. Since some of the most important people in the Embassy were Americans who didn't speak Japanese, they needed someone to teach them how to use the new computer system.

Then, it was normal to backup the computer and turn it off at the end of the workday and turn it back on the next morning. Since there were just two of us in the computer section, we split of the tasks of running and maintaining the computer functions. So in addition to the training, I had the job of starting up the computer system every morning. At night Mr. Itoh would turn off the system and then I'd come in about 6 AM the next day and turn it back on. Sometimes if there was work being done overnight, I'd find the system already on in the morning when I arrived.

One morning in early September I arrived to find the computer system on. When I looked at the logs it appeared there was quite a lot of activity, particularly in the Translation Section. This was back in the days when all the computer programs were stored centrally on the server and each workstation was nothing more than a screen and a keyboard because all the computing power was in the mainframe computer. So from the central computer terminal I could see exactly which workstations were active, and who was accessing which program. Seeing all the activity in the Translation Section, I figured the staff had an urgent deadline on a big report.

About 7 o'clock AM a call came in from a secretary in the Agriculture Section who always arrived early and played a game on the computer. However, there was a bug in the game software and her workstation would freeze up. She would always call to ask me to reset her workstation. I would highlight her workstation on my master terminal and touch the F7 to reboot her machine.

So I did what I did almost every morning and hit the F7 key. But then my workstation suddenly went black and the entire system started to reboot. I realized that I hit the F8 key instead of the F7 key—unfortunately, the F8 key rebooted all the workstations on the system instead of just rebooting hers.

The aftermath

I was just glad it was so early in the morning, before everyone had arrived to work. But then I heard a flurry of activity in the hallway. First Itoh-san ran into the room and asked what happened. I'd never seen Itoh-san in the office before 9 AM. Ever. I explained my mistake and he looked worried and ran out of the room and down the hall. Next, the top administrative guy in the embassy, Mr. Johnson, poked his head in and asked where Itoh-san was. I pointed down the hall. He ran too.

Now I was worried. As the computers were coming back online again I could see that more than 100 workstations were in use on the system. This was not a normal morning. After about 10 minutes, Mr. Johnson came back into the computer room looking really bothered. He sat down in Itoh-san's chair—which he never did—and told me that tomorrow would be Itoh-san's last day. He had just fired him.

He went on to give me the context. During the previous night, a straying Korean Airline, Flight 007—a 747 passenger jet—was shot down by the Soviet Union. All of the information was in Japanese so the translation section had been busy all night. These were still in the early days of computers and there was no automatic save function. So when the system was turned off, hundreds of hours of translation were wiped out. Mr. Johnson told me that Mr. Itoh had admitted to pressing the wrong button and there was nothing he could do but fire him.

Without even thinking I blurted out "Well Itoh-san didn't reset the system. I did. You can't fire him." Mr. Johnson shot back immediately: "Why would he admit to a mistake when he didn't do it?" All i could say, shrugging my shoulders, was: "Because he's Japanese?

In the days following the incident President Reagan was criticized for his delayed announcement of the Korean Airline incident. In fact, without the translations from the embassy, the first government announcements were that the KAL jet had not been destroyed and had landed safely in Siberia. That was simply not true, but the mistake has led to years of conspiracy theory speculation about the passengers being held somewhere in Russia.

Starting to understand a little

In the end, Itoh-san was not fired. He had done nothing wrong. I was fired, but it didn't mean much. It was supposed to be the last day of my internship anyway, which makes Itoh-san's actions even less comprehensible to an American. The job was not my career. I was going back to school the next day, and—don't forget I, was the one who pressed the button! To me, Itoh-san's decision was just stupid. What would possess someone to take the blame under those circumstances?   I have been haunted by the question for most of my life.

It wasn't until I started thinking about the world in 8 Great Goods terms that, for the first time ever, I was able to answer the question in a slightly more comprehensible way. My greatest Goods at the time I worked for Itoh-san were things like: economic Growth, an ethical Belief that honesty is always the best policy, Individuality and Joy. None of those entered Itoh's mind when he took the blame for me. He had to have been thinking purely in Relationships terms. His interpersonal role with me was to be my boss, therefore he was responsible for me. Anything I did was ultimately his responsibility. Given his Greatest Good, he had to take the blame.

Chapter Eleven: Algorithms and Harmony

Once you've really spelled out your 8 Great, you may begin to notice benefits almost immediately. In addition to getting to decisions faster and with less conflict, you will also find that decisions actually stay "made" longer than before. And once you have made clear your most important Goods, you and the people around you are less likely to question the rationale. One of my favorite recent experiences was a CEO reminding everyone in the room that she had a policy against spending on advertising. She reiterated that she personally—and the organization—had never spent anything on advertising. I can assure you that no one challenged her decision the following day or the next week. A few people in the room clearly did not like the policy against advertising—they bravely nodded in agreement with somewhat pained faces—but they understood why that particular decision went the way it did.

A clear prioritization of the 8 Great can become policy. The ordering of the Goods itself can be basis of both strategic and tactical verdicts. And that clear prioritization can establish consistency of action and even "labeling" which may be useful for a person, organization or nation. ("He's the turnaround artist"; "That is a low cost company"; "They are a nation of friendly people.") And the longer these Goods' priorities stay in place the more likely they are to cast their shadow far into the future—even if the decision-making priorities are eventually changed.

Stuck in a Priority

Companies have seen how hard it is to get away from a long held strategic positioning even after trying to change their direction. One of my early consulting assignments was with Sears. The company was trying to change its image in the retail market. There was a real belief among the strategists in the Sears Tower than if the company didn't change its ways, it would cease to exist.

So the top executives set out to design a new strategy with a team of consultants. And in March of 1993, Arthur Martinez, then CEO of Sears outlined a five-pronged approach to the company's new strategy: customer focus, core business growth, cost reduction, responsiveness to local markets, and cultural renewal. Business cards were printed with the five-point strategy for employees to carry with them; posters were hung in offices and in employee areas of Sears stores around the world; and employee meetings were held to get them to understand and adopt the new corporate direction. The new strategy roll out was by the book: well funded, and organizationally supported.

Six months later, a survey was conducted to see how the new plan was being accepted. When employees were asked what they remembered most about the corporate strategy, the most common response was "Protecting the assets of the firm."

We as consultants knew that was NOT one of the five points of the new strategy. In fact, we had no idea where this phrase was coming from. It took more than a few conversations before we started to understand. "Protecting the assets of the firm" (definitely the Good of Stability) had been the battle cry at Sears in the 1960s and 1970s. (A retail strategy of "protecting assets" may explain exactly why Sears fared as it did in 1970s and 1980s!) By the early 1990s this catchphrase had still not gone away, and no six-month program of strategic change was about to wipe that long-term strategic thinking from the collective consciousness of the corporation.

Ultimately, it was an advertising slogan—"The softer side of Sears"—that finally helped customers and employees change the focus of their strategy from "protecting assets" to cultural renewal, customer focus, and responsiveness (much more Relationships, Individuality, and Growth priorities). With a change in focus, Sears turned itself around and runs a very successful operation today.

So be warned: if you create a Good priority and you get buy-in for that priority, it may be with you or your organization for a VERY long time.

Algorithms

There is a big cultural component to all of this as well. Once the Goods come to be ingrained in an individual, family, company, or community, whole algorithms about how to apply the priorities will emerge. Laws are the most concrete manifestation of our national and community priorities.

Rules reflect organizational priorities, and individual codes of conduct and behaviors are indicative of priorities at that level of analysis.

Figuring each other out

We all know just how complex the process of trying to predict how others will make a decision can be from all of our failed attempts. Even couples that have been married for decades will surprise each other sometimes with their choices. Decision-making—even on seemingly unimportant issues—is not an easy algebraic equation.

Second-guessing other people's algorithms is exactly what "governance" is supposed to be. Elected officials are supposed to vote the way their people would vote on issues of great importance. But it is impossible for them to predict how "the people" would really decide. And sometimes the results are far off the mark. Sure surveys are used to try to get at some of what people think, but they are imprecise, and for every survey question, minor changes in the way the question is worded could swing the decision in many different directions.

The Arizona Algorithm

Let's take Arizona State Bill 1070 (SB1070) as an example. This is the law that says government officials are required to ask about the immigration status of any individual they think might be in the country illegally; it opens those officials to criminal penalties and civil lawsuits for non-compliance. In June 2010 a poll found that 55% of Americans supported Arizona's new law. However, at the same time, a separate pool showed that 54% said the new law would lead to discrimination against Latinos. And only 48% thought it would reduce illegal immigration, with 50% saying it would not. So to recap: By democratic majority-rules laws, keep the law, even though we don't believe it will reduce illegal immigration and we believe it will lead to discrimination. Huh?

But look at what happens if we stop relying on public opinion polls and instead use the 8 Great Goods to try to understand an issue.

Complexity and its discontents

In the fall of 2010, I had a chance to moderate the discussion of a group discussing SB 1070. In the audience some people talked about immigrant's family members; some discussed economic hardships; some evoked Nazi images; some waved figurative American flags with every word out of their mouths. Each time a new person spoke up the entire room was engaged—but only until the speaker's side became clear. Then half tuned out, and half started nodding in agreement. You know how the story of one of these debates usually ends: some people leave even more confident in the ideas they came in with—and some leave even more fearful of the other side. The policy debate does not budge, but stress, fear, and anger grow nicely. It's enough to make citizens check out entirely.

I wanted to make this meeting different ... so, of course, I used a trite strategy employed by all moderators: "Let's step back for a moment. This room is full of good, important points of view. The problem is seeing how they might fit together. Can we think of a way to group all the concerns that we've heard so far?"

Trying to be a good facilitator, I didn't let anyone know my biases; for all they knew, I might even really be neutral. So people were actually listening with curiosity, as I began to write down single words: Life. Belief. Relationships. Stability. Equality. There were generally nods all around. People on both sides of the issue were agreeing with all of them—they are all truly good words.

I turned to the participants: "These are all good things. Think about your whole life—not just this issue, not even just politics. As you see it, which one of these good things is most important?" The answers were all over the map. About a quarter of the people raised their hands for Life. Many said Belief. Relationships and Growth got the next most votes, then Stability, and Individuality; quite a few said Equality; a few Joy.

Then, my most important question: "Probably all eight of these good things have something to do with immigration. But for our whole society, in making this one decision, which of the eight is *most* important?" Comments started to flow—but the room felt different. For each comment I put a check mark by one of the eight words. Soon there are many check marks next to just one or two of the words. I stepped back from the board and what I expected to happen did. I looked at the audience. Already a look of comprehension was crossing the faces of some in the room. The rest needed a little more explanation.

What if everyone is really trying to be "good" in this debate? What if the conflict isn't good vs. bad, but good vs. good? And what if we had a way of thinking about that conflict together?

Simple priorities

But can an entire nation really agree on how to rank the Goods? Absolutely not. Our survey of a representative sample of Americans asked them to rank the 8 Great Goods for their personal decision-making. Shockingly, the result was 872 unique patterns—from only 943 respondents. In other words, less than 10 percent shared their particular pattern with even one other person. We all see the perfect mix of goodness in completely different ways.

This brings us back to the troublesome Arizona law. As we saw in that meeting room, there were many perspectives on the issue, and each person might evaluate the whole mix differently, yet with great passion. This has split the state into two camps that really don't understand each other at all. Thousands of people have gathered and marched in favor of and in opposition to the bill. Homes of outspoken advocates, on both sides, have been vandalized. Hate mail has been common. People strongly believe that those opposing their point of view on this law are evil and wrong.

But we *can* get beyond that. Because if we're serious about reaching the best public decision we don't have to agree on the whole list of Goods, or how they play in this particular debate. Instead, we can use the perspective of the 8 Great Goods to focus on what the real, driving trade-offs are. Surprisingly, those may be things we can agree on. Often, certainly in the case of the Arizona law, just two or three Goods are clearly the most central. And that leads to surprising opportunities. Let's run down the list:

Life. The fact is there are no great life-death implications to the immigration law. Yes, illegal immigrants risk their lives to get across the border, but there is very little likelihood of them losing their lives during a deportation. There are potential "livelihood" implications of jobs and the ability to make a living, but no immediate life-death implications.

The one place I found a bit of real "fear for my life" mentality in all of this was in a conversation with a middle-class lesbian couple who would be considered liberal on any political scale, but firmly support SB 1070. They live in a neighborhood that is mostly Hispanic. That is not a problem for them—they chose to live there—but that neighborhood now boasts an increasingly transient and drug-gang quality. The couple blames this on illegal immigration. Shootings and gunfire in the neighborhood have them, to some extent, afraid for their lives.

Growth. Growth is certainly relevant to the immigration debate. The main reason that illegal immigrants come to the US is economic Growth—jobs that pay a lot better than in their home countries. People charged under this law would lose a chance for economic Growth. Illegal aliens' presence in the job market also results in Growth for US citizens; while it may bring down the wage levels for certain job categories, studies show it actually seems to increase wage levels in other categories.

Relationships. The majority of those marching in the streets to overturn Arizona's new law probably value Relationships above all else in this debate. Many of them know and love someone who is an illegal alien. Take Manuel, for example: he doesn't march in the streets, but nothing has made him angrier than this law. As a US citizen with an MBA from a top school and a great job, his position is safe, but his mother and father, who have been living in Arizona as long as he has, a couple of his siblings, and his uncles could be identified and deported at any moment. Another portion of those opposing this law do so because it is just "unkind" to people who live in our communities already. They point out that the law's passage only sends a message of hatred and divides the community.

Stability. Many of those fiercely supporting Arizona's new law do so because they value Stability. True, federal law on immigration is not too different from the new state law. But the law's advocates hope that SB 1070 will send a message to Washington, bringing stronger enforcement, which they assume will mean less law breaking and more Stability.

Joy. Joy has almost nothing to do with support or opposition to SB 1070. Deportation of a loved one would no doubt cause a dearth of happiness, but it is not a motivating force for opposing the law. There are those who support the law out of mean-spirited "fun," but again, a tiny group.

Individuality. There are both conservatives and liberals who oppose the Arizona law because of Individuality, saying things like "No one has a right to ask you or me to 'produce papers.'"

Belief. Belief plays almost no part in the immigration debate, except for the interesting and confused role of the Mormon Church. The Bill's main sponsor was Senator Russell Pearce, who cited the Church's Articles of Faith as part of the rationale for the bill. Mormon Church leaders have officially remained neutral. But the Church's missionary efforts, which largely rely on immigrant populations in the US for growth, are being stymied as word spreads in Hispanic communities that a Church member was the author of this legislation.

Equality. This Good shows us how the 8 Great can cut through the noise and allow some convergence on seemingly endless debates. Many of those supporting the rule that the police check papers see the issue as one of Equality; so do many of those opposing the law. And this leads to head-on conflict. Arizonans who support the bill for Equality's sake don't want to lose out on jobs because someone in the US illegally can work cheaply. Arizonans who oppose the bill for Equality's sake think that it is unfair that someone could be asked to produce papers just because of their skin color or their accent. The people with the biggest gripes about their opponents are those who support or oppose the law for the exact same Greatest Good reason.

Putting it to the test

In the hot-temperature and hot-tempered room of proponents and opponents of the Arizona law, I stood in front at the board where I had listed the 8 Goods in the order in which the group had voted at the beginning of the meeting. The group determined that they were comfortable with the order. The only major disagreement was the idea that Belief (in either a religious or an ethical sense) should come in second place. Tempers flared momentarily, so I asked the group to temporarily leave Belief in second place: "If that ordering has a big influence on the ultimate outcome, we can revisit this debate." Relative calm returned to the room. With the prioritization agreed upon, I turned back to the board and added a separate column and proceeded to write a summary of the discussion just completed:

Ranking of Good	Interpretation of Bill
Life	very slightly FOR
Belief	non-issue
Growth	no real impact—although there is a fear of negative growth driving some opposition
Relationships	strongly AGAINST
Stability	strongly FOR
Individuality	strongly AGAINST
Joy	non-issue
Equality	STRONG arguments on both sides

As I expected Belief, in this analysis, had very little to say for or against the law. So the disagreement over its prioritization meant little.

Stepping back from the board and looking at it carefully, I noted what almost everyone else in the room was already beginning to understand: "Overall, it appears that this 8 Great Goods analysis would argue for opposing the law; with two of the Goods strongly against the Bill and one strongly for it.

Life (which is very, very important) has a very small, but not insignificant role in supporting the Immigration Law."

One person asked: "If Life is such a potentially important swing vote in this decision, could legislation be rewritten to focus on enhancing the enforcement of all laws in neighborhoods where there is an abnormally high threat to life?" Oddly, even the most vehement proponents of the law did not raise their voices against this idea. And there was a sense of general acceptance around the room.

I looked at the group, "Most of you came into this room arguing one side or the other of the equality debate. Equality is important—it is one of the greatest goods in any society—but we all agreed that it may be less important than some other goods on the list."

"Now, some of you probably disagree with Equality's low priority. If the equity issue is still really important to you, I hope that you can at least see that both sides of the equality question are really about good things—the other side is not necessarily evil. If you feel strongly about this issue, you probably want 'equality' for your particular side... but is that really 'fair?'"

"According to our democratically agreed upon prioritization in this room, Society and Stability and Individuality all come much higher than Equality. If we can shift the debate to those Goods that we believe are more important, we may actually resolve this in a way that is satisfactory to all. And we can understand that for the greatest Good of Arizona there may be some different and clearer ways of resolving the great immigration debate."

After the meeting, there was a general atmosphere of understanding—if not acceptance—of the other side's position and a growing appreciation of how much each side ultimately wants to be good.

If we can be clear about our own priorities, and try to understand the priorities of others, it would be a positive first step in understanding the algorithms that drive human behavior. Being explicit about those priorities will make decisions easier, more efficient, and much less conflict-laden.

The Basic Rules of the 8 Great Goods

How do we resolve the inherent contradiction of being in a social world where each of us has such completely different definitions of what is good? How can we agree on anything? How can I keep my personal priorities unscathed when everyone around me believes in something quite different?

These are the basic big questions of all of social life. The 8 Great Goods do not answer those questions, but they do offer a way forward. Here are the basic steps:

1. Know what you want your own priorities to be.

2. Understand that you will have to make trade-offs between the Goods that are difficult and even gut-wrenching.

3. Try to keep your own priorities consistent regardless of context or

the issue at hand.

4. Be willing to try to find ways to achieve your Greatest Good even while a friend or a coworker is trying to achieve their own top priority at the same time.

5. Compromise when you have to, but return to your original priority set as soon as you can.

6. If your environment or thinking changes significantly, do not be afraid to change your priorities, but understand that the people around you will be confused for a while.

7. Realize that even those with different priorities are still trying to pursue a life that is just as good as your own. Always treat them with respect.

Section III

Goods in Countries:
Rules of Top Priorities

John C Beck

Chapter Twelve: Nations and the 8 Great

The great Arizona Immigration debate is a perfect example of how our individual Goods get elevated to social conversations that sometimes result in government policies and laws. Those laws not only reflect our societal prioritization of Goods, but they also become the source of labels, consistency, and harmony for all of us living in any nation on earth. And when we have to make trade-offs between our personal Goods and national Goods, a clear well-stated national or community prioritization can help keep tensions far from a boiling point.

In this section, I'll talk about how nations apply the Great 8. But this discussion could just as easily be about regions, cities, neighborhoods, or even companies. When you apply the Great 8 to larger groups of people, clear prioritization drives understanding and consistency.

In January 2010, I was a participant in an after-dinner conversation with a billionaire, a former ambassador, a Harvard Kennedy School professor, a couple of Lee Kuan Yew School of Public Policy professors, and two young adults. The conversation topic, posed by the host, was a name-the-best-government-in-the-world contest. Okay, it was supposed to be a conversation, but it took on a competitive hue as each person at the table avoided replicating a previously nominated nation. I was near the end of the queue and I can assure you that I was racking my brain as each consecutive contestant usurped my nominee nations one by one.

At the time of this dinner, I had already started my research on the 8 Great, but this one contest/conversation cemented my belief in the relevance of my theory. On my way home that night, I realized that the countries a bunch of pretty bright and well-read experts in their fields listed, just happened to be perfect representatives of the 8 Great Goods.

Making the Switch to Policy

At the time of that dinner, I was a Professor and Senior Advisor at the Lee Kuan Yew School of Public Policy in Singapore. I was a bit of a manatee out of water during my tenure. For 20 years before that I had made a career of teaching MBA students and executives in eight business schools around the world. The students who sat in my public policy classrooms did not look or sound all that different from the groups I had become accustomed to. The national mix was not unlike the mix I had in my business school classes. But the discussions were completely different. It took me a while to understand the dissimilarities, but I finally put my finger on it: business school students all fundamentally agree on the end goal of any decision—public policy students do not.

MBAs measure their success in any case study by economic growth (revenue and/or profit). Students of government (many of whom, like their MBA counterparts, have been in the profession for 5 or 6 years before going back to school) seem to have little consensus around the end-goals. They spend most of their case-study discussion time trying to develop the correct process without a clear end-goal.

Process versus goals

This is not to say that discussions in a public policy classroom were unhappy events. For one thing, they felt less cutthroat: MBAs (and Executive Education participants) will gladly rip each other apart over a financial error or strategically non-competitive suggestion. But my Masters of Public Administration students were actually kind during the discussions. I left the room smiling and feeling good about the give-and-take of the interaction.

Only after I got back to my office, did the feel-good haze clear. Then, I realized that we really decided nothing; or that we came up with a process to study the decision more carefully in the future and involve more people in the decision-making. For instance, once we discussed the case of an educational reform that improved student test scores in inner-city schools by 40%. In an MBA classroom, this would have been an unqualified success story—and we would have spent most of the group's time looking for ways to import the best-practices of this case into other organizations. But for my policy students, there was sturm and drang—the process of school reforms had not been inclusive, it was top-down with "many constituents unrepresented." The process should have been better!

The former state of management science

It was only a few decades ago that state of the art management science was in the same place as public policy is now. The emphasis of good management thinking was process (how to structure the organization, efficiency, management processes). These are all good things—necessary to a high performing company. But if the true end goal of the company is flawed—if a business is pursuing an "unwinnable" strategy—all of the focus on good process will be squandered.

Starting in the 1960s, management scientists began to articulate the need for a match between what the company was doing in the external world (this came to be known as "strategy") and how it was managing its internal world (structure). Before this realization, the term strategy was never applied to business. Now you can't turn around in a company without bumping into a strategy.

The problem in many public institutions and even national governments today is that you can't bump into a true externally-facing strategy even if you turn around a lot. There will be meeting after meeting about how to structure and how to run the process. But the "goal" is usually something as amorphous as "good governance."

Show me the strategy

Successful businesses know their strategy—low cost, best technology, biggest market share, highest customer satisfaction. And companies have been taught to measure against these goals almost *ad nauseum*. But government organizations have few clear goals—and the goals that do exist are not designed to differentiate them from other similar government organizations around the world.

The one national strategy—or Greatest Good—that is used with some real frequency is economic growth. We can debate whether "growth" really is a smart and sustainable national goal in an inherently finite world. But at least this does give some measurable indicator of success.

Not surprisingly, this is the same highest priority Good of many businesses. But they've realized that they have to choose clearly different ways from their competitors to achieve revenue and profitability growth—these are business strategies. And the message of a successful corporate strategy is communicated throughout the organization. Employee's careers are made or broken by their ability to maintain focus on those strategic goals and deliver end results.

Not so in government. While economic growth is espoused as an important "definition of victory" in many nations, not all parts of the government focus on that goal as single-mindedly as they would if they were parts of a large business organization. And, in governments, there is much less consensus that "growth" really should vie with many other Goods that governments want to deliver to their people: stability, equality, individual rights, health, happiness, community building and the right to pursue their beliefs and causes.

That said, there are actually patterns in policy that do emerge in nations. They are not as clear as they should be. If the decision-making process were more focused (something I'll discuss in Section Four), these nations could all be much better at achieving their prioritized set of Goods. But even without strong strategic direction, it is interesting to me that nations have adopted such a differentiated set of Goods as their greatest. I think you'll see in this section, that all of the 8 Goods are viable contenders for producing strong national strategies.

Knowing National Greatest Goods

How can we understand the "Great Goods" of a country? If we are talking about an individual, it is pretty easy to ask them how they prioritize these. And if we are talking about an organization, the leaders of a corporation could prioritize these formally—usually with Growth being the most important. But a country is bigger, less centralized, and less profit driven than a corporation. It seems like it would be harder to judge.

Historical behaviors of governments—laws and policies—are the best way I have found to understand government Goods. That is what you'll find in the chapters that follow. The first nation I discuss—Japan—is a good example of a pattern that you'll see in the other countries that I describe here as well. I want to stay really focused on nations here. As such, when I talk about the

Great Goods of a country, I'm not really talking about the cultural issues—I am focusing more on the legal systems and the decision-making apparatus of the nation.

It is hard to tease apart culture and government in most places. It is a very chicken and egg distinction; a little like the Church and State division that the US Constitution requires. The Founding Fathers, while trying to separate the two, included regular references to God in their state building documents, mottos, and imagery. Culturally, these men were church-going, Bible-reading folk. So a lot of their culture found its way into the government that they were designing. But they were logically trying to draw a distinction. They knew that Head of State and Head of Church were the same in England. And they were doing everything they could to be different from their former oppressor. They wanted the laws—the decision-making systems—of the country to be separate from that of any church.

In these descriptions of countries that follow, I am going to try to avoid the cultural explanation and keep the focus on policy. But you will see: that is easier said than written.

John C Beck

Chapter 13: Life and Japan

It is difficult to say that there is one country that necessarily epitomizes a focus on "life" as its Greatest Good. Every country is about the protection and lives of its people. Every society comes into being—at least in part—as a haven where the strong can protect the weak and everyone looks out for each other. So why would I go and choose Japan as a place where the emphasis is more on Life than on the other Great Goods? Strong cases could equally be made that Growth, Relationships, or Stability are Japan's greatest Goods—strong enough that they warrant a short discussion before we turn to Life.

The Government's Role

If I were writing this chapter twenty years ago, I might have been persuaded that Growth was Japan's greatest good. The country had come from utter destruction to world economic domination in thirty years. People referred to the country as Japan Inc. and corporations as the main players in the society. It seemed that everything was designed for Japan to grow economically. But all of that ended in the early 1990s. Since then economic growth rates have been among the slowest in the developed world. Yet, the lifestyle of the average Japanese person has arguably improved for the last 20 years. Japanese work fewer hours, live in better homes, have more and better cars, commute fewer hours, shop in better stores, and—most importantly—live longer than they did in the 1980s. Something besides Growth seems to be at work in Japan today.

Japanese society is also known for being highly disciplined, orderly, and unflinchingly structured. Japan's trains and subways (even buses, amazingly!) arrive and leave within seconds of the scheduled time. Japanese hierarchy is about as clear cut as any on earth—deference is paid to those older and those who are older (up to retirement at least) are charged with protecting those who are younger and inculcating them with values and behaviors that make them contributing members of nation. If you're the same age as someone else, then you defer to the person who went to the better college or the better high school—there is a meritocratic categorization that every Japanese person knows all too well. So why would Japan's greatest good NOT be Relationships or even Stability—it seems like a rigorously structured society. And one adage that even the occasional visitor to Japan has heard is that the "nail that sticks up should be hammered down." This points to a need for Equality and fairness

These observations suggest that the Greatest Good in Japan might be something other than Life. But mostly, these behaviors are social not governmental. Japanese culture is heavy on social relationships, structure, and equality; but when we look at what the government enforces, it is—more than any other nation on earth—really focused on keeping people alive. Government mandates and policies are written and enacted with more of a premium on Life than any other place on earth.

Legislating against War

It all starts with Japan's Constitution. It is the most pro-life in the world. The basic law of the land is about peace and non-aggression—even to protect its own sovereignty, offensive hostility is not warranted.

The Preamble to the Constitution starts with these words (italics added):

> "We, the Japanese people, acting through our duly elected representatives in the National Diet, determined that we shall secure for ourselves and our posterity the fruits of *peaceful cooperation* with all nations and the blessings of liberty throughout this land, and resolved that *never again shall we be visited with the horrors of war* through the action of government, do proclaim that sovereign power resides with the people and do firmly establish this Constitution."

> "We, the Japanese people, *desire peace for all time* and are deeply conscious of the high ideals controlling human relationship, and we have determined to preserve our security and existence, *trusting in the justice and faith of the peace-loving peoples* of the world. We desire to occupy an honored place in an international society striving for the *preservation of peace*, and the banishment of tyranny and slavery, oppression and intolerance for all time from the earth."

> "We recognize that all peoples of the world have the *right to*

live in peace, free from fear and want."

Then Article Nine of the Japanese Constitution, ratified shortly after the end of the Second World War, takes this even a step further. It formally renounces war and war potential, and specifically forbids Japan from ever again maintaining land, sea, or air forces.

Since then, Japan has actually built up an all-volunteer "Self Defense" force of 250,000 people on land, sea, and in the air. One percent of the country's GDP is spent on this civilian-led force. Japan has now developed one of the most technologically sophisticated militaries on earth.

But, the Japanese population still is largely opposed to war. There is some evidence that younger people (those whose parents don't even remember World War II) are likely to be slightly more hawkish than earlier generations, but still Japan, by and large, is a country that doesn't even like to see their Self Defense Forces deployed in other countries for any military activity. When they are sent abroad to support the United Nations peacekeeping activities, for instance, they are always involved in non-lethal activities. Issues of peace and war are still major drivers of election outcomes in Japan. The ouster of US military forces from the southern island of Okinawa was a campaign promise that helped to elect Yukio Hatoyama and his Democratic Party in 2009; and it was due to his backtracking on that promise that his popularity level plummeted to support from less than 25% of the populace.

War and Peace and War and Peace and …

Culturally and historically, Japan is not necessarily a peace loving society. Anyone who has read about World War II would have troubles thinking of Japan as peaceable place. But the expansionary, imperialistic philosophy that started after Japan opened to the West in the 1870s and culminated in the 1940s, was a 70 year period of aggression following a 250 year period of peace. The Tokugawa Era in Japan, sometimes called Pax Nipponica, was the longest era of peace in any country in recorded human history. This peaceful era immediately followed a period known as the Warring States Era, which you can imagine was a bit less serene. What most people in the world don't realize is that during the "samurai era" of the Tokugawa shogunate, the samurai never really got to fight. They practiced swordplay a lot—but most of their days were spent in tea ceremonies, writing poetry, and (naturally) political machinations. Never did they get to engage in actual war.

It is a bit like there is a Peace-War switch, a light switch if you will, in Japan. When it is on, the light of peace is radiant. Japan is a beacon, and example of non-aggression for the world. When it is off, the culture is belligerent and bloodthirsty.

After World War II, it was not necessarily the Japanese people's choice to adopt a Peace Constitution. Left to their own devices, they may not have. But as the only recipient of nuclear warfare in the world, the Japanese capitulated completely. They fully expected to become the 49th state of the United States.

The mindset of the immediate post war era is exemplified by a story I heard years ago about General McArthur's first triumphal motorcade into Japan. On August 30, 1945—just weeks after the atomic bombs—McArthur landed at Atsugi Air Force Base and then had to drive a few miles to his temporary Occupation Government headquarters. Along the motorcade route, Emperor Hirohito's Imperial soldiers were posted in tight formations along both sides of the road. As McArthur's car would near, the Japanese soldiers would turn their backs to his car. McArthur was reportedly incensed. He expected the soldiers to face him and bow or salute, but turning their backs was a deep insult to him. Later a trusted advisor set him straight. The Imperial soldiers were trained to act exactly this way when the Emperor passed. They would turn their backs and avert their eyes as a sign of respect. But in this case there was an added rationale for their behavior. The Imperial guard was now entrusted with protecting McArthur and as such, they also were turning their backs on the motorcade to keep an eye on the crowds lining the route—a crowd that had recently lost loved ones to McArthur's military. It was not unreasonable to think that someone along the way might be unhappy about his arrival in Tokyo. The soldiers were turning their backs so they could thwart any assassination attempt.

In the two weeks following the end of the war, Japanese military mindset had gone from "kill all Americans" to "save the US general." That is an amazing pendulum swing. Will Japan's pendulum swing back to militaristic warmongering? Yes, probably. But we are less than 70 years into this cycle. If this period of peace is only half as long as Japan's last peace period, most of us will never live to see that change.

Life Goes On and On and On

Perhaps it is this religious and cultural background that has ensured that Japanese cycles of peace have been longer than their cycles of war. Furthermore, it is possibly these cultural beliefs that ensure that government rules and practices have a very pro-life component to them.

Generally, Japanese traditional religious beliefs are life affirming to all kinds of life—human, animal, and even plant. The native religion of Japan is Shintoism, which holds sacrosanct all of nature. To be in touch with nature is to be close to the gods. Natural objects (animate and inanimate) are worshiped as sacred spirits.

Buddhism was introduced to Japan in the sixth century, and the Japanese were quick to adopt the parts of Buddhist teaching that dealt with the spirits of the living and the dead with regard to people and animals. The Buddhist teaching of revering all life as part of a grand cycle resonated with traditional Japanese beliefs. But now the Japanese had even more reason to avoiding hurting or killing a lower life form (or even a lower status human being) because, according to Buddhist teachings, in your next life you may come back in a similarly lowly station. Every living being should be treated with respect.

Japan is certainly not the only culture with deep-rooted beliefs in the sanctity of nature. But it is certainly one of the few modern nations where average citizens maintain a sense of animal and plant deities. And while the Japanese don't report that they are for the most part deeply religious, the idea of natural spirits does stir their imaginations. Hayao Miyazaki's animated shorts and full-length movies often feature these animistic images. The Japanese flock to the theaters in droves to see these films. Miyazaki started in the early 1990s and became known for using young protagonists or children to play key roles in his storylines. Innocence seen through the lens of precocious youth is often juxtaposed with themes of nature and ecology being destroyed by man.

In 2001, Miyazaki launched the most adult and most deistic of his movies. With its release in Japan, *Spirited Away* drew an audience of 23 million. The reviews of the movie were stunning and it cemented Miyazaki's reputation within Japan. An Academy Award for Best Animated Film brought the movie to the attention of even non-film buffs in the West. But on viewing the show, many were non-plussed; the imagery was definitely non-Disney. Sure, there were talking animals, but the animals were of questionable integrity— as likely to eat as they were to shelter the human characters. While Japanese audiences seemed to revel in the animal and plant spirit gods, Westerners found themselves yearning for a clearer wrong and right. For the Japanese, nature is good in and of itself. No matter what form it takes.

A life not wasted is more of a life

It is not just in issues of war and peace that the Japanese government emphasis on Life can be seen. I was first made aware of this when I was just a college student. I was interested in Japanese views of individuality and collectivism and decided to write my undergraduate thesis on Japanese juvenile delinquency as a way to explore that. My research involved riding with a motorcycle gang for a summer; and riding with a motorcycle gang involved run-ins with the law. It was the way the law dealt with the kids in the motorcycle gang that gave me my first glimpse into Japan's focus on Life.

The members of the gang that I rode with were all in their teens and they did some bad things. When they were hauled into a police station and booked, the kids didn't immediately expect they would be jailed because usually they weren't. The most common punishment was to be asked to write a letter of apology and sign it. They were then released to their parents or to their homeroom teacher. Even when they violated the law more than once, they were released after a scare and a formal apology.

I asked the police why they did this. One particularly articulate officer explained with a question: "Why should they spend any of those limited hours in jail doing nothing with their relatively short life?" The hope was that with a catch-and-release strategy, they could move these kids on to productive lives. My experience was that their strategy worked quite well. Of the 20 or more motorcycle gang members that I knew in those days, only one went on to a life that involved adult criminal behavior. The rest, for the most part, became salesmen. The last time I saw these former delinquents, they were in suits and ties and talking about their sales commissions.

Whistling past the death scoreboard

Frequenting neighborhood police stations in Japan while completing my research and walking past them regularly since (there are over 15,000 of these small police boxes in the country!), I was (and still am) struck by the prominent display in front of all of them. A board with moveable plastic numbers announces the number of accidents and accidental deaths in the country the day before and a running tally of the number for the entire year.

In my book, *The Attention Economy*, I found that a profound form of attention is what I call "back of mind" attention—this is routine, almost subconscious attention. (Davenport & Beck, 2001) Companies that want to get more attention to a particular initiative do well to have constant reminders of that issue posted around the work place. It just keeps the initiative in the back of your mind without you devoting a lot of serious thought to it. Initiatives tend to work better if these signals are present.

There must be some deep psychological impact to the Japanese populace of regularly passing police boxes and stations with the death count so proudly displayed. And it is another non-subtle message that the government is working to preserve life—a message that I've never noticed so clearly enunciated by any other government on earth.

Caring about health care

During the US debate about healthcare reform, the Japanese system was often rolled out as an example of one form of government-run health care system. Most Japanese were granted government-health insurance in 1938, making it one of the earlier nations in the world to offer health care to most of its population. Then, in 1958 the law was revised to cover the 30% previously uninsured. Since that time, either employers or the government have covered all Japanese.

There are three broad categories of insurance in Japan: employer-based insurance, national insurance and insurance for the elderly. Primarily, the national government, private employers, and individual coinsurance payments finance these programs, but the services are delivered through a mostly privately-operated hospital and clinic system. All of these programs cover a broad range of services: in- and out-patient care, most prescription drugs, and dental care.

Japan's system differs from the US model in that it is compulsory; has no competition among insurers due to government established reimbursement rates; and patients are free to choose their medical providers.

Today, Japanese go to the doctor about four times as often as Americans—on average 14 times a year. The choice of physician is completely free—no need for a referral from anyone. Walk into any doctors office in the country, shell out a small co-pay, and your visit (and the prescribed drugs) are virtually free. Japanese can expect to be seen—even by the most popular specialists—on the day they choose without a waiting list.

Living and letting live

Being an inhabitant of the most densely populated countries on earth—especially when you consider that most of the Japanese islands are mountainous and largely inhabitable—is you learn to live healthily in close quarters. While medieval Europeans treated bathing as an annual affair, Japanese had already incorporated it into a daily routine—and built a tradition of worshipful relaxation into a visit to the bathhouse. Buddhism connected bathing to purification; mountain spas allowed for Shinto worship of nature while soaking in an outdoor hot spring. And Japan's close quarters made bathing a necessity. The health benefits of a seriously scrubbed society are clear, but a specific law requiring bathing doesn't appear to have ever been on Japanese books. Nevertheless, the consequences of not bathing could result in one of the oddest reasons I've heard for being ineligible for military service. In Japan, you could be denied a spot in the military or receive a dishonorable discharge for body odor. That's right ... during World War II, if you didn't bath for a few days and started to offend your platoon-mates with your stench, you'd be shipped back to an awkward homecoming.

The social emphasis on avoiding the spread of diseases in a dense population can be seen every winter in Japan today. About ten-percent of the morning-commute population on any Tokyo train or bus during flu season can be seen wearing a medical nose and mouth mask. Some wear it because they don't want to be infected themselves. But the vast majority of face mask wearers do it because they are still sneezing or coughing and want to limit their likelihood of infecting their co-commuters and co-workers.

Most Americans would probably prefer to stay home rather than go back to work wearing a face mask before we are completely healed. But the work ethic of Japanese almost demands that you show up at your place of employment as soon as you are able to drag yourself out of bed. Everyone senses a responsibility to work, but there is also a strong right to work.

A surprisingly large—and visible—portion of older men is employed in "traffic directing" jobs. Any construction site or public works project has a handful of people whose sole job is to direct foot traffic around the hazard. In the US, a traffic cone is set out and you are pretty much on your own. In Japan, a truck that is backing up is cause for four or five older gentlemen in highly reflective outfits to wave red flashlights and make sure that there is no harm to anyone in the surroundings. Even a parking lot entrance and exit will usually employ at least one person whose sole job is to ensure that the entering or emerging cars negotiate the intervening sidewalk without threat to pedestrian life or limb.

Hard to live without a livelihood

This right to work is reflected strongly in Japanese employment law. And it exhibits a very different set of priorities than you find regarding employment in the US. Japanese thinking is that an employee is dependent on an employer for life itself. Once an employer hires someone, they have a responsibility for more than a few weeks or months—they are really making a lifetime commitment to that person. You can't fire, reduce the salary of or demote an employee without cause. And if there is cause, you have to punish them according to work rules that have been established by the Labor Standards Office. The only other instance when a salary can be cut or an employee fired would be when the company is nearly bankrupt and all employees (including management) take a cut at the same time.

These laws, as many analysts have noted, really only apply to full-time employees in relatively large companies. And the lifetime guarantee only lasts up to the age of 55. Older, non-permanent, small-company employees actually don't have any of these guarantees. And increasingly, Japanese workers are accepting "temporary employment." Some estimates put the percentage of non-permanent workers under the age of 35 at about 20%. These workers are known as Freeters (combining the English word "free" with the German word for worker: "arbiter") or NEETS (people Not in Employment, Education, or Training). They do actually work, but they are not "officially" employed. So they are not officially exempt from layoffs. Often these non-permanent jobs pay better hourly wages than permanent jobs, and there is not the obligation involved in being a permanent, full-time employee. During an upturn in economic growth, companies often hire temporary employees first and then after assessing the situation (to make sure the need for additional staff is long-lasting), they will convert some temporary jobs into permanent jobs. But every employer in Japan understands the obligation involved. Once employees are full-time, it is impossible to fire them just because economic growth slows or sales are sluggish. In this way, the livelihood of the employee—not the interests of the shareholders—is the ultimate objective of a Japanese corporation—Life not Growth is the top priority.

Working to death

The intersection of life and work is not more obvious anywhere in Japan than in the concept of *karoshi* (kah-roe-she), or "death from overwork." Just the fact that a particular term has been developed to describe this phenomenon in Japan may make you think that there is a real problem. And while there is no doubt that Japanese employees tend to stay late at the office—later than their American counterparts, there is a social aspect to these later hours that is not found in many American firms. My experience in consulting with and working for Japanese firms is that Japanese employees are much more likely than Westerners to go for drinks and dinner with their coworkers—usually at a bar or café near the office. A common pattern is then for the employees to go back to the office after the social outing.

Especially with the downsizing of workforces in the US over the last decade, there is plenty of evidence that the average American worker spends almost as many hours and at least as much effort in the office as do the Japanese. The main difference is this: If a Wall Street broker is found in the morning slumped over his computer, it will be called a heart attack. If a Japanese banker is found under the same circumstances, it will be labeled *karoshi*, and an investigation into workplace practices will be launched.

Karoshi was labeled in the late 1980s and since then almost 40,000 Japanese have been deemed to be its victim. That large number pushed bureaucrats to structure the Japanese pension system to offer benefits to the families of karoshi victims. And following the 2008 death of a 30-year-old Toyota worker (who had been putting in 80 hours of overtime a month), the Japanese courts insisted that Toyota change its work processes to ensure no more *karoshi* among its workforce. No similar pension benefits have been granted to workplace death survivors in the US. US courts don't push corporations to redesign the employment practices to keep employees from overworking. Again, in Japan, we see the obvious emphasis on Life rather than on economic Growth.

Life Begets Longer Life

All of this emphasis on life and living conspires to give Japan the lowest infant death rate and highest life expectancies (an average of 82 years) in the world. But of all the Japanese, it is those on the island of Okinawa who can claim the longest lives. The Japanese government claims that 457 Okinawans are at least 100 years old—that is 34.7 centenarians for every 100,000 Okinawans; by far, the highest ratio in the world. (By contrast, the USA has about 10 people over the age of 100 for every 100,000 in the population.) And Okinawan oldsters appear to have far lower rates of dementia and hip fracture than their U.S. counterparts. Some Okinawan centenarians claim they are still having sex, but researchers can't confirm that. But a few individual stories are truly amazing: martial artist Seikichi Uehara was 96 when he defeated a thirty something ex-boxing champion in a nationally televised match and Nabi Kinjo became a local legend when she hunted down a poisonous snake and killed it with a fly swatter. She was 105.

Okinawans benefit from all the usual Japanese Life priorities—the "peace Constitution," the health care system, the employment guarantees, and the cultural emphasis on life and living.   But Okinawans also lay claim to better nutrition (they eat a quarter of the salt and sugar of other Japanese) and a relatively stress-free existence—with year-round warmth and sunshine, short commutes to work, and few corporate jobs.

Disaster Planning on Shaky Ground

Maybe it is centuries of living in one of the most physically vulnerable geographies on earth that makes the Japanese so focused on Life. The earth can shift beneath your feet at any time in Japan. While developed countries in the West—those focused on Growth and Individuality—move more and more budgetary resources away from governments, one thing the Japanese learned from the great Hanshin earthquake in 1995 was that more centralized control is actually better for saving lives. The Self-Defense Forces in Japan were given authority to deploy automatically in case of a disaster without local political authorities calling for that help. And fire response coordination was centralized in Tokyo and Kyoto rather than with local fire departments. Japan's government and her companies have for years, sacrificed Growth opportunities to invest in better and safer construction and disaster planning—all to save one extra human life.

The Japanese reaction to the awful earthquake, tsunami, and nuclear disaster in Fukushima in the spring of 2011 was even more telling. Some friends of mine have held up the actions of the government in not providing more oversight to the Tepco (Tokyo Electric Power Company) power plants as a key piece of evidence that Growth, not Life, is really Japan's top priority. And I can see how they come to that conclusion: there is no doubt that individuals in the government and in companies in Japan put their careers and financial gain ahead of safety at the Fukushima electrical plant.

But in their defense, before the disaster (caused by the worst earthquake in Japan's recorded history), international nuclear agencies regularly found Japanese reactors in complete compliance with global standards of safety. President Obama and Republican leaders alike praised Japan's nuclear safety record. (Sheppard, 2011)

The events after the disaster are more telling still. The Japanese government exerted its right to protect life in the country by nationalizing Tepco's power business. By contrast even in the worst days of the 2010 Gulf oil spill, there was never any talk of BP's US interests being taken over the American government. Before the Fukushima disaster, France and Japan were the major proponents of nuclear power—and the only two corporations building nuclear plants (Areva and Toshiba) are, not surprisingly, based in these two countries. It makes logical sense that Japanese, having borne the brunt of a nuclear meltdown, would have a stronger reaction to the disaster than the French. But the contrast could not be more profound. The French have announced in the months following the Fukushima meltdown that they will increase the number of nuclear power stations in their country; meanwhile the Japanese are looking at ways to phase completely out of the source of 30% of their country's electrical power.

It is interesting to note that Germany (which relied on nuclear for 20% of its total) also decided to close down nuclear plants following the Japanese disaster. Maybe Germany should be a candidate for best exemplar of Life, right up there with Japan. The two nations do have the relatively recent shared history of the massive loss of life which may make the Good of Life even more dear to each.

The Flip Side of Japan's Life Culture

I suppose I can't end this discussion of Life in Japan without a short detour into suicide in Japan. Japan is one of the only countries in the world where suicide is still considered an honorable act. It is not illegal and, to many, it is considered respectable. Many non-Japanese have come to be familiar with the Japanese terms for suicide—*seppuku* and *hara-kiri* (introduced to the US by military personnel with the pronunciation "Harry Carry" after World War II). Official statistics show that about 30,000 Japanese per year kill themselves. That puts the suicide rate among the top ten countries in the word, and by far the highest rate among developed nations. Over 70% of these are men, many over 60 years old, but a disturbingly large number of 30-somethings as well—one common pattern is that they are jobless, and deep in debt to loan sharks. And suicide is the leading cause of death among those under 30 years old. Some still adopt the traditional samurai method of death by sword, but stepping in front of trains, falling from tall buildings or cliffs and drug overdoses are also common. But it is one traditional method suicide that brings us back full-circle to the cyclical nature of life. It was not uncommon for older people in Japanese history—those reaching the point of complete dependence on their children—to just wander off into the mountains and never be heard from again. In highly urbanized Japan, this is somewhat more problematic. But there is still a place, even for this form of suicide. It is called the Aokigahara Forest—a dense forest with literally breathtaking views of Mount Fuji and signs posted along the most common paths reading "Please reconsider" and "Consult with the police before you decide to die." About 70 people a year make this place their final return to nature.

Perhaps it all comes back to the definition of life in Japan. Life is protected and cherished like it is in no other country. But once a life is no longer seen to have purpose or meaning, it is unusually common for an individual to put an end to that life not worth living.

Chapter 14: Individuality and the United States

The United States of America is my nominee for the country that best epitomizes Individuality. In my speeches and conversations about this topic, someone in the audience almost always challenges the countries I've offered as the best examples of a particular Good. But the US is one of only two countries (the other one I'll discuss later) for which no one has offered a better alternative. The US is all about Individuality.

America's history of individuality started early—very early—with the first pilgrims escaping religious persecution in England and in the process escaping their families and friends. The American Revolution rejected societal hierarchy as a god-given right and cut Americans off from their history and ancestry. Every wave of immigrant since has been willing to leave behind security and all of their societal ties in a bid for greater economic opportunity (Growth) and independence (Individuality).

In fact, the first time the word "individualism" was used according to the Oxford English dictionary, was when Henry Reeve who was translating de Tocqueville's *Democracy in America* in 1840 found that there was no good word in English for Toqueville's French word "individualisme." So he basically kept the French one. Tocqueville's definition of American individualism was as good a definition of this concept as you are going to find: "a mature and calm feeling, which disposes each member of the community to sever himself from the mass of his fellow-creatures and draw apart with his family and friends that he willingly leaves society at large to itself ... individualism is of democratic origin." (Tocqueville, 1840)

Anti-Social Genes?

The word "individualism" sprang from the New World almost as if the concept itself was brand new. But anthropologists agree that individualism has been around a lot longer than societal bonds. Pre-humans were not very good a suppressing their individualistic needs—that is one of the reasons they were "pre-humans." A big part of our being classified as humans is that we learned to form long-term relationships. Sure there are herd animals that work well together and primates seem to bond in small groups as well. But humans are among a handful of life-long-mating, family-based, individual-needs sacrificing species on earth. An ape that thinks he is up to challenging the ape group leader will. Most humans who know they are physically capable of overpowering the current leader of their group choose to submit instead.

Those who dig up and understand the meaning of bones, tell us that *homo habilis* made a transition to *homo erectus* and males and females of the species started to be of about the same skeletal size. Scientists speculate that this physiological change may have signaled a change in social structure as well and many of them believe this is about when our human ancestors started bonding for something more than pure survival. That was the beginning of human kind.

Over the following million years, we have built and lived in communities. Many of the most frightening stories of lore have been about individuals (or even small groups of individuals) who venture off alone from the community onto the ocean or into the woods. To be where people were not was a truly frightening specter to most humans. During our long human history, biologists would argue that natural selection has favored those who have been the most domesticated. The genetic lots of the village daredevil and the village couch potato (or its ancient equivalent) would have been quite different.   The argument goes that the seafaring adventurer of a teenager might never have had the chance to procreate; meanwhile the homebody teen would have been more likely to produce a passel of kids. (Now we know this is not entirely true because the ne'er-do-well sailor might have impregnated a different woman every day while the faithful husband would only get a chance at procreating every nine months. But the safety-conscious man would, on average, have lived longer. And he would have provided for his children—unlike the scallywag.)

Studies on animals show that if you're selecting for domesticity, you can create a whole society of domestics in a relatively short number of iterations. Dmitri Belyaev started an experiment with 100 female and 30 male wild silver foxes. He selected for traits of docility and in a surprisingly short period of time—just thirty-five generations—most of the foxes were behaving just like dogs. These wild, fierce, mean animals became "lap foxes."

Even with all our bonding tendencies, in every community of people there were always those who didn't quite fit in—the loners, the weird, the strange, or even the mentally ill. These people didn't have any lower sex drive than the socialites did and, chances are that throughout human history, they probably interbred often with others of their ilk, keeping a strain of anti-social, individualistic behavior alive and well in all communities.

Escapees in America

One quick glance at the history of the peopling of the United States and you have to wonder if we didn't tap pretty deeply into the individualistic gene pool that existed in Europe (and more recently Asia). Those most connected to the familial, communal, or national societies would have been poor candidates for the allure of emigration to the United States of America. Those in any given gene pool with the most individualist tendencies—not afraid to stake a claim to land in the middle of nowhere and cultivate it on their own; hopeful for wealth and a new start to life by traveling alone to work a railroad job or pan for gold—are the gene pool that has created America.

Even our evangelical bent betrays our individualism—we believe that we have the right to talk directly to God and no formal hierarchy of saints or priests should stand in our way. The religions that have prospered in the last few decades are those without formal structure where the preacher is hired or fired by a congregation wanting to hear entertaining messages of hope, prosperity, and individual success.

More individualistic over time

Even though they had to have been pretty individualistic to come to the American continent in the first place, the colonists probably did not universally feel the need to severe ties with their home lands. John Adams famously calculated that at least one-third of Americans at the time of the Revolution were opposed to it. Historian Robert Calhoon estimates that only about 40 to 45 percent of the white populace would have been actively supporting the Patriots. (Calhoon, 2000, p. 235) The black slave population would have almost universally opposed the war enticed by emerging British policy to free all slaves. And it wasn't just fear of losing to the Brits that drove the loyalists, Robert R. Palmer estimates that about sixty thousand people emigrated after the war; a larger proportion of newly minted Americans left the country than the proportion that emigrated during and following the bloody French Revolution.

There is a pretty good argument that we've become even more individualist over time than we were at the time that the country was born. Our constitutional amendments have, for the most part, offered *more* individual rights. The most important removal of rights, the Eighteenth Amendment which prohibited alcohol, was overturned just 13 years after it was passed. Individual rights were accorded blacks and women by these amendments. Even more electoral power was accorded to all individuals by the 17th Amendment which made a popular vote the mechanism by which Senators would be sent to Washington (stripping the power of state legislatures to determine their senators).

Not uniform

This is not to say that all Americans are individualists. There is obviously a big range. In fact, in my 2009 survey, only 8% of Americans claimed that Individuality was their Greatest Good (38% said Life and 27% said Belief). But this chapter is not about individual priorities, it is about government policy. Eventually individual priorities do have a huge impact on governmental decisions. All it takes is a few people dying as the result of a government policy and that policy will be changed—and usually rather quickly. If anything threatens to interfere with someone's right to worship, government will work to preserve that right as well. My argument here is not that Life and Belief aren't important governmental decision criteria in the US, but that Individuality may be even more important in American national policy.

Let me give you an example. We as Americans will gladly send our military into other countries to defend individual freedoms—we seem willing to sacrifice Life for the preservation of Individual rights. It is the same with Belief. Religion or a particular ethical standard is important to many of us individually. But it is the *right* to worship that is key to government decision-making. We protect an individual's *right* to worship as one chooses—even if those individual beliefs come into conflict with each other.

One place where the normally strong trend toward Individuality seems to break down a bit—at least in voting patterns—is in US urban areas. Those who live in large cities in the US are the most likely to vote for the most liberal—least Individualistic—agenda. Perhaps this is because of their physical proximity to other people. Urban dwellers rub shoulders with the less fortunate every day; they see the negative impact on their own lives when others are struggling.

In an international context

So how does the US compare to other countries in the world on individuality? Legal scholar Barbara Bennet Woodhouse points out that the US cultural and legal system which prioritizes individuality at the top may be responsible for the fact that the US is the only nation in the world not to ratify the UN Convention on the Rights of the Child. (Woodhouse, 2008) The US government is the only one in the world that sees this law not as a commitment by the government to assist and support children, but rather as government interference into an individual's right to raise a child as he or she sees fit. This emphasis on individual responsibility can result in some sad consequences for those not able to fend for themselves. In a United Nations Children's Fund (UNICEF) Innocenti Research Centre study in 2005, the US had a higher percentage of kids living in poverty (21.9%) than all but one (Mexico) of the twenty-six OECD countries in the study.

But at the same time, the world has become more open to the notion of American one-person-one-vote democracy. In 1900, not a single country in the world had universal suffrage. By 1950 there were twenty-two countries with universal voting rights. By 2010, eighty-nine countries in the world (making up almost half of the world's population) are real democracies. In other words, over the last 110 years, nations around the word have placed Individuality as an increasingly high priority in their decision-making process.

Real crises and Individuality

In most countries, the strong pull of Relationships has been slowly matched (or at least balanced) by a focus on Individuality. But in a place like the United

States where the founding ideals were, from the beginning, so much about Individuality, how do you create a society that actually binds people together?

It is interesting that Herbert Hoover made the term "rugged individualism" famous in 1928, shortly before he won the election and shortly before the US plunged into its worst economic crisis:

> "We were challenged with a ... choice between the American system of rugged individualism and a European philosophy of diametrically opposed doctrines of paternalism and state socialism. The acceptance of these ideas would have meant the destruction of self-government through centralization ... [and] the undermining of the individual initiative and enterprise through which our people have grown to unparalleled greatness." (Hoover)

Americans voted for this point of view during the pre-crisis "happy days," but Hoover's individualistic policies didn't help bring America out of the depression and some say they even hurt. After the next election, Franklin Roosevelt introduced, perhaps, the least individualistic set of policies in US history.

The times when we, as a nation, have been willing to pull together have been moments of national tragedy or crisis. The Revolutionary War was the start of it all—a time when individuals agreed with each other (for the most part—although the biggest Constitutional battles through our history have been over issues that our Founding Fathers could not agree on themselves) to separate themselves from a much bigger and more powerful society. All American legislation which has been meant to support the weaker (and less well off) among us has been passed when we were all feeling vulnerable— the Depression, World War II, the aftermath of Kennedy's assassination and 9-11. At times like these, even the most individualistic among us have given up some "rights" in the hope that someone would come to our rescue and protect us—we hoped that somehow the nation could make things better.

But if it isn't a real crisis...

In the wake of new laws on welfare, social security, civil rights legislation, gender equality, our society actually did get stronger. Our willingness to work together as a nation and as communities (whole communities, not just the people who looked alike), created an era of growth and growing equality in the US. From the 1920s to the 1970s, inequality in wages and living standards in our country dipped; we became more alike than different—geographically, racially, sexually, and economically.

But with the crises gone, we naturally revert rather quickly to our individualistic ways. We want the nation—big brother—out of our way. This tendency is exacerbated by economic discomfort (which hasn't quite turned into crisis) for most of us in the country. As overall economic growth rates have slumped in the US, we want to hold on to what we have. We are individualists after all. Our culture (and possibly even our genes) predisposes us to move farther away from each other, put up fences, break out the guns, and ardently protect what we have.

But most of our country is God's land of Individualism. And if history is any guide, it will remain that way until the next crisis makes us realize how important we really are to each other.

John C Beck

Chapter 15: Relationships and Growth: Switzerland and Singapore

Switzerland (Relationships)

It may seem odd that I chose Switzerland as my example of a country focused on Relationships. After all, it is a nation that fiercely adheres to the advice of its most popular saint, Nicholas of Flüe (1417-87): "Don't get involved in other people's affairs."

Certainly, Switzerland's foreign policy has been anything but sociable for nearly 500 years. The country has in effect been neutral since 1515. And after the Napoleonic Wars in 1815, this neutral status was formally guaranteed by all the great powers of Europe. Thus, Swiss neutrality has deeper roots than any of Europe's other major neutral states: Sweden (1815), Eire (1921), Finland (1948) and Austria (1955).

The first melting pot

When it comes to its internal relations, Switzerland has been a melting pot of groups who might naturally be enemies. It is the first nation that brought together three different language groups—French, German, and Italian—with all three being national languages. This shows a tolerance for differences in neighbors and a respect for individual differences.

In a 1980s survey of Swiss attitudes toward fellow countrymen, Sociologist Carol Schmid—in *Conflict and Consensus in Switzerland*—found that unlike Canada where French-speakers and English-speakers tended to overestimate the percentage of same language speakers in their country, the Swiss all underestimated the percentage of their countrymen that shared their native language. (Schmid, 1981) This, perhaps, is evidence of a surprisingly naturally "outward" looking culture in what has always been characterized as such an insular place.

Taken from this perspective, even Switzerland's foreign policy can be seen in a different light. Because Switzerland was never willing to form an "exclusive" relationship with any country (they didn't join the United

Nations until 2002—even though Geneva is the second largest headquarters for UN staff after New York City), the nation has, throughout its modern history at least, been rather inclusive of all countries. Switzerland relies on bilateral agreements—which treat every country pretty equally—rather than alliances with any group of countries. It was really only after all of its surrounding neighbors had joined the EU that Switzerland made any moves in that direction at all—and still there are no plans to meld completely into the EU. From this "inclusive" perspective, we can see that to join the EU fully would mean forming relationships with other European nations at the risk of alienating some non-European countries. Swiss policy seems to value a relationship with the whole earth more than with any other specific country.

Political relationships

Switzerland's government has had to allow for diversity and conformity through its "direct democracy" voting system. There is no other system on earth like it. There are officials elected to a national parliament on a representational, not a majority basis (so that minority parties and positions are represented in congress) and they discuss and draft laws. Most laws that parliament enacts are subject to a referendum and citizens can vote directly for or against the legislation.

Although, most of the power of government in Switzerland remains at the local, or Canton, level. There are 26 Cantons of vastly different population sizes (from 15,000 to 1.2 million). All Canton laws are subject to a direct vote. And there is no rule that Cantons must have uniform laws or legal systems. However, this is where the importance of relationships becomes clear. Because so many Swiss live in one Canton and work in another, there is a need for some uniformity. Canton governments will meet informally with each other and align their legal systems with the neighboring Cantons. This informal system yields a fair degree of uniformity throughout the country, but is not required.

Switzerland has long been known for its consensus politics. The Swiss Federation Council is composed of seven people and serves as the cabinet and a collective presidency—with the actual job of the President (largely a symbolic and ceremonial post) rotating in one-year intervals among the members of the Council. From 1959 to 2003, there were always two members of the three largest political parties and one from the smaller Swiss People's Party. From 2003 to 2007, there was speculation that with the shifting Council seat, Switzerland may be seeing an end to consensus politics as the People's Party picked up an extra Council member; but in the 2007 election the system reverted to the traditional balance.

And, according to a 2009 survey, the Swiss seem as consensus minded as ever. Eighty percent of the population favors cross-party cooperation and want cabinet seats based on "appreciation of key Swiss values and institutions." Also, half of the population believes that the cabinet is either working well or very well. (Geiser, 2009)

Business relationships

There is an argument that some of the secular societal norms that have driven Switzerland have actually emerged from a religious sect, Calvinism— upon which sociologist Max Weber's *Protestant Ethic* was predicated.

Another argument for Switzerland's tight and precise societal interactions argues that Switzerland was—for a long time—a relatively poor country surrounded by richer and more powerful neighbors. Swiss society developed rigorous codes of conduct and behavior to reduce risk. To this day, Swiss companies have a reputation for being slow to change, but ready to follow— to the letter—rules that ensure high quality delivery of goods and services.

So in Swiss companies, you find corporate goals that tend to be more relationship oriented than in other countries. Swiss banks are all about client-banker relationships. There is a level of trust that develops between a Swiss banker and patron that is unlike any other model in the world. And even the laws for the banking industry are geared much more toward the social relationship than banking laws in other developed countries.

Furthermore, it is not just the personal Relationships issues that are beneficial to businesses in Switzerland. The nation as a whole offers many relationship advantages to companies from around the world. In a 2009 study, consultancy Arthur D. Little reported that 269 headquarters were transferred from abroad in the previous six years. Sixty percent of these were European or EMEA (Europe, Middle East and Africa) headquarters and

40% of them were global headquarters. Americans were the most likely to relocate a regional headquarter to Switzerland, while many European firms moved their global headquarters to Switzerland. The report notes that a low tax regime is one of the attractive aspects for relocating companies, but even more important may be the Relationships-based attractions of the country. Swiss employees rank first in the world in motivation, second in the world for attracting skilled foreigners, and third in the world in labor-employer relations. The education system in the country is ranked 4th in the world for primary education and 6th for higher education. . (Arthur D Little, 2009)

It is probably little wonder then that the biggest and most important gathering of business elites in the world takes place every year in Davos, Switzerland. It is a society well positioned to naturally protect the press-wary upper-crust of the world as they hobnob with each other.

Neighborly relationships?

When my partner and I were considering a job offer in Switzerland, the one "negative" that we heard about the place over and over again was concerning the "neighborliness" of neighbors. The most common story which I would have thought was just urban myth given the number of times we heard it—if everyone hadn't insisted it happened to them personally—was the "noise after 10 p.m." problem. Having a party, playing the television too loudly, doing laundry, or even flushing the toilet after ten o'clock in the evening brings the potential of a visit from the local police apparently. Neighbors rarely ask you to curtail the behavior first; they just call the police hotline. My favorite variant of this story was the American who hosted a party and invited his neighbor from the building, the neighbor came and enjoyed the food and spirits for a couple of hours. Then, at 10 p.m., the neighbor left the still lively party, went back to their apartment and apparently called the police to come and close the noise down.

Another common story was about cars getting ticketed or towed. Parking spaces are tight and clearly demarcated in Swiss cities and people warned us that if you park even an inch or two out of the lines, you are likely to pay the price. Since the neighboring parking spots are all your neighbors and people you see everyday, you think someone would just knock on your door and ask you to move the car, but that doesn't seem to be the case very often.

These incidents seem to be a clear indication of the primacy of societal norms and the socially sanctioned enforcement of those norms. The idea behind them is to allow individuals to coexist peacefully and civilly while the police enforce the rules rather than expecting neighbors to do the "heavy lifting."

Family relationships

The role of the family is the basic building block of Swiss relationships. Most countries only give lip service to this notion, but the Swiss put their rankings where their mouths are in an OECD study of the well-being of children in 21—mostly well-to-do—nations where Switzerland ranked fourth overall. In their consideration of "family and peer relationships," only Italy, Portugal, and the Netherlands had higher rankings than Switzerland. And in "subjective well-being," Switzerland was second only to the Netherlands. (Adamson *et. al.*, 2007)

In the Survey of Health, Ageing and Retirement in Europe project, 25% percent of Swiss respondents with a living mother report that they regularly gave her practical help and care. This is lower than the 45% in Italy or the 35% in Spain, but Switzerland and Belgium have the highest rates among the more northern European countries. (Börsch-Supan & et al, 2008) The elderly in Switzerland had the best quality of life—based on a measure than included both socioeconomic and social factors like care and informal help—of any in Europe.

Regardless of—or perhaps because of—Switzerland's isolationist past, today's Switzerland is one of the most cosmopolitan and sociable of nations. This is a country that hosts corporate global and governmental headquarters—by definition recognizing the society of all countries in the world. By not forming an alliance with any one country, Switzerland is able to befriend all countries. And, in the process, has become more focused on human ties (family, community, national, and global) than any other nation on earth.

Singapore (Growth)

As we sat around a dinner table in Singapore with a group of very smart people all making their best effort to describe the best government on earth, it is perhaps not surprising that Singapore came up as an example. Interestingly, the person who proposed Singapore also noted that three years earlier, he would have said Ireland. But sadly, Ireland's star had already risen to its highest level and dropped from the sky before that conversation. But for the purposes of this section, Ireland would have been a more "pure" form of a government built around the Good of Growth. After being Europe's basket case economy for years—and some would argue centuries—the 1990s were a particularly great decade for the country. From 1990 to 2008, Ireland grew at a rate of 5.5% per annum making the country one of the most attractive business headquarters and manufacturing bases in the world. But the Global Financial Crisis was the end of the Ireland's appeal and many of the economic policies that created her boom were directly responsible for her bust.

Singapore, on the other hand, had one bad year in 2009, but recovered about as quickly as any nation on earth from the recession. By the first quarter of 2010, the economy was growing at over 20% per annum!

Need for Stability

Singapore's historical Good has not always been Growth. In fact, here was a great story of a country making a transition from one Good to another—at least as its highest priority. I actually attended graduate school in Singapore in the early 1980s and therefore have three decades of experience of mentioning Singapore to friends and family around the world and then noting how they respond. The most common response—to this day—is confusion over where Singapore is located. Many believe it is a city in China. The next most common response is a reference to Singapore Airlines—which is very fair in this context. The national airline has been one of the most important drivers of Growth for the last 40 years. It is, for my money—and according to almost every survey—the best airline in the world. Those with a little more knowledge of Singapore are likely to mention the punishment by caning for graffiti and the fines for chewing gum. These are indicative of the legacy of Singapore's longstanding focus on Stability.

Singapore ceded from Malaysia in 1965 as a mainly Chinese city that was rankling against being a part of a nation which was mostly Malay. The break was clean and without much violence. But the worry of ethnic strife among Singapore's Malay and Indian minority was a constant fear of nation-builder Lee Kuan Yew. Many of the early social policies in the country were a direct response to this fear: government housing was designed to break down traditional ethnic villages and neighborhoods; government control of newspapers contained any rabble rousing; and the government to this day is highly secretive about its actions. One colleague of mine at the Lee Kuan Yew School of Public Policy in Singapore quipped that there was more publicly available data about then still-closed Myanmar's government than there was about Singapore's.

The country has been controlled by a set of fines and publicity campaigns from the early days. While less ubiquitous today than even ten years ago, it is still jarring for many tourists to see the number of "Do Not" signs (red circles with diagonal slashes) prohibiting a variety of behaviors with a dollar figure below the sign advertising the amount of the fine for breaking the law. My favorite is the one found in public restrooms. If you are caught not flushing the toilet, a fine of S$150 can be levied. Chewing gum in the country was once a fineable offense, now the sale of gum is simply prohibited; however, it is still available if you are trying to stop smoking and your doctor gives you a prescription for nicotine gum.

The government controlled population policies, immigration policies, the press, nightlife, and gambling—all for fear of losing control. Stability was the norm in the country until the new millennium.

Shift to growth

While Growth was always an important Good for Singapore, it was not the top priority. Nevertheless, there are strong signs that the pendulum has finally swung in just the last decade.

Singapore prides itself on its strong economic growth rates and turning itself into a developed nation from its rather impoverished beginnings in just three decades. The World Bank's "Doing Business" survey regularly ranks Singapore as the best country in the world for unrestricted business transactions. Early political leaders in Singapore realized that the nation's future depended on its ability to encourage trade through its ports and airports. Business has always taken a front seat in Singapore.

However, a bunch of really smart planners—Singapore pays its government employees market-competitive salaries and is regularly able to attract the best and the brightest citizens to these jobs—realized that for growth to continue in Singapore the population would need to continue to grow rapidly. After discouraging large families in the 1960s and 1970s, the government made an about-face and actually gave large tax benefits to highly educated parents with growing families. Prime Minister and Oxford University graduate, Lee Kuan Yew's policies and philosophies on this topic were decried as eugenics in most of the world, but those articles were censored in Singapore and it never became much of a topic there. In addition, the tax incentives were never able to raise population growth enough to create the manpower necessary for the growth rates the government was targeting.

Finally, immigration policies were relaxed. In 1988, only 9000 permanent resident permits were issued. For most of the 1990s, that number increased to 25,0000 a year. Currently Singapore is adding almost 100,000 new residents a year.

As one of the most attractive locations for expatriate headquarters in the region, some of that annual population growth is highly transient. International executives and their families take three to five year stints in the country and then leave after the assignment is over. But, compared to other expatriate cities, Singapore retains a high number of these who decide to stay after their assignment and find a job as "local" staff.

The manufacturing sector is surprisingly quite strong for a developed nation. But the workers are drawn almost exclusively from guest workers and from recent immigrants. In their drive to create a high growth economy, Equality has not been one of Singapore's overarching concerns. In fact, in recent international comparisons, Singapore is one of the most inequitable nations in the world from both income and wealth perspectives. The gap between the haves and have-nots is greater than in any other country in Asia—and it is one of the highest in the world. While the odds are increasingly against them, the high growth rates do give even the poorest Singaporeans hope that they can rise to tycoon status in one generation of hard work.

Tourism still accounts for a large percentage of Singapore's economy, driven by a great airline. But in the government's efforts to create a clean, stable environment for their citizens, they also have been criticized for making the nation too "sterile." Tourists—and expatriates alike—complain that there is nothing interesting to do in the country. Singapore, like most port cities in the world, had a colorful nightlife for the first 150 years of its history. But in their efforts to "control" the people and ensure that bad elements couldn't gain a foothold, the policies on entertainment became puritanical. For years, nightclubs were mostly banned; casinos were not allowed; and gay bars were shuttered. That has all changed.

Perhaps one of the biggest symbols of Singapore's shift from a society focused on Stability to one focused on Growth is the Marina Bay Sands Casino & Resort towering over the rest of the skyline. It is one of two major all-inclusive casino resorts that opened in Singapore in 2010. The Sands is the second most expensive casino in the world—after the MGM Mirage's City Center in Las Vegas. It is expected to pull in US$1 billion annually in profit.

One large driver of economic growth during the last decade has also been the property market in Singapore. In the 1960s the government began a scheme to house its population in high-rise public-built housing. Today almost 80% of the population lives in affordable government-constructed buildings—some of them extremely luxurious. Ninety-one percent of Singaporeans own the condominium or home they live in—the rental market is almost negligible, really only serving the expatriate community. A government program that was originally meant to give its citizens an affordable basis for building property equity and stability has been turned into a wealth building exercise.

Property speculation is one of the most popular pastimes on the island as families trade-up. During a ten-year period from 1995 to 2005, more than half of Singaporean families traded up to better housing stock. The residential property price index shows that even on an inflation-adjusted basis, values are almost 250% of what they were two decades ago in Singapore. Over the last twenty years, income has played an increasingly smaller role in Gross Domestic Product in Singapore with wealth taking a larger position.

With real growth that averaged almost 5% in the '00s—and even with two short recessions caused by the dot-com bust and the financial crisis— Singapore is the best example of a developed nation that can boast Growth as its Greatest Good.

John C Beck

Chapter 16: Stability, Belief and Equality: China, Israel/Saudi Arabia, and Norway

In this chapter, you will get a three-in-one: not because these are unimportant Goods or unimportant countries. Rather the link between these countries and the priority of their Greatest Good is quite straightforward. The policies that these governments have adopted in promoting each nation's Greatest Good are unmistakable. Rather than deal with each of these in too much detail, I will hit the high points in describing my favorite nominees for countries boasting the Greatest Goods of Stability, Equality, and Belief.

China and Stability

Those of us in the West cannot think of China without some image of a strong, unyielding central power passing through our minds. The Chinese government's first and foremost goal is Stability; without control and security, nothing else about the country will work. This has been the case throughout the Middle Kingdom's history. Perhaps the greatest symbol of China is the Great Wall and this was nothing but a bid for Stability in a world threatened by chaos from the Mongols and the Manchus.

The second strongest image of China is probably of the rapidly emerging economic prowess of the nation and its people. Indeed, a very important goal for the country is economic growth—but in China's case, Growth is in service of Stability not the other way around.

China tried Stability through pure communism until the 1970s, but the model—particularly as an isolationist model—didn't work. I remember doing a textual analysis of China's Sixth (1981-1985) and Seventh (1986-1990) Five Year plans when I was a graduate student—looking for the number of times that the Chinese characters for Socialism (社) and Economics (経) were used in the official reports. This was long before automatic text readers existed, so I became the human text reader. It was a tedious job going through the reports page by page looking for these two characters, but the findings were interesting. I found that the Economics character use increased by about 30% between the two reports and the Socialism character only increased slightly. Economics was not substituting for Socialism, rather, I theorized at the time, an increased emphasis on economics seemed to require a simultaneous reemphasis on Socialism—this to maintain Stability.

China's focus on Stability is perhaps best exemplified by the Tiananmen Square rebellion in 1989. To ensure that the current government structure continued unaltered, the Communist leaders at the time authorized the use of deadly force to put down the student led revolt. Hundreds of people died in the bloody massacre. But according to one possibly apocryphal story it was not just the leaders of the current regime who were concerned about Stability. The story goes that the leader of the Communist student organization in China was planning to throw his support behind the students in Tiananmen Square until he heard that because of unusually dry conditions, the fall harvest was predicted to be unusually low. This leader didn't mind a little chaos in the country, but political chaos on top of a famine would be too much to handle, he believed. He called off his organization's support of the protests and days later, the tanks rolled into the Square and hundreds, if not thousands, of students were killed.

The priority of Stability and control before growth is pretty clear in a number of recent decisions that the Chinese government has made as well. Google's decision to pull out of China is a prime example. However, there are also a number of examples where companies that wanted to do work in China and employ Chinese workers decided not to because of technology transfer requirements. The Western firms didn't want to open up their technology to the Chinese government, and therefore were not allowed to establish business entities in the country. So, it seems that China has been willing to forgo some economic growth to maintain control of the country.

Stability is not an uncommon goal for any government. Nevertheless, when Stability rises to the top priority for a government, that nation will inevitably run afoul of some definitions of "human rights." Even countries like Singapore, where a large majority of the population was sanguine about the government's stability interventions, there was a lot of international pressure for a political system change. Generally after a period of political strife—often accompanied by bloodshed—people are quite happy to accept a government focused on Stability and endure loss of rights particularly if it means that the killing will end.

Rwanda is an excellent example of just such a nation. Paul Kagame was the military leader who imposed a rule of law on the country. While he instituted a constitution that guaranteed democratic elections, there are reports of less-than-democratic election practices within the country. Even though this outrages many of us in the West, it does not bother a large percentage of the Rwandan population—they just don't want a return to the genocide and civil war of two decades ago. If Kagame can keep them from that fate, then they are supportive. As a new generation of Rwandans with little or no memory of those atrocities comes to adulthood, the need for Stability will be replaced by another Good. But Stability will always be near the top of any government's priority list.

Norway and Equality

Like most of its Scandinavian neighbors, Norway prides itself on equality. And the country works hard to make it happen. Few countries in the world have as little income disparity as Norway—it is derided as a socialist welfare state by some. But Norway came through the most recent Global financial crisis in much better shape than most other developed nations. Meanwhile, drug addicts are supplied free drugs and the unemployed eat their meals at the taxpayer's expense. How does it do this?

Norway's laws on equality and anti-discrimination are about as stringent as anywhere in the world. One good example of this is the law—established in 1985—that 40% of all public committees (including the boards of public companies) be populated by women. It took almost 10 years for the quota to be met; and today almost 45% of all board members in the country are women.

At the time this law was put into place, many argued that it wouldn't be good for Growth: that installing unproven women to oversee public and private corporations would lead to corporate disasters and unprofessional oversight. After all of these years, there are no corporate losses tied to the fact that women are equally represented on the board.

Some say that Norway has just been lucky in economic terms: policies of equality should not naturally lead to economic success and Stability, and really Norway has only the fortune of North Sea oil to thank for much of its success— earning and estimated $66 billion from oil in 2012. Yet, the UK has had a lot of oil revenue as well and has never found itself as economically well off as Norway. Furthermore, when it comes to equality, the UK and Norway are on opposite sides of the scales. In the 2009 book *The Spirit Level*, authors Wilkinson and Pickett found that the UK is among the most unequal industrialized countries on earth, meanwhile Norway is among the most economically equal. (Wilkinson & Pickett, 2009)

Where does all this focus on equality come from? How does a society come to this? It is perhaps deeply embedded. Norwegians have always adhered to an ancient property code called *allemansretten* or "every man's right." Under this code, public access to wild areas was guaranteed. Property could not be tied up in private hands except in cities and agricultural areas. For the rest of the land in the country, everyone had equal access regardless of station or rank.

But it wasn't just traditional social rules that set Scandinavian countries on their current path toward prioritizing Equality as their Greatest Good. In 1766, Sweden enacted the equivalent of a Freedom of Information Act that ensured all Swedes had equal access to government information. Since that time, more than in any other region on earth, the Nordic countries have developed a broad network of public libraries to grant everyone in the nation fair access to knowledge.

This focus on equality yields some interesting societal results. For instance, in the 2000 World Values Survey, on the question "Can most people be trusted?" 55 to 65 percent of people living in Finland, Sweden, Denmark, and Norway said "yes." This compares to only about 16% of people in Latin America; in Brazil, with its particularly high levels of inequality, only 3% could agree with that statement. . (World Values Survey Association, 2000)

This result is not surprising. If government policies demand that the society as a whole is tasked with the welfare of each individual, a natural trust will build: "I know that you'll take care of me if things go bad for me" and vice versa.

There was a time when religious Belief was the Greatest Good for almost any country on earth. For most of recorded human history, most nations *were* belief-based entities. The Pope reigned over the Holy Roman Empire. The King of England was the head of the Church of England. China's and Japan's Emperors were Gods in human form. State religion and national priorities were pretty closely aligned. Emerging capitalist and communist nations of the 19ᵗʰ and 20ᵗʰ centuries took pride in the notion that Belief could be a personal, and not necessarily a community, priority. And just as Belief had nearly been wiped out as a top priority in most nations, two new forces arose that have become epitomes of modern nations with Belief as their Greatest Good. Israel was born as a religious state in the wake of the horrors of World War II's holocaust; and the notion of Islamic nationhood got its start in Egypt in 1928. Until twenty-two year old scholar and schoolteacher Hassan al-Banna formed the Muslim Brotherhood, there was never any organized effort to build national governments around Islamic law. Moreover, as this organization grew in membership (to more than 500,000 members a decade after its founding), the rhetoric took on an increasingly nationalistic tone. Today there are 57 member countries in the United Nations' Organization of the Islamic Conference. Not all of these countries are run completely by Islamic law, but customs and teachings of the Qur'an do openly influence their political discourse and legal affairs.

Saudi Arabia

When I ask people anywhere in the world to name a country based on Belief, the first answer is inevitably "Saudi Arabia." There may be other countries where the religious basis for the nation is equally developed, but Saudi is large, influential (because of oil), and has adopted one of the strictest interpretations of Islamic Law that it has incorporated into its national laws.

Sharia Law

In Saudi Arabia, the constitution of the country is the Qur'an, the sacred text of the Islam faith. The system of laws is derived from Islamic laws of *sharia*, meaning "path" in Arabic. Within the Muslim world several countries use *sharia* as a source for their laws. Compared with other countries such as

Kuwait, Bahrain, Yemen, and United Arab Emirates, Saudi Arabia employs the strictest interpretations of this law.

The First Article of the Constitution states: "The Kingdom of Saudi Arabia is a sovereign Arab Islamic state with Islam as its religion; Allah's Book and the Sunnah of His Prophet, Allah's prayers and peace be upon him, are its constitution, Arabic is its language and Riyadh is its capital."

The presence of other religious worship in the country is outlawed. Christian worship services held at the American Embassy were discontinued in the 1990s; symbols of any other religion's imagery (crosses, Star of Davids, or images of Buddha) are not allowed; entering tourist luggage is searched and bibles and bottles of alcohol are confiscated. All Saudi citizens must be Muslim.

Rules that aren't in the Qur'an

While there is regular talk about some of the strictest rules being relaxed in the future in Saudi Arabia, the path is fraught with problems. For instance, in 2006 women who didn't like leering men selling them bras pressured the government to pass a law prohibiting men from selling women's undergarments. The problem was that mall owners and shopkeepers, who were male, did not think it was right to employ female retailers in the same environment. So apart from a limited number of women-only malls in the country, it has been almost impossible for women to buy lingerie.

The 2011 protests that toppled governments in Tunisia, Egypt and Yemen had effects in Saudi Arabia but minor ones. Signed petitions asking for change in women's rights and election of local officials were delivered to the King but, the most signatures any of these petitions had was only 400. Days of Rage were declared in online sites but no crowds emerged. Nevertheless, there has been some loosening of the restrictions on press reports of discontent with the government. But a March 2011 report in the Al-Riyadh newspaper of a verbal attack on a government minister shows how deeply embedded Belief is as the greatest Good in this country. The minister was chided with the words, "Khoja, fear God in your ministry."(Miller, 2011)

A few months back I did some executive education programs in Saudi Arabia. When I presented the concept of the 8 Great Goods to them, everyone in a room of 40 executives agreed that Belief was the greatest good. One participant suggested that all the other priorities are determined by the teachings of the Qur'an. Everyone agreed with that. But when I asked them to rank their personal priorities, everyone ended up with different rankings after ranking Belief as number one. While the Qur'an may explicitly give a priority for the Goods, in that group of corporate leaders, each person was interpreting that prioritization in very individual ways.

Israel

Israel too is a religious state, but Jewish codes are less rigidly enacted and enforced than Islamic laws in Saudi Arabia.

In Israel there is more tolerance, partly because the basis of law in Israel is British Common Law—a remnant of the British control of Palestine in the early 20th century. But there are some laws in place even now in Israel that reflect Jewish codes rather strictly. Pigs, for instance, cannot be raised on "holy soil" according to the law; and because the State of Israel is the "holy land," pig farming is outlawed—unless you can get around the law; which is exactly what enterprising entrepreneurs have done. If you can keep the pigs from actually touching soil, you are legal; thus, some smaller pig farms are built on wooden planks ensuring that pig hooves and holy land never intersect. One of the biggest pig farms—boasting over 10,000 pigs—doesn't have to worry about planks; it has discovered another loophole. It is a research kibbutz where the animals are raised for research. Obviously, it would be bad form to waste the pig meat when the research is over, so the pork (amazing amounts of research must be done everyday because the kibbutz produces A LOT of pork) is sold to grocers all over the country to cater to non-kosher Jewish and Muslim customers.

The basic educational law states that one essential purpose of elementary education is to teach the values of Jewish culture. Local Jewish religious councils have their budgets paid for by national and local government coffers; other religions get no help. And probably most importantly, the immigration policy is designed to accept any Jew from any nation to settle in Israel. Non-Jews must go through a separate immigration process.

For the most part, Israeli law allows non-Jews to live in the country and follow the rules of their own religion. In fact, one-fifth of the population is non-Jewish. Nevertheless, Israel is a country where the highest priority is Belief. Any law that would directly contravene any deeply held Jewish cultural norm would probably never be allowed to pass.

When national Belief leads to conflict

We've seen it before. During the decades of terrorism and civil warfare in Northern Ireland, the fight was about religion—Catholic versus Protestant. National borders became important symbols of religious differences.

The same seems hold true in the Muslim-Jewish holy wars. As I discussed earlier in the book, conflicts between the Goods can be intense. But when people give top priority to the same Good but interpret it in completely opposing ways, the outcome can be particularly bloody. This is what we see with Belief. National systems based on belief are tremendously unifying—God and nation are one—but they can also lead to levels of international strife that are unmatched when the conflict is over prioritization of the other Goods.

Chapter 17: Joy and Bhutan

It was just thirty years ago that Bhutan opened up to the forces of change and modernization. Until then the country offered only rugged isolation to its citizens. The Bhutanese were almost entirely dependent on the environment around them for both food and clothing. Since the 1970's, Bhutan has gone through a series of national development plans that have changed the country's landscape—literally by replacing animal-made paths with man-made roads. With such a visible display of change and development it may seem strange that this chapter isn't about Growth or even some kind of national Stability. But the emphasis in this Himalayan nation is not Gross National Product, instead they have created their own measure: Gross National Happiness. The government evaluates decisions based on whether any change will increase the overall Joy of the population. The national philosophy is based on the conviction that happiness is the single most important aspiration of its citizens. And because of this conviction, the government's primary role is to meet this need. Bhutan—the youngest democracy on earth—explicitly chooses Joy before every other issue on the list.

I visited Bhutan—for the second time in my life—in the summer of 2010 to advise the government on designing a high-level governmental think tank. I followed on the heels of a consulting firm—McKinsey—which had been working on the same project, but had been asked to leave after they developed a proposal that ... well ... just didn't include enough Joy.

And it wasn't just the stories about my predecessors that convinced me that this is a top priority; I saw it in almost every action of the government and the Bhutanese people. Let me give just two examples:

Lords of the flies

During my visit, I was asked to sit in on a meeting of top cabinet officials and other government bigwigs where they were trying to make some spending and budget decisions. The first thing that struck me about the meeting was that, of course, everyone in the room was wearing the traditional (and national) Bhutanese outfit called a *gho*—a knee-length robe, tied at the waist by a cloth belt, that wraps around the body and extends to the knees where knee-length socks cover the remainder of the leg. The Prime Minister and cabinet members all sported *ghos* that were made of beautiful, heavy fabrics. To see all of these decision-makers file into the wood paneled meeting room dressed in their national garb was awe-inspiring. The room was air-conditioned, but it soon became clear that the windows had not been closed long. As the Prime Minister who sat in the seat next to mine began to talk, I noticed that a fly had landed on his face. Then more gathered on him. As I looked around the room, I noticed that all of the ministers had several flies on them. But no one was making any attempt to shoo the flies away. This being a devotedly Buddhist country where every sentient being is to be respected, the most overt behavior I observed was face scratching or arm brushing ... temporarily dislodging the flies. Of course, in any other country, the room would have been sprayed, disinfected and insect zappers would have been strategically placed around the room. But not in Bhutan.

From their behavior, you might think that Life would be the obvious greatest Good. However, the point of the story here is really not about the flies. It is really about the content of the meeting. Every time a point was raised for doing something new, or spending money, or even discontinuing a project currently in place, the first question posed by someone in the room was: will this make our people happier? Joy was always the standard for ultimate decision-making. Maybe they were looking out for the Joy of the flies as well?

Tunnel to nowhere happy

Later that day I was on my way back to the airport—a two-hour winding drive from the capital city, Thimpu. In looking at a map, I had been surprised to see that Thimpu was actually not that far from the airport, yet the road to the airport formed a V. During the ride, I asked my host from the Foreign Service if I was right in believing that the airport was actually quite close to the capital city as the crow files. He told me that the departure city and the airport were in parallel canyons and really only about 10 or 15 miles from each other. I mused that a tunnel would not be unreasonable at some point in the future.

My host—a young man who had lived in Thailand for many years—gave me a quizzical look and asked a question I'll never forget, "Why would we want to do that?"

A number of responses flashed through my mind: there were the advantages of infrastructure development and efficiency; a rail line would introduce eco-friendliness by removing truck traffic from the highway and reducing automobile pollution; shorter travel times would make the country more attractive to tourists. But for the life of me, I couldn't come up with any argument for why the lives of the Bhutanese people would be happier if they had a tunnel.

In the end I capitulated with a mumbled: "Maybe it isn't such a good idea after all." With that, I settled back into the car to watch the beautiful scenery of rivers, trees and villages go by on my two-hour ride to the airport. And then I had an epiphany: where I come from, we take vacations to see such beautiful scenery; but in Bhutan, you get to see it every time you go to and from the airport.

Gross National Happiness

The idea of Gross National Happiness (GNH) began in 1972 when newly crowned Jigme Singye Wangchuck took the throne at a mere 18 years old. The youngest monarch in the world set to work modernizing the tiny kingdom of Bhutan with his inspired vision of balance and progress. However, initiating an ambitious development plan for the Land of the Dragon —as it is known by the locals—came with a caveat. The young, but wise King maintained that development proved nothing and increased nothing if peace and happiness did not remain the focus of the country. So he began spearheading the philosophical and technical framework of GNH.

There is some folklore suggesting that the King first coined "Gross National Happiness" as an off-the-cuff remark. But he and those around him liked how it sounded and soon it was being structurally defined. A GNH society, King Wangchuck said, "means the creation of an enlightened society in which happiness and well-being of all people and sentient beings is the ultimate purpose of governance."

The rationale for beginning a measurement system of GNH in the first place was because of the prevalence of the GNP measurement in the rest of the world. Bhutan and its leaders wanted a way to at least internally measure how the country was doing on this from year to year.

There obviously would be no international comparison ... but in a country that does not spend a lot of time thinking about national competitiveness, this fact doesn't bother them much.

It was no small task to create a quantitative index capable of measuring a population's happiness. It took almost 30 years to form the infrastructure to support the philosophy. The Centre for Bhutan Studies along with the GNH Commission were formed to work out the nitty-gritty details and it wasn't until 2008 when a GNH measurement system was officially adopted by the government.

There is a lot made of Bhutan in the press on the measure of GNH that is being developed. I'll explain this in a little depth here, because if any country decided that a particular Good was its greatest, it could then begin to develop a measure of that Good. But I explain all of this with a big caveat: internally, at the highest levels of Bhutan's government, there is still a debate ...

Four pillars

There were four pillars that were explicitly laid out in the early 2000s: economic self-reliance, environmental preservation, cultural promotion, and good governance. And the government sees them all as a huge success, particularly environmental preservation: in the last decade, the forest cover of Bhutan has actually increased while it has dropped almost everywhere else on earth.

However, some things really important to the Bhutanese people were not accounted for by the Four Pillars; for instance, in this Buddhist nation, opportunities for meditation are highly valued—so, "time use" was included as one of the domains. The four pillars were divided into nine domains:

1. Psychological Well-being: Government policies and services are determined based on increasing the collective level of satisfaction and quality of life.

2. Time Use: In contrast to GDP, which tracks a countries ability to produce goods, GNH tracks how the population spends their non-working hours. Activities like sleeping, community participation, religious activities, and leisure contribute to a rich and meaningful life. Just because income isn't being generated doesn't mean these activities should be any less valued.

3. Community Vitality: This is essentially the same thing as Relationships; it measures the nature of societal ties, and sense of belonging.

4. Cultural Diversity and Resilience: I'll go into this in more detail later; essentially this domain is about preserving a communal sense of identity and being able to correctly assume the core values of the society.

5. Health: This is physical well-being, but also knowledge about health related issues like the transmission of HIV and good breast-feeding practices.

6. Education: Beyond providing quality education to school age children, this domain measures whether education creates buy-in to the goal of collective well-being.

7. Ecological Diversity and Resilience: This monitors the pressure that development is putting on ecosystems and identifies appropriate responses.

8. Living Standard: This is beyond just income level and measures the sense of financial security. For example, is there an ability to make household repairs or contribute financially to community festivities?

9. Good Governance: Bhutan is doing a lot in this area. Not only is this about good governance practices but also how people perceive the government in terms of efficacy, honesty and quality.

You'll notice these nine domains are basically nine goals that the Government has identified as necessary factors toward happiness. They hint at what the policy-makers grapple with—how to first identify, then turn societal Goods into actionable policy?

Measuring happiness

Identifying and protecting key determinants of happiness is the function of the nine domains. This is accomplished through a series of indicators—both objective and subjective in nature. Objectively, more hospitals have a more positive influence on happiness than fewer hospitals. Subjectively, with lower instances of tuberculosis people perceive that they are healthier and thus happier. Combining into one metric the self-report of experiences and the objective statistics—government officials believe—helps paint a more accurate picture of all around happiness. And as this is measured annually, it allows for a feedback loop to evaluate progress and self-correct policies according to the GNH indicators. It's also a telling representation of the Buddhist philosophy of interdependence and accountability. Examples of questions include:

- How much do you trust your neighbors?
- During the past few weeks, how often have you felt the following moods/ emotions? (Choices include anger, guilt, selfishness, pride, calmness, empathy, forgiveness, contentment, generosity, disappointment, sadness, and frustration.)
- Indicate the importance that you assign the following principles in life: family life, friendship, spiritual faith, compassion, self-development, reciprocity, responsibility, freedom, material wealth, financial security, career, success, and pleasure.
- Do you take part in local festivals and community events?
- Do you know the names of candidates from your constituency in different political parties?

According to the last national census, the reported levels of happiness among the Bhutanese people are quite impressive:

Not Very Happy = 3%
Happy = 52%
Very Happy = 45%

Life is too short not to be happy

It's only fair though to acknowledge some inherent tension between Joy and the other Goods in Bhutan. Time is a precious commodity in Bhutan. If you consider that the average Bhutanese life span is a mere 66 years—that's up from 46 years, which was the norm in 1977—Life seems like it would have premium status among the 8 Great Goods. But it's the shortage of Life that makes Joy so important. The Bhutanese know that a life spent in pursuit of material goods is futile, because ultimately you can't take any of it with you. Over 1,000 years of Mahayana Buddhism influence has shaped the belief system of the country. Bhutanese faith stresses individual development, sanctity of life, compassion for others, respect for nature, social harmony and the importance of compromise over material rewards.

A 54-year-old Bhutanese man who was living in Singapore—which is incidentally the 10th most expensive city in the world and the epitome of Growth—reported that he hadn't been seduced by the glamour of the big city. He couldn't wait to return to Bhutan, even though he would most likely never own more than a dozen cows, a small plot of land, and an old, broken-down car. He compares Singaporeans to people who try to drink salt water to quench their thirst. In his mind, their emphasis on Growth will never lead to Joy—you can always have more, so you can never be truly satisfied.

In 2005, the nation's fourth king, the one who came up with the idea of GNH, announced that the kingdom would become a democracy. When he stepped down, an election would be held for a prime minister and a government would be formed. His son would still be King but would have no formal power. He reasoned that he knew his son was a good man and would rule justly as a King, but he didn't know if his grandsons or great-grandsons would be good people. In the long run—he believed—a democratic government would yield more consistently positive results than a monarchy. In his drive to make sure that his people lived in Joy, he gave them the rights of Individuality that come with democracy.

The world is watching

Bhutan is increasingly being recognized by the world for its innovative vision of change and growth. The idea of GNH has caught the attention of academics, politicians, and economists alike, who are beginning to see the disconnect between happiness and material wealth. Already four International Conferences on Gross National Happiness have been convened in different countries and is propelling the idea of GNH into more mainstream developmental theory. Canada, Australia, France, and most recently Britain have begun looking at ways to incorporate the values of GNH into their public policy and programs. In November 2010, Prime Minister David Cameron unveiled a plan to measure Britain's happiness in addition to GDP as a measure of national success.

Bhutan's influence is also being felt in ways beyond GNH. In 1985, Bhutan was one of the countries responsible for establishing the South Asia

Association for Regional Cooperation (SAARC). Along with Afghanistan, Bangladesh, India, Maldives, Nepal, Pakistan and Sri Lanka, the very first objective of the Association is to promote the welfare of the peoples of South Asia and to improve their quality of life. After 25 years, the 2010 Declaration of SAARC emphasized a greater focus to uphold traditions and values and pursue people-centric development. Perhaps indicative of Bhutan's growing influence on the outside world.

A cultural identity worth saving

Bhutan is also cognizant of the importance of Cultural Diversity and Resilience. Cultural values have been crucial in buffering against the hostile outside world (read "bad western influences").

TV is only broadcast during limited hours and the Internet is still not pervasive; nevertheless, television and the Internet are increasingly becoming a part of everyday Bhutanese life. One of the most interesting concerns that I heard voiced on the influence of external media involves a plant found lining almost every road in the Kingdom. Cannabis is considered a bothersome weed by most of the population—but very contented cows do enjoy munching on it. Access to western media has been introducing Bhutanese youth to other uses of the plant. According to one source, the strain found in Bhutan is not particularly strong, and so not much of an intoxicant. However, that doesn't seem to be stopping Western-influenced young people from trying.

In spite of the country's development and willingness to participate on a global level, tourism is tightly managed, and travelers may only enter with a registered travel agency. Visitors are required to spend an average of US$250 a day and visa permits are carefully managed to ensure that tourists most willing to pay enter first.

My first visit to the Kingdom was on a whim. In 2006, I realized that I had 10 days magically free in my schedule. My partner and I considered where we'd like to go that we'd never visited before and Bhutan came to mind. We made contact with a high-end hotel in the country; they arranged our visas; and less than a week later we were on a plane. As far as I was concerned, Disneyland lost claim to the title Magic Kingdom as soon as I had set foot in Bhutan.

John C Beck

As a daily, personal reminder of heritage, the King instituted the policy of *Driglam Namzha* (Etiquette and Manners) in 1988, which required all citizens to wear traditional clothing while in public. The King further established the requirement of teaching *Dzongkha* (the national language) in schools.

The government is undertaking a campaign to do inventory on the abundance of oral traditions, songs and dances that enrich the everyday lives of the Bhutanese. Festivals and ceremonies are highly revered as expressions of identity and bring to life the communal values and beliefs. The stories they tell depict the eternal struggle between the forces of good and evil. As this beautiful country is caught up in a world spinning with visceral distractions, Bhutan preserves its cultural values from the dizzying tug of the Internet, mobile phones and cable TV. It balances modernity with its firm stance on what its end goals are. Bhutan knows: endless happiness is worth preserving. And the government is determined to do just that—above all else.

Really?

So how happy are the Bhutanese really? In general studies of satisfaction or happiness levels from country to country, Bhutan actually scores very well—but not at the top. In a 2007 study from Adrian White of the University of Leicester, Bhutan ranked eighth out of 178 countries in Subjective Well-Being (a measure used by psychologists since 1997). And Bhutan was the only country in the happiest top 20 to have a very low GDP.

In my first meeting with the Prime Minister he told me that he likes the term Gross National Happiness not only because it is a substitute for Gross National Product, but also because of the meaning of the words "gross" and "national." Both words imply that this is not about the happiness of one person or one group of people. Rather, gross means "all" or "total" and national means in all geographies of the country. So what he is trying to pursue is the happiness of everyone in the totality of the country. That is a tall order given the remote primitiveness of many of the villages in this tiny country, but a worthy goal nonetheless.

Applying a measure to the other Great Goods

How do you get everyone to the same understanding of the 8 Great Goods?

First you have to get everyone to agree on the meanings—that could be done with training or an educational campaign. But, it is more than just basic definitions. It really helps if there is a way to measure the Good in question. You can see the complications in trying to measure—productively—something as seemingly straightforward as happiness or Joy. If it is too simple a tool, there is still a lot of room for individual interpretations of the data. If it is too complex a tool, people may think they understand what it means, but really have no clue. Take GNP for example, even government employees and academics who use the term GNP all the time, probably do not understand all that is involved in measuring it.

That is the risk that the current Bhutanese government faces. The measurement tool they are developing may be technically correct, but it will be difficult to really understand. What happens when the GNH measurement says everything should be all right, but the people aren't feeling it? In a democracy, the tool must be a fair reflection of what people themselves are sensing about their world, or it will be quickly discarded as a useless tool.

There is no other country besides Bhutan that can claim Joy as their greatest good. But it is interestingly the one Good that stands the best chance of substituting for Growth as a metric of success. In a fascinating day-long meeting sponsored by the Bertelsmann Group in Singapore in 2010, I watched as academics, government officials and business practitioners from around the globe struggled with the issue of "if not growth, then what?" The conclusion was that Bhutan's example of happiness as a metric may be the only real alternative. Happiness is, after all, something on which we humans can all agree.

John C Beck

Section IV

Goods in Practice:
Leading Good Organizations

John C Beck

Chapter 18: ACDC Leadership

In the previous section, I explored the ways that the Greatest Goods of nations are expressed through their policies and decision-making. It was a descriptive tour of countries around the globe. But rather than describe a wide variety of business organizations in this section, I plan to be a little more prescriptive. Here, I will recommend actions to make your organization (corporate or philanthropic) more aligned with clearer priorities of the Greatest Goods.

The nations I described earlier have stumbled or debated their way into their current policies. Nations really do not have to change those strategies very often. Companies—which normally have the Greatest Good of Growth—are likely to want to change lower level priorities more often than governments. In this section I offer some ways to lead organizations more effectively through the 8 Great Goods.

We, as humans, should be pretty damn proud for our ability to organize big groups of people to complete a shared task. It is partly what separates us from the animal kingdom. The outputs of our most ambitious big projects have come to be known as the Wonders of the World. Rome ruled the Western world because of its ability to control large armies. Britain dominated the seas and maintained imperial holdings all over the globe due to their ability to coordinate large numbers of people.

It should be of little surprise then, that business organizations have become such a source of human pride. The capitalist system gives both wealth and power to those best able to funnel the activities of thousands of people to create and support desirable products and services. The story of successful organizations is *really* the story of successful leaders.

Good Leaders and the Great Goods

There is an argument that the measure of leadership greatness in most organizations is Life—or at least "longevity." Many of our corporate or government leaders are lauded more for the number of years they spend in power than for their actual output. Often senators get introduced as "the three term senator from the great state of ...." more than they get introduced as "the senator who pushed through civil rights legislation or fiscal reform or ...."

Of course, there is an understanding that if these leaders are not running an organization very well, they will be replaced. Therefore, longevity is a proxy for success in other ways, I suppose. But for most of the greatest leaders throughout history, the Good they are remembered for was more than just their "time served."

Abe Lincoln is not known for having been less than a five-year president, he's also known for having held the country together; FDR was president for a long time, but he stared down a couple of pretty major obstacles during his time: an economic disaster and Hitler. Steve Jobs will probably not be known for his long tenure (in two separate terms) at Apple, but rather as the founder and creative force behind the Macintosh computer, iTunes, the iPod, the iPhone and the iPad. Joe Forehand won't be known for his five years as a CEO nearly as much as he'll be known as the guy who took Accenture public, changing its name from Andersen Consulting—and therefore distancing the company from its parent company, Arthur Andersen which stopped operating only one year after Forehand's company made a clean split. In terms of the 8 Great Goods, Lincoln held a nation of Relationships together, FDR focused on Life and Stability, Steve Jobs is about Joy, and Forehand created an Individuality for his company that allowed it to thrive.

It is pretty easy to attach a Great Goods label to any good organizational strategy. But it is still incumbent on the leader to create and nurture that direction.

ACDC Leadership

Good leaders all have a few things in common that they want their people to do well: focus, alignment, decisiveness, and flexibility. Those four characteristics go a long way toward making an organization good and the only way for that organization to get to good—let alone beyond that, to great—is with a leader or leadership group that can make these four things happen. My mnemonic for the skills to do this is: ACDC Leadership (Attention, Culture, Decision, and Change).

But I must pause for a moment to address your concerns about the use of the acronym ACDC. I don't know which of the common meanings of ACDC flew into your mind first when you read this, but all of the most popular meanings might apply pretty nicely to great leadership as well.

AC/DC: energy. Alternating current and direct current: the two basic forms of transmission of electrical energy. Being a great leader requires plentiful and appropriate energy to power an organization.

AC/DC: standards. One of the first great commercial standards battles was over electrical standards. Thomas Edison installed direct current electrical systems in city centers around the US and worked tirelessly to protect his patents for this system. But the alternating current system supported by George Westinghouse and Nikola Tesla proved to be better for long distance transmission and—theoretically, at least—safer. Interestingly, the installation of alternating current generating equipment at Niagara Falls in 1896 was a major turning point in the standards battle. Eventually the entire US converted to AC; however, the last direct current transmission in America— one run by Con-Edison in New York City—was not terminated until 2007. Like the AC/DC standards battle, good leaders must supply the standards for their organizations and, in the case of conflicting standards, make hard choices about which should be used.

AC/DC: the rock band. This music group, from Australia, started in the early 1970s and has sold 200 million albums since. They are rock stars. If you are going to be a great leader, you need to sell yourself like a rock star—in a functional rock band.

AC/DC: flexibility. AC/DC usually means that a device can use both forms of current and switch easily back and forth between the two. As a leader you need to be flexible enough to still be effective no matter what environment you are in.

AC/DC: bisexuality. AC/DC became a euphemism for bisexuality in the 1960s. I'm not suggesting that good leaders need to be bisexual—although there is nothing wrong with that—but I think great leaders are able to be a bit ambiguous at times ... allowing their follower to feel like they are always on "their team."

With the standard meanings all explained in terms of leadership ... whew! Let's now consider the meanings that I'd really like to attach to these letters.

John C Beck

Chapter 19: A: Leading through Attention
(where do we focus?)

A good organization is a focused organization—one composed of people who know what they want to achieve and how to get there. A good leader is someone who can help the organization get that focus.

Mission statements and values statements are two tools that leaders have long—and successfully—used to direct the attention of employees. As a young consultant, I sat in on a number of mission/values statement meetings of top executives. To me, these meetings felt like hours—sometimes days—of group editing. Often lengthy debates occurred over where to place a comma or whether the word should be, for instance, "honesty" or "integrity." So it was a surprise to me when I found out that mission/values statements are considered two of the most valuable tools in executives' managerial quivers. The consulting firm Bain and Company has been conducting a study of the most successful management tools on an annual basis since the early 1990s. In each of those years, mission/value statements have been ranked consistently among the top two or three tools. Business leaders report that they find these managerial tools are really useful at focusing attention. Once it was put in those terms, I started to understand the popularity as well. All those hours that corporate boards and top executives spend in what looks like semantics arguments may be more than that. They may actually be working through some misunderstandings that exist and trying to get clarity for everyone in the room— so that everyone can focus on the same thing.

My one qualm remaining with organizational value statements, in particular, is that they list a lot of "values" that the organization should have, but not in a way that is actionable. Many corporate values statements end up being a mere laundry list of laudable characteristics; you can be sure that in any values statement you come across these days there will be something in there about protecting the dignity of employees and being environmentally green. Those are, indeed, important and good values; I wholeheartedly support them. But what if "green" and "dignity" come into conflict with the company's goal of making a profit? Do you still value them? What if they come into conflict with each other? Which one is more important?

I've raised these questions before in meetings and been shushed with a curt "Our people must be capable of doing all of these things." I don't mind any company setting stretch goals for their employees, but no one's brain can pay attention to more than one thing at a time. You may be able to switch your focus pretty rapidly from one thing to another, but in any given instance, it is on just one thing. And, the brain pretty quickly prioritizes conflicting tasks and will devote resources to the one that is more important. So, unless you are cultivating a new species as your workforce—I've been in companies where it really did feel like they thought they could do that—you probably need to help employees prioritize. As a leader, your job is to focus employee attention in a way that drives them to achieve the goals of the organization.

A leader's attention

But this prioritization of your employee's attention all starts with getting your own mind focused on what is most important. As a leader, your attention actually ends up being the focus of attention for your employees. If you don't have your mind trained on the right things, you really can't expect your subordinates to stay focused.

In a study I conducted over ten years ago, I found that subordinates will pay inordinate amounts of attention to where the attention of their leaders is focused. And subordinates will then put their own attention on the same issues that their superiors are finding important. (Davenport & Beck, 2001) We are all hierarchical beings, so we like to please those above us. We've learned over millennia that paying attention to what more powerful people care about will make them less likely to want to kill us—and may even earn us a reward if they think we are more like them.

How does this all work? We know that successful CEOs really do care about what they urge their employees to do: Steve Jobs cared deeply about design and usability; Jack Welsh really did want to be number one in everything. These are traits of leadership attention that allowed attention to be pointed to the right issues throughout the organization. But, sometimes even a laudable leadership focus can take an organization down an untenable path.

Harvey Fellman was long-term CEO of a successful consulting firm. He personally held Relationships as his Greatest Good—naturally and smoothly focusing on the ties that bind one person to another—and he was brilliant at it. A major part of his leadership style was in helping employees when the vicissitudes of life cropped up. By being there for employees at their time of need—problems with children, elderly parents, divorce, even deaths of loved ones—he created miraculous performance among his employees and consistent loyalty throughout his tenure as CEO and beyond. The company felt like a "family company" even though it was a corporation with multiple shareholders.

Everyone in the company took their cue from Harvey and worked hard at forming tight, collegial—even friendly—relationships with others. In-company dating was not frowned upon—in fact, it was celebrated. Married couples worked together on the same teams—separated only if a workplace difficulty cropped up.

It was a joy for everyone to work in a company where there was not a clear up or out policy and profitability was explicitly subordinated to human relationships. When the company was in its infancy—as was the consulting industry—a good company that could attract and keep good people was the key to economic growth. But over time the industry's growth slowed and Fellman's company never was able to shift out of the Relationships focus to something more economically viable. Given his company's focus on keeping employees happy with each other, the increasingly challenging economic environment was not obvious to most of the employees of this company until it was almost too late. What had been created was the corporate equivalent of French royal court behavior. Everyone wanted to get the relationships right and had stopped thinking much about anything else.

Before he knew it, Fellman was being edged out of the company. And the group taking over would not be his handpicked successors. But they *were* the group that was most able to shift the emphasis to Growth and interestingly, have been able to keep some of the focus on Relationships at the same time—probably because the culture, a topic addressed below, was so imbued with this thinking. After five years of really painful changes and restructuring, the company is back on a profitable course again.

Another leader of a small, but influential organization—lets call him Ivan—found himself constantly at odds with his most important employees. He is a handsome, and very charismatic CEO—young for his position and highly focused on connecting with the most important people in the world. He has made a bit of a name for himself by focusing on issues of Equality: "how people should treat each other." This topic aligns nicely with his personal prioritization of the 8 Great Goods: he cares about it deeply. But it never has been a major focus of the organization where he works. The most talented people in his organization and his customers were interested in Growth. Needless to say, equality and growth often find themselves at odds with each other. He talks to his Board members, employees, and customers about Equality all the time. But they have trouble relating to his cause célèbre. Nonetheless, during his tenure as CEO, attention throughout the organization has been diverted to Equality and, sadly, the bottom line has suffered.

Attention Exercises

I've said that leaders will get attention no matter what; and the issues that leaders pay attention to will also get a lot of attention. But if, as a leader, you have a set of pet issues that need the attention of the whole organization, you probably want to highlight those.

1. Take one—or a set—of the 8 Goods and let everyone know that is your emphasis. Make it explicit.
2. Periodically survey your people to see if they are paying attention to the same Goods that you think are important.
3. If there is a disconnect, ask why. Maybe there is a need for a lot more communication to help followers understand the priorities that leaders would like for the organization. And, just maybe the leaders' priorities to change.
4. If the Goods of leaders and followers are too similar, ask yourself if you may be overly focused on that one good and need to introduce others into the priority mix.

Chapter 20: C: Leading through Culture (who are we?)

As you can see from the stories about Harvey and Ivan in the previous chapter, the focus of a CEO and the organization quickly morphs into culture. But culture is even longer lasting than attention. An individual or an organization can decide to pay attention to something new or different. It is not easy to switch at first because our "attention synapses" have learned to focus the brain on certain things. But it can change relatively quickly. Culture is another animal completely. Once in place, its effects can last for decades.

The "buck stops" with leaders for creating, nurturing and altering the culture of their organization. The mechanism for setting the culture is clearly attention but, with culture, a leader has more levers to pull than with attention. The only way to alter the attention of an organization is really for the leader to adjust his or her own attention. Organizational culture can be molded in many ways, but always from the top. Have you ever seen a company with a great culture that was rotten at the top?

If you can accept the argument in the previous chapters—that the 8 Great Goods work as priorities for whole nations—then the importance of the 8 Great in organizations should be much easier to fathom; after all, organizations are smaller, more focused, with a clear cut decision-making process.

What the survey said about organizations

In December 2009, I surveyed 1000 Americans and 1000 Japanese about their 8 Greats. (I should note that part of the reason for this survey was exploratory: I was trying to categorize the Greatest Goods and there were only seven that I had identified then—you'll notice that the names of the goods were different as well.) The choice of Japan and US for this initial international survey was a careful one. I've been designing and conducting cross-cultural surveys since I was a college student. In every international survey I've ever done, the Japanese are always at the opposite end of the results spectrum from the US. Consequently, I often start a series of international surveys with these two countries—then I know what the global extremes are likely to be.

Organizational Greatest Goods in Japan and the US

Percentage of respondents who listed each Good as their organization's highest priority

	Life	Society	Growth	Individuality	Joy	Belief	Fairness
Japan	7	19	49	8	2	1	15
US	15	10	42	7	4	12	11

And, on this survey—as in all of those in the past—there were significant differences in results from country to country. Interestingly, on any survey or interview I've given on this question, respondents felt like they could answer the question quite easily. Usually they spend a lot less time on the question of Greatest Goods for their organizations than they do when trying to rank their own personal priorities.

One of the important findings, but not surprising in a way, is that Life is rarely perceived by employees as the Greatest Good of their companies. In most business organizations, Growth is the greatest good. In both US and Japanese samples, Growth was king in organizations.

There are three important observations from this chart. One is that because Belief is so high in the US compared to Japan, it skews the remainder of the less highly prioritized Goods. Individuality appears to be a higher Good in organizations in Japan than in the US, but without the effect of Belief, this would be less pronounced.

The second fascinating difference is that Japanese organizations emphasize Life less than those in the US by a two to one margin. This would seem to fly in the face of my argument that Japan is the most pro-life country on earth. But the difference is in the unit of analysis—nation versus organization. Japanese corporations are so controlled by national law on the issue of Life that they don't have to pay much attention to it. Moreover, because Japanese law actually prosecutes corporations for employees dying on the job or being fired without cause, corporations are widely perceived as the "bad guy" on the issue of Life— to a much greater extent than in the US.

And finally, the most important point of the chart is that Growth is by far the highest priority Good of nearly a majority of organizations in the US and Japan. This is not at all surprising given that the goal of business organizations in capitalist societies is to make money and get bigger. What is surprising is that more than 50% of the respondents *didn't* see their organization's greatest good as Growth. (Do note, however, that about 15% of the respondents from each country held jobs in government or education and therefore would be less likely to see Growth as their organizational Greatest Good.) In Japan Equality and Relationships themselves are two big foci of organizations. In the US the emphases are really mixed. And, Joy is the top priority of a very small number of organizations in either country.

It would be fair to argue that the second and third tier Goods of organizations help differentiate businesses from each other. For instance, the Marriott hotel chain wants to make money—and does. Everything I've seen of their strategy and culture suggest that Growth is their top priority. What many people don't know is that the Marriott Corporation was founded, and is run by, a Mormon family. To most Marriott customers, the most obvious sign of Belief being one of chain's Greatest Goods is the fact that a Book of Mormon can be found in the nightstand drawer at all of their properties. But a clear signal that Growth (also known as revenue) is a more important Good to the Marriott Corporation—and has been so for decades—is the fact that this alcohol-forswearing Mormon family for many years (particularly while it owned HMS Host until several years ago) sold more liquor than any other single corporation in the world. The Belief priority did not get in the way of making money. I once asked a Mormon friend of mine, many years ago, why this apparent contradiction didn't bother him and he told me: "If they didn't sell alcohol they wouldn't make as much money and wouldn't give as much to the Church in tithing."

In a follow-up to the 2009 survey, I asked an additional question to 1100 Americans in 2012. I wondered how bosses in companies were perceived, versus the top leadership of the firm. I hoped to get a little more nuanced view of what "companies" were perceived to be in the first set of surveys. Remember that the labels for the 8 Great Goods has changed since my 2009: so now we have Equality instead of Fairness, Relationships instead of Society, and Stability has been added.

What I find interesting—but quite predictable—about the difference between "organization" and "my boss" is, happily, that "my boss" is more human. Immediate bosses care more about life, relationships, belief,

Greatest Good of one's organization and one's boss among US respondents
Percentage of respondents who listed each Good as the highest priority

	Life	Relation-ships	Growth	Individu-ality	Joy	Belief	Equality	Stability
My Boss	14	13	29	7	5	12	6	14
Organization	9	10	41	5	4	9	7	15

individuality and much less about growth. But they also are not much more interested in joy than the organization and actually care less about Equality, Stability, and Growth.

Fit and Satisfaction

One of the more interesting results of the survey is the strength of the tie between an individual's own Greatest Goods and one's perceived Greatest Goods of their organization. In my survey of people around the world, there is a strong, statistically significant relationship between the congruence of individual and organizational 8 Great priorities and job satisfaction. And, it is not just job satisfaction that is badly affected by a mismatch between personal and organizational Good priorities; satisfaction with community, leisure activities, and even family life are all thrown out of whack when personal priorities are significantly different from those that surround you at work everyday.

The chart on the next page requires a little explanation. In this chart I chose just to analyze the approximately 1000 American respondents in my 2009 survey. My hypothesis was that job satisfaction would be higher if there was a closer fit between an individual's prioritization and the prioritization of their organization. What is represented in the chart is the point count difference between a respondent's priorities ranking of each Good and their perceived ranking of the Goods for their organization. So for instance, if I think Joy is my greatest good, it would get a 1 ranking, and if I think my organization places Joy last, it would get an 8 ranking. The difference, or delta, is 7 points. I simply summed up the delta between personal ranking and organizational ranking for each of the Goods to come up with the My Ranking to Organizational Ranking Delta. In the United States, the average delta was 18.1.

In the chart, I compare the deltas of those who are satisfied with various aspects of their lives to those who are dissatisfied with those aspects of their lives. My hypothesis that there is a big delta between personal and organizational Greatest Goods was confirmed—but even more interestingly, those who report larger differences in Good priorities from their organizations also find themselves less satisfied with their family, their community, their leisure lives and the success-level of their organization.

One word of caution, because this was a survey, we don't know what the organization's actual prioritization was, all we were able to capture was an individual's perception of those priorities. And there is a possibility that people who are disenchanted with their organization are likely to see the priorities of the firm as quite different from their own. But the fact that there was no correlation between My-Org Delta and the respondent's satisfaction with health, spirituality, or even personal financial success makes it harder to turn the causality in the other direction.

The important point here is that there is a significant drop in satisfaction the greater the disparity between an individual's priorities and those of their organization.

	My to Org Δ
Job Satisfaction	17.7
No Job Sat	18.9
Family Satisfaction	17.8
No Family Sat	19.5
Community Sat	17.6
No Comm Sat	19.2
Leisure Sat	17.8
No Leis Sat	18.9
Sat with Org Success	17.8
No Sat Org Success	18.7

Making a job decision without the 8 Great Goods

I saw this link between individual and organizational priorities and satisfaction up close and personal a few years ago. At the time, I didn't have the 8 Great Goods to guide me but, I naturally didn't make my decision to take a job in Japan lightly: I'd been talking to the founder of the school for four years; there were six months of negotiation on the contract; and I had spoken to a dozen or so of the top people before I actually decided to accept the job offer. You'd think I would have uncovered the basic seeds of incongruence during all of these conversations. And to some extent, and perhaps at some subconscious level, I knew something was not quite right for me; so, I made sure there was a one-year opt-out clause in the contract. I was never able to pinpoint my discomfort, and ended up signing the contract.

I took the job, partly, because I thought there was pretty good fit between my priorities and the school's. At the time I made the decision I didn't have these words but, in retrospect, this is what I was thinking:

I've always been one who values Joy and learning in life. And, I care about family members and organizations (Relationships) and Individuality. Economic success and even Life itself are farther down my priority list.

I thought there was reasonable congruence between my Greatest Goods and my new employers'. Most universities highly value learning for the Joy of learning—I assumed this was the case for this school as well. I was concerned that Japanese companies are loath to put Individuality above Relationships. While I've studied Japanese society my whole career, this worry had been a deterrent to my taking jobs in Japan in the past. But in this job decision, the man hiring me for this job—the founder and owner—was a self-avowed maverick who had left the big, bad Japanese corporate world to start something that would allow people to be themselves. My contract allowed me to set my own work hours and even my own place of work—I could work from home as often as I liked.

I know that most organizations don't put Joy as high on their priority list, but my new boss reveled in the fact that he left work every day at 5pm to go swimming with his children and spent a month or more every summer in Australia so his kids could learn to speak English. He even talked about the frequent parties that the company held. During the hiring process, one of my first interactions with my team was a raucous evening of drinking and laughing. I expected a lot of fun!

Since the school was mostly for-profit, I expected that Growth would be important as well. It was rarely expressed in monetary terms in the meetings I attended before hiring on. But there was a clearly expressed goal—to be the best school in Asia in the next 10 years. And that, too, was an ambitious goal that fit with my own interests in trying to push limits and achieve greatness.

So what could possibly go wrong in terms of a fit of my personal and the corporate Great 8? Joy, Individuality, Relationships and Growth—there was a pretty complete fit!

The Real Goods

A few months into my new job I talked about my problems at the school to friends in America. I usually tried to do this with some anecdotes, and I, naturally, expected my friends to be appalled by what my new employer was doing to me. Their response was baffling. They tried to look sympathetic but there was no true empathy. Even their questions felt like recommendations for me to try harder: "Isn't this just a cultural issue?" "Maybe if you stick with it, you'll find it isn't so bad?" "Don't a lot of Japanese companies work like that?" "Can't you try to fit in better?" My anecdotes were not communicating my discomfort. I was unable to explain why the lack of fit that I was feeling was driving me to a place of real unhappiness. I didn't have the words. Now I do. Now I even have a chart! (on the next page)

For the sake of argument, let's assume that Life is the Greatest Good. I'm taking the job partly because I'd like to have the money to stay alive and my new employer would like me—and the other employees—to stay alive for obvious reasons. If we remove that great Good from the comparison, my next six Goods (at this point in my evolution, I hadn't yet included Stability in my conceptualization of the Goods) were roughly in the following order: Joy, Relationships, Individuality, Equality, Growth and Belief.

Before I joined the organization, I expected my new Japanese employer to prioritize major decisions in approximately the following order: Growth, Individuality, Joy, Relationships, Equality, and Belief.

Seven Great Goods (without Life)	My Personal Order	Expected School Order	Survey Results Order	Δ My to Expected	Δ Expected to Results
Relationships	2	4	1	2	1
Growth	5	1	4	4	1
Individuality	3	3	7	0	4
Joy (including Learning)	1	2	6	1	5
Belief	7	7	2	0	5
Equality	4	6	5	2	1
Stability	6	5	3	1	3
				10	20

In other words, there was a respectable congruence—If I just add up the point differences between my personal order and my expected organizational order, I get a delta of a 10 point difference (see the chart below). One of the biggest differences that I expected was in Growth. I place a fairly low emphasis on acquiring more money or stuff. But, because I was going to work for an educational corporation—albeit a partially not-for-profit company—I was comfortable with a focus on revenue and growth. You would expect Growth to be the number one Good in many companies.

Almost a year after leaving the job, I asked seven people who worked at this university to rank the Greatest Goods there. If I had only had the wisdom to do a quick survey when I was interviewing for the job!!! Then, I would have known to ask an entirely different set of questions, and I probably would have decided to forgo the opportunity all together. My respondents—on average—thought that the 8Greats for the school were: Relationships, Belief, Stability, Growth, Equality, Joy and Individuality.

Looking at the chart, can you see how different my own and my expectation of the prioritization of the Goods are from the reality of the organization? No wonder I was generally unhappy in my job. When the Goods of an organization are that far from the ones that we personally profess, it is likely there will be some tension. And in this case, I was completely blindsided by a couple of the priorities. I really believed—based on everything that I was told—that

Individuality was an important priority to the university. But in my after-the-fact survey, the employees rated Individuality as dead last. And Belief came in first place!!! At a place like Notre Dame or Brigham Young University, I might expect Belief to be first place, but this was entirely unexpected. I actually had a sense that there was a religious affiliation to the university during my early interviews. I even asked the founder if he was part of some evangelical Buddhist sect. He denied having any affiliation or even any strong belief in religion. So, I was surprised to find, after I joined, that at many organization off-sites and gatherings, we were asked to read from Neo-Confucianist texts. In my interviews, the founder was technically correct to say that there was no "church affiliation," but there was a very strong belief system. If I had just done this survey before I joined the organization, I would have armed myself with a broader set of questions during my due diligence period. Finally, it was significant that not even learning was a huge priority at this university.

I came into the organization expecting a place where we could discuss how the individual employees could uniquely contribute to the future. I started right off proposing innovative new solutions to grow the school to become Asia's Number One. But, I didn't give proper obeisance to—nor did I even understand—the belief system in place, one that emphasized Japanese tradition, social cohesion and hierarchy. I was just in the wrong place and I felt it in every conversation I had and in every meeting I attended.

Culture Exercises

1. Ask your employees what they believe others in the organization perceive as the Great Goods.

2. Ask your most important customers and clients what they see as your Great Goods.

3. If these are different from what you would like to see as your Great Goods, what decisions and changes do you need to make to ensure that your culture is perceived as the culture you want to nurture?

John C Beck

Chapter 21: D: Leading through Decisions (how should we decide?)

In my descriptions of national Goods earlier in the book, I tried to keep the focus off of culture and mostly on decisions—in the form of laws—that a country supports. But the correlation between the decisions that are made and the culture of any group of people should logically be quite high. And, indeed, if you examine studies done on organizational culture and decisions, the two are indeed highly correlated. From corporations to government organizations to hospitals to fire fighters, study after study shows that culture has a huge impact on decisions in organizations.

Decision-making is the clear realm of the leader in any human group. It is the most explicit role of leadership. Attention will focus on the leader whether the leader wants it or not. A leader may task others to create a culture or to direct change—but if the leader doesn't support it completely, it will not happen. An organizations' leader must make decisions. Many decisions may be delegated to subordinates, but when the subordinates disagree, the leader is left to make the final decision. US Presidents have noted the importance of this leadership role with memorable quotes like: "The buck stops here" (Truman), "I am the decider" (G.W. Bush) and "In any moment of decision the best thing you can do is the right thing, the next best thing is the wrong thing, and the worst thing you can do is nothing." (T. Roosevelt).

Even Napoleon got into the quote books on this topic: "Nothing is more difficult, and therefore more precious, than to be able to decide."

The whole point of prioritization of the Goods is about decisions. Even if your personal prioritization isn't explicit, you are still subconsciously using some kind of a hierarchy to make decisions. If you are doing any form of group decision-making, however, subconscious is not a good idea. It causes chaos and disagreements where there need not be any; the more explicit the prioritization, the better. So, in any organization, all decisions can be streamlined with a clear, well-communicated prioritization of Goods.

There are lots of models of decision-making—there are whole academic disciplines devoted to understanding decisions: organizational behavioralists, psychologists, sociologists, and brain scientists—all hard at work on the issues. In other words, lots of people have tried to understand how we come to a conclusion about what we are going to do.

But when it comes to good bases for organizational decision-making, I think there are really 3Cs—Clarity, Consistency, and Candor.

Clarity

One thing that is pretty evident, if there is not a clear end goal—aim or mission—then groups of people will dither for a long time over every single decision.

One of the clearest decision-making apparatuses I've ever experienced as a consultant was in a project that I was doing for Walmart. We were supposed to be coming up with ideas for an advertising campaign for the company. The group I was working with was extremely clever. Great ideas were emerging. We believed we had notions that would reposition Walmart and really sell well to the American—and even foreign—public. But, once we met with the Walmart executives, we heard a broken record—that given my years of teaching about the company, I had oddly not anticipated: "How much will that cost?" "Will it be clear that we are low cost with that message?" "We want simple ads that show we are low cost." "Will that idea take the focus off of our low costs?" Every sentence out of the Walmart executives' mouths was about "low cost." It was their religion. It was their culture. It was their ultimate Good. All decisions had to take cost into account—and usually cost was the ultimate factor in those choices.

In too many organizations—even businesses where you might think the "almighty dollar" would usually be the final arbitrator—the bases of decisions are muddled or non-explicit. This leads to a lot of faffing around.

Consistency

In the case of Walmart, the "cost" criterion is both clear and consistent. But not all organizations do both of the first two Cs equally well. Clarity is an important first step in achieving consistency, but it is not enough. I've seen many organizations where there was a shared—and clear—understanding at the top of the organization that the basis of decision-making would change under certain circumstances. For the people lower in the organization—those who are not in on the inner circle; these departures from stated norms can be nerve-racking.

I consulted in a company that did a great job of hiring really amazing people into its ranks. It promised lots of autonomy (Individuality) and opportunities for innovation (Joy). These same people loved the clarity of the message and the opportunities that were presented. Once they were in the firm, however, it was a different story.

We all have seen or heard of the pre-hire lies that attract good people who find that once they are on the inside, the truth is far different from the recruiting hype. But, that was not what was going on in this case. Here, there were indeed people at or near the top of the firm who were basing their decisions on Joy and Individuality—Stability didn't rank very high in their decision-making. But between those top people who did a lot of the recruiting of the "high potential" staff and the newly hired staff, there was a layer or two of people who had completely different decision-making Goods. They rightly perceived that the company was hiring potential future stars who were meant to leapfrog them to the top of the organization. Their completely understandable response was to become focused on Stability and Equality—"If I can't get my ideas heard a level above me, then neither can you." The recently hired new employees were leaving in droves. The message at the top—and to the world—was clear: "We are a company that is all about innovation and new ideas—we welcome mavericks." But, that message was not applied consistently throughout the ranks.

Candor

You can be clear ("Relationships is the most important Good") and consistent ("Relationships are what everyone makes decisions on in this organization") and still be pretty dishonest.

And it is even worse when decision hypocrisy comes into play—you know, where decisions made are said to be based on one thing, but it is really something else that is most important. Decision hypocrisy just makes employees crazy. The most common version—which you've probably experienced more than once in your life—is the "Decisions are based on the bottom-line profit ... but (sotto voce) it is really all about power" hypocrisy. This is the one where the Board and shareholders are led to believe that money is the ultimate criterion, but really good ideas, good opportunities, and important cost-cutting are lost because someone is trying to hold on to their job or get an important promotion.

In a 2010 *Sloan Management Review* article, Peter Tingling and Michael Brydon call what inevitably results from this, "decision-based evidence." A decision is made first on the basis of one Good and then resources are dispatched to make up the evidence to support the decision based on a different Good. The authors conclude that this is not always bad. If the audience for the evidence is external to the organization, then it may be a necessary evil. But they warn that this process should not be used to convince internal constituencies. Those inside the company just have too much access to information to ever believe the bogus evidence. (Tingling & Brydon, 2010)

But the key is that the internal messages must be honest. (I would actually go a step farther than this and argue that for long-term organizational health both internal and external messages should be consistent and candid.) And the only way out of a dishonesty trap is with honesty—a hard nut to crack in a corporate culture riddled with duplicity. In fact, if your culture is riddled with dishonesty, it is unlikely that you'll ever realize that your priorities are not clear or consistent. So, in many ways, without real candor, it is unlikely that your organization will achieve any of the 3Cs.

Decision Exercises

1. Ask a dispassionate third party to look at a string of decisions that you and the organization have made in the last few weeks/months:

2. What do those decisions say about your priorities?

3. If you look at your boss' and your subordinates' decisions—small to large decisions—what are they prioritizing? Is their decision based on the same Good as yours?

4. Ask your people if they believe there is any duplicity in the decision priorities. If there is, is it a "necessary evil" or is there a way to create a system with more of the 3Cs?

Chapter 22: C: Leading through Change (how do we become something different?)

Maybe I always thought that change was an important component of leadership ... I really can't remember any more. But, I do remember the moment when my current appreciation for the link between the two became really clear to me. For four years as a graduate student, I was a research assistant to John Kotter at Harvard Business School. He was interested in what made leaders into leaders and wrote and researched a great deal on the topic—eventually he was named the Konosuke Matsushita Professor of Leadership at Harvard.

A few years after he was named *the* leadership guy at HBS, I realized that he was no longer talking a lot about leadership. He was spending a lot more time talking about "change." I was puzzled by the shift, but the answer was simple. He told me: "I finally distilled the essence of leadership down into what leaders really do. What a real leader does is changes the way that other people do things."

Kotter had written an early book describing the differences between leaders and managers. And when you think about it, getting people to do the same thing over and over again is management; getting people to do something different is truly leadership. It is one of the best definitions of the difference between those two words that I've ever heard.

Thus, good leaders have to be leaders of change.

Not all organizational changes will involve a change in the prioritization of Goods. I've seen plenty of companies that have gone through some sort of wrenching change—as the company decides to globalize, for instance. The greatest Good is still Growth, but the determination has been made that growth can't come from the local market any more, so there needs to be a new external focus for the corporation.

But, often a big change involves a shift in what the organization is ultimately trying to accomplish. And the more explicit this shift is, the better.

Changing your organizational Goods

While countries can change their goods and sometimes do, the priorities of nations usually stay in place for a much longer time than they might for organizations. The inertia of a nation is just much greater than for a company. With really strong leadership, even countries can change their focus—especially in the face of a crisis or a major opportunity.

But, there are some other good reasons why you see major strategic changes in an organization. For instance, customers may have new needs; new technologies may be emerging; or competitors are getting stronger. Sometimes the shift in prioritization of Goods comes because new leaders take over and with them come new priorities.

However, there is one prediction I can make without fear of refute. If you don't regularly reassess the priority of your Goods and either recalibrate or re-emphasize your current prioritization, I know that over time your organization will become one that emphasizes Stability over all else.

For some organizations, Stability is exactly the Good they should emphasize. I want my electricity utility to be highly focused on stability—well ... I suppose I want them to emphasize Life or safety first, but after that stability. I want to be sure that I get my electricity in an uninterrupted way. I don't want them to be tinkering with the system as they try to grow their revenues or profits. I just want to pay about the same amount every year and get the same services.

Even so, there are other organizations that would not choose Stability as their most important strategic goal and yet they find themselves making decisions based primarily on that basis. This is what is known as bureaucratization. As individuals, we like to have some assurance of stability in our lives. When a large number of individuals in an organization are all seeking that stability, you get lots of routinization and boundary building. And, it is hard to hack your way out of the icy block of bureaucracy. So, as a leader, you need to constantly assess and assert your 8 Great Goods.

Thunderbird School of Global Management

One of my favorite examples of an organization that has been struggling with identity—partly because they don't have a clear set of 8 Great Goods priorities—is a school in Glendale, Arizona called Thunderbird School of Global Management. I've been associated with the organization for two decades and have watched it go through a major change of Goods from which it never really recovered.

Thunderbird was established in 1946 at a decommissioned air base in the Arizona desert. The charter of the original school was to teach students—many of them recently discharged military men on the GI bill—foreign languages and cultures to ready them for jobs outside of the US. The classroom buildings and dorms were just the old barracks and hangers from the air base that were repurposed for educational programs. The control tower building, for instance, became the "student union."

Through its first 40 years, the school took a very practical bent—lots of language classes, along with culture, business and government courses often taught by recently retired practitioners. This strategy was all about Relationships—helping students to better connect to the world around them and become valuable contributors to our increasingly global society. Students claimed that one of the most valuable parts of their time at Thunderbird was the socialization with students from so many different nationalities who became friends for life. The entire program was very human relationship centric.

And, it developed a strong reputation—especially outside of the US. When I took a job at Thunderbird in 1994, a colleague from Brazil informed me that he thought Thunderbird was better regarded in his country than was Harvard.

When I first visited the campus, the education, students, and teachers were all in stark contrast to Harvard Business School where I had been educated. I was, honestly, enthralled with the fact that I could sit in a corporate strategy course team-taught by a really smart theoretician and a recently retired IBM executive. The conversations became real world based applications of the theory they were learning. It all seemed so … relevant.

In the early 1990s a new president was brought in with a much more traditional academic background. Until that time Thunderbird was a big hit with students, but it was not so popular with professional educators. The way to prestige in academia was with lots of publishing in academic journals and this was not the forte of the average teacher at Thunderbird. So a new class of academics was hired—mostly young folks but, from good schools—with a strong potential—and deep interest—in publishing.

Since rankings of MBA programs were based to a large degree on the publications and reputation of academic personnel, Thunderbird's star began to ascend quickly. When *US News & World Report* started ranking "International" business programs, Thunderbird became a perennial list topper.

Over the next few years, the school made some wrenching changes. In terms of the 8 Great Goods, the school moved from a focus almost exclusively on Relationships to one on Growth and Individuality. The master's degree, which had been called an MIM (Master's of International Management), was dropped in favor of an MBA degree. The language requirement for real proficiency in a second language was abandoned. And the third of the school that had focused on International Policy was almost completely dismantled—the professors, for the most part, "outplaced".

The focus of the curriculum was business, students were no longer encouraged to take jobs in not-for-profits or governments upon graduation—it was argued that the lower salaries in those professions kept the schools' rankings low—and there was increasing emphasis on the discipline of finance which helped graduates in finding jobs on Wall Street—where the high salaries help drive up rankings. While students would still congregate at the on-campus Pub for socializing, the professors, for the most part, did not. The professors became more traditionally academic—sequestered in their offices trying to pound out the next academic article and eschewing Master's level teaching because it interfered with their research. The introduction of an Executive Education program at the school added further Growth focus to the faculty. Executive Education paid faculty members a lot more than teaching the master's students. And, the revenue from those classes went mostly into faculty pockets rather than to the school itself.

Meanwhile tuition for the MBA program went up—to very near Harvard Business School levels—but enrollment went way down. When I first joined Thunderbird, there were about 1500 master's students on campus. When I reconnected with the school in the mid-2000s, the campus felt like a ghost town. There were only about 500 students on campus at that time.

The decrease in head count—regardless of higher tuition—was wreaking havoc on finances. By the time a new president came into the school in 2003, the school was hemorrhaging almost $10 million a year. What had once been a very self-sufficient business model based on Individuality, had turned into a financial wreck when the priorities changed to Growth and Individuality.

A shift like this need not necessarily have such dire consequences. In fact, you would expect a focus on Growth would usually lead to better financial management. But, in this case, individual faculty members reaped the harvest of a Growth emphasis—some of them making as much as a half million dollars a year while the school was sinking into receivership.

Furthermore, there was another important incongruence. The students were still coming to the school based on its reputation for an emphasis on Relationships. Sure they came to get an MBA, but Thunderbird students were not your usual group of MBA students. They were former peace corps volunteers, missionaries, nurses, writers, and philosophers who were surprisingly—for MBAs—much more interested in traveling the globe and in making the world a better place than they were in making a buck. The priority of the students never changed to an emphasis on Individuality.

This disconnect between what Master's students wanted and what Thunderbird offered became a source of tremendous tension.

Under the direction of a new president, the school stopped losing money, but still was not anywhere close to being in good financial shape. Also, the rankings of the school continued to drop. Interestingly, the highest overall ranking the school ever achieved in the Business Week MBA list—number 25—was in the mid-1990s when Thunderbird wasn't even offering an MBA! Since then, overall rankings of the school have slipped. The School managed to retain good rankings in Global education and regularly did very well on Wall Street Journal rankings that looked at the quality of students and the student's reputations among employers. The school has continued to attract students who want to be different from the usual MBA, and employers have appreciated that.

The new president of Thunderbird recognized this too and continued to try to edge the focus of the faculty away from Individuality and Growth—in both curriculum and behaviors—but the president was a natural Relationships-based leader who wanted consensus for change. That consensus was not forthcoming and the stand off between student (customer) priorities and school (faculty) priorities continued until the board needed to find yet another new president.

Starting a new organization (Kotter International)

I started this section talking about John Kotter and his theories of change, but it was interesting to be a fly on the wall in some of the meetings with him and his team as he was starting up his company, Kotter International. John has always been a bit of a nonconformist, rankling at any system or process that tied him down too much. Academia is good for that kind of individual freedom. Unless you are on the administrative side of higher education, you can actually create a lot of autonomy for your career. But now, for the first time, Kotter was trying to start a company of his own. With the first couple of employees, he gave them the same the autonomy that he had always fought for in his career. But as the company grew, he realized that there had to be rules. In fact, Stability was a more important Good than he'd ever realized when he was just doing things on his own. His employees couldn't be inside Kotter's head all the time, and they were all creative, talented people themselves. So, rather than having them out selling and delivering dozens of different products as the Kotter "system," he quickly discovered that he was going to have to create a standard and hold everyone to it. I watched as Kotter had to make the shift quickly from Individuality and Joy to Stability, Relationships, and Growth. And while this was a necessary change in his new firm, the irony was not lost on him: Here was a company that was all about telling clients how to change and it had adopted Stability as its greatest Good.

Choice Humanitarian

The toughest wars, debates and disagreements come when the combatants are supporting a different version of the same Good. Religious wars, ethical disagreements, economic model diatribes, and tribal clashes are all examples of different interpretations of the same Goods. Changing from one version of a Good to another version can be equally challenging. That is what I found myself in the middle of as a Board member at Choice Humanitarian—a non-profit charity for poverty alleviation and village development based in Salt Lake City, Utah.

I was invited onto the Board of the organization at an interesting turning point in their history. They had been founded by Mormons and developed a network around the world based on connections to Mormon missionaries and communities. Everyone on the Board—I found when I started talking to them—was Mormon. But the CEO had a notion that the Relationships of Choice Humanitarian should not be the Mormon community but, rather, the world. One of their country managers was by that time a non-Mormon and they had decided that they wanted to expand their Board—and their fund raising efforts—beyond the confines of Utah. I had grown up Mormon but had left that belief system behind long before, so it was thought that I might be a good "bridge" to a bigger world for them.

The first efforts to make the change were almost comical. I'll never forget the offsite in Mexico where a group of teetotaling Mormon retirees had a day of leadership training led by two non-Mormon gay men. After a tense afternoon session in which one member of the Board was reprimanded by the gays for his sexist ways—he consistently interrupted and talked over the one woman Board member every time she tried to add anything to the discussion—the dinner conversation was commandeered by one of the consultants who expounded on the finer points of brewing a truly great beer.

Eventually a non-Mormon CEO was hired and the Board expanded to a handful of non-Mormons. But it was a rocky road. Board votes on new initiatives tended to split Mormon versus non-Mormon. And the new CEO was concerned that the cultural gulf between the two societies might be too great for the organization to bridge.

And he was right.

Eventually the non-profit reverted to its largely Utah roots. Making perhaps a fair assessment that for consistency and uniformity of decision-making,

Choice Humanitarian needed to retain its focus on Mormon Relationships. It had tried valiantly to shift its definition of Relationships, but failed.

Other organizational priority shifts

I'm sure the difficulty, yet necessity, of changing Goods can be seen not only in the company stories that I've watched personally. Just look around at some of the big companies that have seen changes in their histories. You probably have some pretty good stories yourself. And there are plenty in the news on an almost daily basis.

In an earlier chapter I talked about Sears trying to change its strategy. It was basically moving from an emphasis on Stability ("Protect the Assets of the Company") to Relationships (customer focus).

Toyota had long been known as a car company devoted to quality control and safety (Stability and Life). New management and an increasingly international Board pushed Toyota to focus more on Growth in the last decade. During the car company's safety and recall crisis in early 2010, the company's new CEO, the 53-year-old grandson of Toyota's founder, was quoted on the front page of The Wall Street Journal as saying: "Toyota's rapid expansion in recent years attracted much praise from outside the company, and some people just got too big-headed and focused too excessively on profit." (Wall Street Journal, 2010) The elevation of Growth in their priorities had caused problems that created the first economic loss for the firm in 50 years. Now the company admits that they have re-elevated their focus on quality, longevity of the firm (Stability) and the sanctity of Life as their primary goals.

Remember, none of this is to say that Growth is unimportant to Toyota or any other firm; just that priorities can and do shift.

Another case that I watched from the inside—but if you read the papers at the time, you probably know about it too—was the shift from Andersen Consulting to Accenture. Arthur Andersen, an audit firm that sadly saw its demise during the Enron scandal, had its start—as do many accounting firms—as a company and culture focused on Stability. There is not much that happens in the business world that is more about Stability than accounting and audit rules. This is the place where companies have to show that they comply with the law of the land. And the auditors are there to make sure that the companies do just that—or at least look like they are doing that. From this foundation of auditing, a consulting firm—Andersen Consulting—got its start. But Andersen Consulting was not, at the beginning, anything like the McKinseys or the Bains of the world. Andersen's consultants were not advising CEOs about broad, far-reaching strategic views. The firm's bread and butter was in computer system implementation and the reason that Andersen Consulting was better than almost anybody else doing this kind of implementation is that they had a rule book—which was a damn good rule book—called Method/1. This was such a rigid process—much like a good audit—that the New York Times called Andersen a "culture of clones" in a 1992 article (September 6, 1992). In addition to the focus on Stability, there was also Relationships—very little mid-career hiring and a feeling that you were part of the Andersen Consulting family when you joined the partnership. Also, Equality mattered a whole bunch—career paths were clearly laid out. No one got a promotion inside Andersen until they had the proper tenure with the firm—no matter how talented they were.

In the early 2000s, the firm split with Arthur Andersen formally and changed its structure from a partnership to a listed corporation. Suddenly, the culture and the priorities also shifted significantly. Growth became the main focus, but there was also more focus on Individuality—and individual merit—than in the past. Accenture has been very successful with this strategy. The firm has tripled the number of employees and more than doubled its share price since it made the shift in Good prioritization.

It should be obvious from the stories above that organizational changes in priorities can happen, but they are tricky. Some happen quickly—particularly when there is pent up "demand" for the change or there has been a crisis that drives an organization to redefine itself. Some intended changes never quite "take" and the organization reverts to the safety of an old set of priorities. But to be successful, the leadership of the organization must be involved. And the more explicit the change is, the better. If you can let your people know that you're shifting from a Stability focused organization to a Joy based organization and, if your actions are consistent with that message, you stand a much better chance of making the change successfully.

Change Exercises

To see if your change efforts can be improved by using the 8 Great Goods, try the following exercises:

1. As a leader, prioritize your own personal 8 Great Goods. What is most important to you personally? If you have a leadership team in place that is helping you to lead, ask them to list the priorities they believe are in place in the team.

2. Ask your employees what they think the organization's 8 Great Goods are. If you are the leader of the organization, employee's perceptions of your priorities and the organization priorities will probably closely align. But if they are different, that should be cause for an interesting discussion about why your decisions and the organization's Goods are different.

3. Ask your employees and customers what priorities you and the organization SHOULD focus on.

4. Meet with your people and discuss how you can make decisions that will better reflect what the organization's Goods should be. If you are saying that your priorities are one thing, but your decisions are reflecting another prioritization, how do you change your decisions to make the two align?

5. If you are in the middle of a change effort in the organization, how would the change be characterized from an 8 Great Goods perspective? Would your employees be able to tell you how the Good's prioritization would change based on the efforts you have initiated?

Chapter 23: Your Life ... from Goods to Greatest

In any good academic book, this is where you would find a few paragraphs telling you that more research is necessary. Clearly, this is not a good academic book. Of course, I do believe that what I am describing here is scientifically verifiable. But I want this to be useful to you and those around you—not to a bunch of analysts.

So let me suggest in these final pages, some unscientific, non-academic "research" that you can conduct as you incorporate 8 Great Goods thinking into your personal, organizational and community life.

Do you know your 8 Great Goods?

I hope that some point along your way through this book, you have taken the time to actually write down your priorities. I also hope that you've gone back to that prioritization more than once to see if your behaviors reflect your espoused priorities. It took me multiple attempts at prioritization before I settled on an order that I thought was really "me."

Are you happy with your 8 Great?

Once I settled on a prioritization that made me really comfortable, the strangest thing happened: I was no longer reprioritizing my 8 Great, I found that the 8 Great were reprioritizing me.

I found myself using the list to make almost all of my decisions. When some difficult—or, for than matter, even trivial—issue was making me pause to consider options, I could think through each of the issues in the decision in terms of 8 Great Goods. Fitting all of the issues into the 8 Goods took a little getting used to, but once I had my categories, the decisions—even the really difficult ones—became clear and easy.

How consistent do you think you are with your priorities?

One day recently, I was deciding if I really needed to make a trip to the East Coast. The trip was to see some colleagues of mine to discuss business issues—most of these people I consider personal friends too and I had not seen them for a while. Additionally, there were some purely fun reasons for making the trip. Since I own my own company and the cost of the trip would ultimately come out of my own pocket, I found myself leaning toward cancelling the trip. The meetings could be done almost as well by phone or Skype, I reasoned; no need to incur extra expenses.

But then I felt sad. I was really looking forward to seeing my friends, both business and personal. Most importantly, I realized that I was violating my own prioritization of the 8 Great. The whole reason for cancelling the trip was because of Growth and Stability ("saving for a rainy day"). Growth and Stability are rather low priorities on my personal list; while Joy (having fun) and Relationships (being with people I like) are high on my list.

With this realization, I made my airline reservations and confirmed my appointments—and started contacting other people I wanted to see there. I was happy and excited to see old friends and make new contacts. And, I got an odd rush just knowing that I was being true to my own 8 Great priorities.

It ended up being a great trip—better even for business than I expected it would be.

What are your organization's 8 Great?

The assessment of your organization's Goods will be based on the way people have interacted with you. You will also find that corporate policies probably play a big role in what you think about your organization. Generally, this assessment of your organization's Goods will be easier than figuring out your own personal priorities ... unless you are the boss.

If you are one of the top leaders of the organization, you'll find yourself dithering and unsure about the priorities. You'll naturally want to make all eight equally important. You'll predictably argue that there is no need to prioritize and that each decision should be made on its own merit. If you are strongly resistant to setting a clear prioritization for your organization, I suggest you go back and read Chapters 2 and 9.

How do the organizational 8 Great compare to your personal priorities?

If you're like most people in our surveys, you'll tend to overemphasize the differences between your own priorities and those of your organization. If you are a non-religious person, you'll probably dwell even more on the quasi-religious overtures of your organization. If Equality is not really all that important to you, you may end up believing that your organization does more than necessary to make everyone feel equal. If your organizational Goods are in the exact opposite order as your own, you may have made a scapegoat out of the organization. Try to take a dispassionate look.

What do your coworkers think your organization's 8 Great are?

Your own view of the prioritization of the organizational Goods may change a bit after you see what your coworkers think the organizational priorities are. If no one else sees the organization's top priority as Belief—but you do, you may rethink your own assessment. Now, of course, it could simply mean, that no one else has noticed a pattern that is obvious to you. But it *could* mean that you are overemphasizing certain policies and actions. Recalibrating your own view of organizations and people around you is a worthwhile activity in and of itself.

Is there a dysfunctional mix of priorities in your organization?

If the leaders of the organization are trying to create a place that is diametrically opposite to the priorities of most of the people who work there, the workers' natural priorities will probably eventually win out. This has been the downfall of so many companies and even countries. Hire a bunch of people who are all individualists and then get them to try to work together and you'll have problems (GE in the 2000s). Hire people who are really focused on Relationships and Life and their natural focus on profitability will be lacking (Japan). The Arab Spring riots that toppled governments in Tunisia, Egypt, Libya, and led to a bloodbath in Syria and unrest elsewhere were all about the conflicts among Stability and Individuality and Equality and Belief. In companies, even when a coup is not successful, workers can often exert their Goods to stall progress if not change the priorities completely.

What if you don't have the same priorities as your organization?

Your organization will be more productive, creative, and reflective of your customers if it is composed of individuals with a variety of 8 Great priorities. Just because you want Growth, you do not want everyone in the place to be solely focused on Growth—it leads to serious dysfunction. You need a nice balance of employees who at least accept—if not embrace—the organization's top level Goods priorities. But you want them all to have their own view of the world—and as leaders or followers in organizations we need to be able to celebrate those differences.

Should you try to change the priorities of your organization or your community?

If you really believe organizations or people around you would be better off with a set of priorities closer to your own, you should use every persuasive tool in your arsenal to change minds. There is a lot of learning in this kind of dialog—it makes us all better.

But once an organization or a family has decided, constant agitation for change will decrease efficiency, effectiveness and harmony. What you can do is set up a time period with your company, spouse or friends when those priorities *can* be revisited. Every year along with New Year Resolutions, for instance, you could ask the question: should we think about changing priorities based on our experience with the old set of priorities from last year?

When is it time to bail?

When you have tried your best to fix priority incongruence and cannot, it may be time to leave. But the 8 Great Goods give you one additional tool that most career or marriage counselors may not offer. Don't think about a switch until your association with a particular person or organization is blocking you from achieving your Greatest Good. (Or at most, your top two Goods.) For instance, you may be a person who ranks Stability as your top Good and Joy much further down then the list. You may find that you are not happy in your job but it does give you a predictable long-lasting income. In that case, you should not leave that job. If however, you are mostly a Joy person and

Stability is a lower priority, *and* you are not happy in your job, you should seriously consider finding employment elsewhere.

What if my community and I don't see eye to eye?

Sometimes you may even have to leave your current community to be able to achieve your personal Greatest Goods. In our increasingly globalized world, it is relatively easy for us to relocate to another nation that could provide a better environment for the Goods that you value most.

A recent political debate made us question, for the first time in 15 years, where my partner and I should live. Arizona is notoriously conservative. Currently, there is a move afoot for the most liberal part of the State to secede and form a separate state or territory. Without that liberal influence, the part of Arizona where we live would become almost intolerable. We started discussing whether we would have to move, should Baja Arizona (yep, that's the name they're using!) become a reality.

From a purely philosophical point of view, the inexorable answer seemed to be that we would have to move. But when we listed our top Goods to see what impact a liberal secession would have on them, the answer was quite different from what we expected. Our top priorities are Relationships (each other, family, and friends), Joy, and Individuality. None of these would be terribly impacted by a Baja Arizona split. In fact, there is an argument that Individuality may even be enhanced. Now if Equality or Belief (in liberal causes) were our very top priorities, we might need to move. But until we laid out our Greatest Goods as our criteria, we were leaning toward focusing on less important issues.

If there is not a good fit, however, you should consider a move. I have known Individualist Japanese who have moved to the US for more of that Good. I know Growth-oriented Europeans who have moved to Singapore. I know Relationships-based Americans who have moved to Switzerland. All with very positive results. If it is difficult for you to achieve your top priorities where you are right now, there is a place in the world that may be a better fit.

Can understanding my Goods make me a better person?

The whole point of this book is to get you to think in a new way about how your mind and the minds of those around you work. That understanding will help you to be more clear about your own purpose. It will also help you to communicate your needs better to those around you. And, in the process, you may learn some really important truths about those you interact with regularly—family, coworkers, neighbors—and even yourself.

If—in even a small way—this book helps your to achieve your Greatest Good, I will have achieved my goal in writing it in the first place. That brings me Joy (my Greatest Good) and I look forward to the new Relationships (my second highest Good) that will inevitably spring from interacting with those of you who find value in what I have written.

Bibliography

Adamson, P., Bradshaw, J., Hoelscher, P., & Richardson, D. (2007). "Child Poverty in Perspective: An overview of child well-being in rich countries. Retrieved from UNICEF-IRC: http://www.unicef-irc.org/publications/pdf/rc7_eng.pdf

Arthur D Little. (2009). *Headquarters on the Move.* Retrieved from Docstoc: http://www.docstoc.com/docs/119318303/Headquarters-on-the-Move

Attwooll, C. (2009, August 5). *"Jumping genes" create diversity in human brain cells, offering clues to evolutionary and neurological disease.* Retrieved from Salk Institute: http://www.salk.edu/news/pressrelease_details.php?press_id=372

Börsch-Supan, A., & et al. (2008). *"Health, ageing and retirement in Europe 2004-2007" 2008).* Mannheim Resarch Institute.

Bach-y-Rita, P. (2001, September 1). "The Seeing Tongue" . *Science News* .

Bana e Costa, C. (2001). The use of multi-criteria decision analysis to support the search for less conflicting policy options. *Journal of Multi-Criteria Decision Analysis* , *10*, 111-125.

Barbalet, J. M. (2001). *Emotion, Social Structure and Social Theory: A Macrosociological Approach.* Cambridge University Press.

Beck, J., & Wade, M. (2004). *Got Game.* Boston, MA: Harvard Business School Press.

Boaz, & Ciochon. (2004). *Dragon Bone Hill.* USA: Oxford University Press.

BT. (2003). *Just Values: Beyond the Business Case for Sustainable Development.* London: BT.

Calhoon, R. M. (2000). Loyalism and Neutrality. In J. P. Greene, & J. R. Pole, *A Companion to the American Revolution.* Malden, Mass: Blackwell.

Damasio, A. (1994). *Descartes' error: emotion, reason and the human brain.* London: Vantage.

Davenport, T., & Beck, J. (2001). *The Attention Economy.* Boston: Harvard Business School Press.

Donald, M. (1993). Human cognitive evolution: What we were, what we are becoming. *Social Research , 60.*

Dunbar, R. (1998). The Social Brain Hypothesis. *Evolutionary Anthropology .*

Epley, N., & et al. (2009, December 2). Believers' estimates of God's beliefs are more egocentric than estimates of other people's beliefs. *Proceedings of the National Academy of Science .*

Face Research Laboratory at the University of Aberdeen in Scotland. (n.d.). Retrieved from http://faceresearch.org/

Fitzpatrick, B. J. (2009). Rapid fixation of non-native alleles revealed by genome-wide SNP analysis of hybrid tiger salamanders. *BMC Evolutionary Biology , 9.*

Frager, R. (1970). Conformity and anti-conformity in Japan . *Journal of Personality and Social Psychology , 15*, 203-210.

Gazzaniga, M. (2008). *Human: The Science Behind What Makes Us Unique.* New York: Ecco Books, Harper Collins.

Geiser, U. (2009, Sep 3). *Swiss still attached to consensus politics.* Retrieved from SwissInfo.ch: http://www.swissinfo.ch/eng/Specials/Cabinet_Election/Background_and_Analysis/Swiss_still_attached_to_consensus_politics.html?cid=9790

General Social Survey. (2008). *General Social Survey.* Retrieved from NORC: http://www3.norc.org/gss+website/

Gloss, T. (2008, August). Decision Making, Rationality, and Reason. *Observer , 21* (7).

Goldberg, E. (2001). *The Executive Brain: Frontal Lobes and the Civilized Mind.* USA: Oxford University Press.

Gomez-Beldarrain, M. (2004). Patients with Right Frontal Lesions Are Unable to Assess and Use Advice to Make Predictive Judgments. *JCN , 16.*

Haidt, J., & Joseph, C. (2004). Intuitive Ethics: How Innately Prepared Intuitions Generate Culturally Variable Virtues. . *Daedalus , 138*, 55-66.

Hamer, D. (2004). *The God Gene: How Faith is Hardwired into our Genes.*

Hoover, H. (n.d.). *Herbert Hoover, "Rugged individualism Speech" (October 22, 1928).* Retrieved from Pinzler: http://www.pinzler.com/ushistory/ruggedsupp.html

Klauss, & Bass. (1974). Group Influences on Individual Behavior across Cultures. *Journal of Cross-Cultural Psychology , 5* (2), 236-246.

Koten, J., Wood, G., Hagoort, P., Goebel, R., Propping, P., Willmes, K., et al. (2009). Genetic Contribution to Variation in Cognitive Function: An fMRI Study in Twins. *Science , 323* (5922), 1737-1740.

Lawrence, P., & Nohria, N. (2002). *Driven: How Human Nature Shapes our Choices.* San Francisco: Josey-Bass.

Levy, A. (2006, February 1). *Brain Scans Show Link Between Lust for Sex and Money (Update1).* Retrieved from Bloomberg Press: http://www.bloomberg.com/apps/news?pid=newsarchive&sid=a45yNOnzzWq0

Li, S., Mayhew, S., & Kourtzi, Z. (2009). Learning Shapes the Representation of Behavior Choice in the Human Brain. *Neuron , 62*, 441-452.

Maslow, A. (1943). A theory of human motivation. *Psychological Review , 50* (4), 370-396.

McClelland, D. (1987). *Human Motivation.* New York: Cambridge University Press.

Miller, D. E. (2011, March 7). *SAUDI ARABIA'S LEADERS LOOSEN GRIP, PROMPTING PROTEST.* Retrieved from The Media Line: http://www.themedialine.org/news/print_news_detail.asp?NewsID=31549

Mitani, J., Watts, D., & Amsler, S. (2010). Lethal intergroup aggression leads to territorial expansion in wild chimpanzees. *Current Biology , 20* (12), R507-R508.

Olds, J., & Milner, P. (1954). "Positive reinforcement produced by electrical stimulation of septal area and other regions of rat brain." . *Journal of Comparative and Physiological Psychology , 47* (6), 419-27.

Porter, M. (1996, November). "What is Strategy" . *Harvard Business Review .*

Rydin, Y., Thornley, A., Scanlon, K., & West, K. (2004). The Greater London Authority - a case of conflicts of cultures? Evidence from the planning and environment policy domains. *Environment and planning c: government and policy , 22* (1), 55-76.

Schmid, C. (1981). *Conflict and Consensus in Switzerland.* University of California Press.

Schwartz, S. (2006). Value orientations: Measurement, antecedents and consequences across nations. In R. Jowell, C. Roberts, R. Fitzgerald, & G. Eva, *Measuring attitudes cross-nationally - lessons from the European Social Survey.* London: Sage.

Sheppard, K. (2011, March 14). *Obama Touted Safety Record of Japan's Nuclear Industry.* Retrieved from Mother Jones: http://www.motherjones. com/mojo/2011/03/obama-touted-japan-nuclear-safety-fukushima

Shiv, B., & Fedorikhin, A. (1999). "Heart and mind in conflict: The interplay of affect and cognition in consumer decision making". *Journal of Consumer Research , 26.*

Shweder, R. A., Much, N., Park, L., & Mahapatra, M. M. (1997). The 'Big Three' of Morality (Autonomy, Community, Divinity) and the 'Big Three' Explanations of Suffering. In A. Brandt, & P. Rozin, *Morality and Health.* New York: Routledge.

Sohn , E. (2010, December 16). *The No-Fear Woman (And What Her Brain Reveals).* Retrieved from Discovery: http://news.discovery.com/human/ fear-fearless-brain-emotion.html

Streidter, G. (2005). *Principles of Brain Evolution .*

Tingling, P., & Brydon, M. (2010, June 26). Is Decision-Based Evidence Making Necessarily Bad? *Sloan Management Review .*

Tocqueville, A. d. (1840). *Democracy in America* (Vol. 3). (H. R. translation, Trans.)

Tricomi, E., Rangel, A., Camerer, C. F., & O'Doherty, J. P. (2010, February 24). "Neural evidence for inequality-averse social preferences". *Nature .*

Tulving, E. (1985). Memory and Consciousness. *Canadian Psychology , 26.*

University of Glasgow. (2010). Retrieved October 2012, from University News: http://www.gla.ac.uk/news/archiveofnews/2010/march/ headline_145327_en.html

Wall Street Journal, "Toyoda concedes profit focus led to flaws" March 2, 2010.

Wang, Coble, & Bello. (2006). *"Cognitive-Affective Interactions in Human Decision-making: a neurocomputational approach.".* Retrieved from Proceedings of the 28th Annual Meeting of the Cognitive Science Society: www.csjarchive.cogsci.rpi.edu/proceedings/2006/ docs/p2341.pdf

Wilkinson, R. G., & Pickett, K. (2009). *The Spirit Level: Why More Equal Societies Almost Always Do Better.* Allen Lan.

Woodhouse, B. B. (2008). "Individualism and Early Childhood in the U.S.: How Culture and Tradition Have Impeded Evidence-Based Reforms". *Journal of Korean Law , 8*, 135-160.

World Values Survey Association. (2000). Retrieved from World Values Survey: www.worldvaluessurvey.org/

Wrangham, R. (2009). *Catching Fire: How Cooking Made Us Human.*

Zahariadis, N. (2005). *Essence of Political Manipulation: Emotion, Institutions, & Greek Foreign Policy.* Peter Lang Publishing.

John C Beck

Index

A

B

C

Colorado 68

D

Damasio, Antonio 44, 46, 47, 49
Dickinson, Emily 51
Donald, Merlin 46
Dunbar, Robin 58

E

Ecole Polytechnique Federale de Lausanne 44
Epley, Nicholas 61
Equality vii, 10, 25, 27, 28, 29, 50, 59, 60, 61, 67, 68, 77, 85, 88, 90, 104, 107, 108, 109,
    120, 148, 151, 153, 154, 180, 183, 184, 187, 188, 193, 203, 207, 209

F

Face Research Laboratory 54
Ferrari 16
France x, 86, 90, 131, 165
Freeters 128

G

Gage, Fred 59
Gamers 40
Gandhi, Mohandas 59
Gazzaniga, Michael 45, 214
GE Capital 3
General Social Survey 67, 214
Giese, Jeanne 51
Gigerenzer, Gerd 93
Gomez-Beldarrain, Marian 56
Got Game 40, 213
Greene, Graham 61
Gross National Happiness 159, 161, 165, 167
Growth vii, xi, 2, 26, 27, 36, 54, 56, 63, 69, 76, 77, 80, 81, 84, 88, 90, 100, 102, 104, 106,
    108, 116, 119, 128, 129, 130, 133, 141, 146, 147, 149, 150, 151, 153, 159, 165, 168,
    173, 179, 180, 182, 183, 184, 187, 188, 195, 198, 199, 200, 202, 203, 206, 208, 209

H

Haidt, Jonathan 49, 50, 56
Harvard Business School 28, 36, 38, 195, 197, 199, 213, 214
Harvard Kennedy School 113
Hoover, Herbert 138

I

Individuality vii, 8, 26, 27, 29, 50, 58, 61, 67, 68, 75, 77, 85, 88, 90, 91, 100, 102, 104, 107, 108, 109, 130, 133, 136, 137, 138, 165, 174, 182, 186, 187, 188, 189, 193, 198, 199, 200, 203, 207, 209

Innocenti Research Centre 137

Ireland 146, 158

Islam 155, 156, 157

Israel vii, 151, 155, 157, 158

J

Jacob, François 54

Jamaica 8

Japan vi, 72, 73, 97, 116, 119, 120, 121, 122, 123, 124, 125, 126, 127, 128, 129, 130, 131, 132, 155, 181, 182, 183, 186, 207, 214, 216

Jigme Singye Wangchuck 161

Jobs, Steve 174

Joseph, Craig 49

Joy vii, 6, 26, 27, 28, 36, 37, 55, 61, 62, 63, 75, 76, 81, 85, 89, 90, 100, 104, 106, 108, 159, 160, 164, 165, 168, 174, 183, 184, 186, 187, 188, 193, 200, 203, 206, 208, 209

Juvenal 26

K

Kagame, Paul 153

Khmer Rouge 3

Knutson, Brian 55

Kogure, Masa 26

Koten, Jan 59

Kotter, John 195

L

Lady Gaga 17, 18

Lawrence, Paul 36

leadership 35, 70, 107, 116, 130, 148, 152, 157, 161, 173, 174, 175, 176, 177, 178, 179, 180, 181, 183, 191, 195, 196, 201, 203, 204, 206, 207, 208

Lee Kuan Yew 113, 147, 148

Lee Kuan Yew School of Public Policy 113, 147

Life vi, vii, 1, 7, 24, 25, 26, 27, 29, 36, 50, 51, 52, 61, 63, 67, 68, 76, 77, 78, 79, 81, 82, 83, 85, 88, 89, 90, 104, 105, 108, 119, 120, 123, 124, 128, 129, 130, 131, 132, 136, 160, 164, 173, 174, 182, 186, 187, 196, 202, 205

Lincoln, Abraham 174

London School of Economics 39

M

Malaysia 147

MapQuest 18

Marriott 183
Maslow, Abraham xi, 27, 28, 35, 36, 82
Max Planck Institute for Human Development 93
Max Weber 143
McArthur, General Douglas 122
McClelland, David 36
McDonald's 17
mental model 17, 18, 19, 20
Miyazaki, Hayao 123
Moniz, Antonio Egas 48
Mormon 33, 62, 107, 183, 201, 202
multitask 15, 19
Muslim 155
Muslim Brotherhood 155
Myers-Briggs 71

N

Napoleon Bonaparte 191
Navy 1
neocortex 58
New York City 11, 142, 175
Nohria, Nitin 28
Northern Ireland 158
Northwestern University 49
Norway vii, 151, 153, 154

O

Orton, Bill 33
Oxford University 148, 213, 214

P

Porter, Michael 38
prefrontal cortex 15, 44, 45, 46, 47, 49, 60, 63
prioritization x, 24, 36, 37, 39, 40, 68, 69, 75, 76, 79, 81, 89, 91, 93, 96, 97, 98, 101, 108, 109, 113, 157, 158, 178, 180, 184, 185, 188, 191, 195, 196, 203, 204, 205, 206, 207
prioritizations 14, 70, 88, 89, 97
Protestant 143, 158

Q

Quayle, Dan 32

R

Relationships vii, 4, 24, 25, 26, 27, 29, 36, 50, 56, 68, 75, 76, 77, 79, 80, 84, 88, 90, 91, 100, 102, 104, 106, 108, 119, 120, 138, 141, 143, 144, 163, 174, 178, 179, 183, 186, 187,

University of Toronto 48
University of Virginia 49
University of Wisconsin 43
Utah 33, 201
Uzbekistan 7

V

values 13, 30, 31, 32, 33, 34, 35, 36, 37, 77, 119, 143, 149, 157, 163, 165, 166, 167, 177, 186
Vietnam War 12

W

Wade, Mitchell 40
Walmart 192
Washington DC 3, 33
Welsh, Jack 178
Westinghouse, George 175
Wrangham, Richard 56

Y

Yahoo 18

Z

Zahariadis, Nikolas 97

John C Beck

New Teachers, Less Smoking and Demerits Start Off 74-75 Year

Teachers and students switch clothes for a day

Bicycle And Car Equal Confusion

Majorettes and Poms Do Their Own Thing

When quotations are used in heads, single quote marks, rather than double, are usually used, to save space. The following head has used double quote marks.

"You haven't seen nothing yet"

Headlines are not to be written as announcements as in the following examples

Here They Are: Queen Candidates

Other headline rules that should be followed include:

(1) Do not editorialize except in editorial heads.

(2) Do not abbreviate days and months unless specific date is given. For example "January" by itself should be spelled out, but it is satisfactory to write "Jan. 17."

(3) Do not repeat key words in a head or forms of the same word.

(4) Do not begin a headline with a verb.

(5) Use Miss, Mrs., Ms. or Mr. for adults.

(6) Use strong verbs, forceful and dynamic. All headline

ferring to. In most schools, there are many people with the same last name, so it is usually best to use first name or first two initials of a person if possible for clear identification.

There should be a verb expressed or implied in all heads and each head should have a subject. The first two heads below have no subjects and the third one has no verb. Thus, all three heads fail to feature the complete idea behind the story.

1. ## Check into Mental Health

2. ## Offers 14 Courses

3. ## Junior Achievement

Forms of the verb "to be" should be omitted in headlines, as they are generally passive in nature. The verb "to be" may be used, however, to indicate future tense. A newspaper staff should decide whether they are going to use "to be" or "will be" for future tense and stick to one or the other for consistency. The verbs "is," "are," "was," and "were" should not be used in headlines. Generally they are space fillers and serve no useful purpose. The verbs "is" and "are" can be understood verbs in headlines; however, they are often passive and should be avoided. The following head could have been written, "Volleyball First." The word "is" is simply a space filler.

Volleyball is first

Verbs should be written in the active voice rather than the passive. In other words, the subject should be doing the action. The following headlines are all passive as indicated by the "-ed" verbs.

49 *honored by WMA honor society assembly*

Meeting Planned For Teachers

35 Seniors
commended

The headlines could have been rewritten in the active voice. For example:

> WMA Honors 49
> Teachers Plan Meeting
> Principal Commends 35 Seniors

Each of the revised headlines has been rewritten so that the subject is doing the action. The WMA honors, the teachers plan, and the principal commends.

Only present and future tenses are used in headlines. The passive voice almost always tends to imply past tense. In the three above headlines the verbs "is" or "are" could be understood in each one, making the headlines present tense, but that does not eliminate the passive voice. Present tense is used for both present and past stories, and future tense for future stories.

Numbers may be used in headlines in Arabic form unless they begin a line, in which case they should be written out. This is particularly true of the first line of a headline; headlines are written like sentences, and sentences should not begin with a numeral. The following headlines should have their numerals spelled out.

3 Come To Learn English
6 Achieve Merit Rating
3 AFS students experience new school

Only well-known abbreviations are used in a he abbreviations are used without periods in most case lowing headlines should not have periods after the ations, and it is doubtful that most readers would l E.E.E. is or what I.S. is. Most schools, however, d P.S.A.T. test and many have a D.E.C.A. chapter, sc breviations are more readily understood. P.E. is a abbreviation for physical education. However, reme abbreviations should not be followed by periods.

D.E.C.A. reaches for the top

Parkway offers E.E.E.

I. S. begins a new year

P.E. Adds Coed Classes
P.S.A.T. test
to be given
October 22

The words "a," "an," and "the," are space fillers in mo *and should not be used.* If they are part of a title, it i factory to use them. The word "a" in the following he could have been eliminated without changing the meaning head. Don't use "a," "an," or "the" just to enable the cha count to fit.

A Frustrated Lot Speaks Out

The word "and" is also a space filler. A comma could been used to substitute for it in the following heads.

writers must have a good knowledge of synonyms in order to get strong verbs in the headline and in order to vary word usage so that headlines on the same page do not contain the same words. Writers who have a large vocabulary can probably think of their own synonyms, but all writers should familiarize themselves with *Roget's Thesaurus* and *Webster's Book of Synonyms*. These books are extremely helpful for finding synonyms for any word.

(7) Do not hyphenate words between lines.

(8) Avoid question heads.

(9) Introduce new information in each deck.

(10) Every head should be a complete sentence. Keep in mind that some words in a headline can be left understood.

HEADLINE STYLES

There are two basic styles of headlines. The "Traditional Style" uses capital letters for all words except prepositions and conjunctions of four letters or less. If a preposition or conjunction begins a line it is also capitalized.

Learning Resource Center Integral Part of Program

The other style is usually referred to as downstyle. Three types of downstyle are in use today. The most common style capitalizes the first word of the headline and all proper nouns as in the following example. Proponents of this style argue that heads are easier to read if written like a normal sentence.

Harriers continue to win in pursuit of District title

Varieties of the downstyle capitalize only the first word of the head or use complete downstyle with no capital letters as in the following example.

new group forms to better
daily class announcements

HEADLINE TYPES

There are at least seven different types of headlines. They are: Flush Left, Dropline, Inverted Pyramid, Banners or Crosslines, Hanging Indention, Kickers or Taglines, and Boxed Heads.

Flush-Left Heads are the most common, probably because they are the easiest to write. Each line of the headline is set flush left with the column or columns it is to go across and should come within two counts of the maximum allotted. In general, a headline takes on better appearance when the bottom line is just as long or longer than the top line. At the same time the top line should not be more than two counts under the maximum either; it provides poor appearance if it is too short, as in the following example.

Booster Club
To Hold Pie Supper

The following headline also is poor in appearance, because the bottom line is definitely short.

Lampoons take
League title

The following headline looks good, due to the fact that each line is the same length. This is not always possible to accomplish.

Golfers vie for title;
look to state tourney

Dropline Heads are usually two lines in length with the top line flush left and the bottom line flush right. Each line should be the same character count. Therefore, if the top line is two counts short of the maximum, the bottom line will also be two counts short. If the head is three lines long, the top line will be flush left, the middle line centered, and the bottom line flush right. This head is difficult to write, as unit counts need to be precise.

Conservative view
of editorial issue

VanDyne offers explanation
for student payroll problems

Three or more lines of type are necessary for a true *inverted pyramid headline,* although some papers use only two. The first line of an inverted pyramid head completely fills the column. The second line is centered and indented the same number of units on each side, and the third line is centered under the second line and decreased by the same number of units on each side.

English Class
Launches
Glider

Redwings to host
district tourney

Crosslines are one line in length and completely fill the columns allotted. *Banners* are also one line in length normally, but they are designed to go completely across the page.

Juniors to elect Jam royalty

Three lines of type are required for a *Hanging Indention* head. The first line completely fills the column. The second line is indented one em. An em is a printer's measure the size of the letter "m" in whatever size and style of type is being used. The third line would be indented two ems.

Youth Orchestra
wins   medal
in Berlin

Kickers or taglines may be used to introduce the main head. The information in the kicker should be different from that given in the main head (usually one-half the point size and one-third the length) and should contrast with the main head. If the main head is roman (type that is straight up and down), then the kicker should be italic (slanted type). Kickers are usually underlined, and the main head is slightly indented, as in the following example.

Kirkwood Highlights

SC 'Game Night' Tonight

Boxed heads are normally used to keep heads from being run together on a page if it's necessary to place them side by side, or they are used for emphasis to attract a reader to a story. It is possible to place a complete box around a head, but that tends to separate the head from its story. A three-fourths box is best, as shown in the following example. Note also that headlines don't always have to go at the top of a story. The first example below shows that the headline is placed to the left side of the story. It is set inside a box, but that is not necessary.

**Greenhouse
will offer
new scene**

FM stations alter music styles

And That's
The Way
It Is . . .

Grafner serves United Way

Subheads are used to break up long, gray columns and to help guide the reader through the story. They are usually three or four words in length and they should have a subject and a verb. They are usually slightly larger than the body type. For example, eight-point body type might use 10 pt. subheads.

Some school newspapers use *jump heads,* but most do not because of the small size of school papers. Jump heads are the headlines used to go above a story that is continued on another page. Generally three or four words from the headline at the beginning of the story are repeated in the jump head.

It is also possible to use more than one deck for headlines. A headline that contains a complete idea is a deck. A deck may be one or more lines (never more than three). Hanging indention heads and inverted pyramid heads are usually second-deck headlines. Most school newspapers use only one-deck headlines because of their size. The following is an example of a two-deck headline. "Spirit Week begins today" makes up the first deck and "Class of '76 presents their 'Grand Ole Jam' " makes up the second deck. Don't confuse decks with lines. A two-line headline does not mean a two-deck headline.

Spirit Week begins today
Class of '76 presents their "Grand Ole Jam"

All newspapers should be provided with a headline schedule by their printers. The size of head to be used on a story should be dictated by the importance of a story and by its placement on a page. The more important stories usually are placed high on a page and get the larger heads. Sometimes there are several stories of equal importance, so they should get close to the same size head, if not the same size.

The size of headlines varies according to the printer's available type. Generally a 72-point (approximately one inch high) headline is the largest. For most school papers a 72-point headline is too large. A common headline size to use for the largest on the page is either 36-point or 48-point.

In selecting headline sizes, a headline writer must also be aware of headline families. Headline families should not be mixed on a page unless they complement each other. Most headline families come in roman and italic type. They may be used together on the same page, but a writer should not use some headline type faces with serifs and some that are sans serif. A serif type has a small decorative line across the end of a stroke used in forming a letter. A sans serif type face is one without the decorative stroke.

SERIF

The Mess

SANS SERIF

The Messe

As already mentioned there are several types of headline families. The ones below are only a few of the types available.

BODONI

The Messenger Offers Complete Gra

BODONI ITALIC

The Messenger Offers Complete Grap

UNIVERSAL CONDENSED

The Messenger Offers Complete Graphic Fac

UNIVERSAL CONDENSED ITALIC

The Messenger Offers Complete Graphic Fac

FUTURA MEDIUM

The Messenger Offers Com

FUTURA MEDIUM ITALIC

The Messenger Offers Com

DOM CASUAL

The Messenger Offers Complete Graphic Facilit

DOM CASUAL ITALIC

The Messenger Offers Complete Graphic Facilit

BRUSH

The Messenger Offers Complete G

MURRAY HILL

The Messenger Offers Complete Grap

In the above examples the headlines in Bodoni type have serifs, so they should not be used on the same page (and probably not on a two-page spread) with the Universal Condensed. The Universal Condensed type and the Futura Medium type do complement each other, so they could be used together, although it is probably best to use one or the other.

Below are the Universal Condensed type faces in both roman and italic, showing you point sizes ranging from 14 to 72. The first two numbers above each headline indicate point size. The second two numbers are a printer's code standing for Universal Condensed, and the number in parentheses stands for the character count per column width. For example, the headline marked "3070 (11 ct)" means that the headline is a 30-point headline. The 70 indicates Universal Condensed, and the character count per column width is 11.

Universal Condensed

1470 (21 ct)
The Messenger Offers Complete Graphic Facilities for

1870 (18½ ct)
The Messenger Offers Complete Graphic Fac

2470 (14 ct)
The Messenger Offers Complete

3070 (11 ct)
The Messenger Offers Co

3670 (9½ ct)
The Messenger Offers

4870 (7½ ct)
The Messenger O

6070 (6 ct)
The Messeng

7270 (5 ct)

The Messe

Universal Condensed Italic

1471 (21 ct)

The Messenger Offers Complete Graphic Facilities for

1871 (18½ ct)

The Messenger Offers Complete Graphic Fac

2471 (14 ct)

The Messenger Offers Complete

3071 (11 ct)

The Messenger Offers Co

3671 (9½ ct)

The Messenger Offers

4871 (7½ ct)

The Messenger O

6071 (6 ct)

The Messeng

7271 (5 ct)

The Messe

Selection of the proper headline family can mean the difference between a neat appearance and a sloppy one. Proper usage of a headline schedule can bring orderliness to a newspaper layout. Not following the headline rules could cause an overall haphazard appearance. Following them can bring a final paper that the entire staff can be proud of.

EXERCISES

(1) Find two examples of each type of headline from any newspaper. Mount them on white paper, label, and bring to class for discussion.

(2) Count the following headlines and point out any errors.
- (a) Science Fair to Be Held
- (b) Seventh Graders Dance
  To Music of Jazz Combo
- (c) Scott, Speziale, and Baker
  Win Class Presidencies
- (d) North Defeats Maplewood
  In First Game, 42–38
- (e) 'THE ART OF KEEPING UP WITH YESTERDAY'
- (f) Fire Investigation Held
  In R-9 District
- (g) Chorus Assembly
  To Be March 17

(h) Mike Schwarz
Wins Contest

(i) Decorations Beautify Halls
At Christmas Time

(j) Panel Discusses Teenagers
At PTA Monthly Meeting

(k) Teachers Choose
Pupils of Month

(l) North to Be Represented
At KU Summer Camp

(m) School Levy Vote
Today In District

(n) Discount Prices
At Rummage Sale

(o) Orchestra, Chorus
To Hold Concerts

(p) Class to Tour
Post Dispatch

(q) Journalism Week
To Be Celebrated

(r) Robin Hoods Rob People Blind!

(s) Help Teachers Help Themselves
Give Bottles, Don't Apple Butter

(t) March 32 Plays Tricks on People
Blades Removed, Horsefood Served

(u) Cheerleaders Brief Girls
On Basic Fundamentals

(v) KUATT Members Cause Trouble
Slow Down North's Track Team

(w) Boy Wins Bet;
Pepsi Can Shot

(x) GAA Sponsors
Volleyball Game

(y) Increase In Tax Levy Needed

(z) Macaroni-Eating Record
Set by George Jones

(3) Analyze ten headlines in a major newspaper and discuss whether they abide by the headline rules or not.

(4) Write two-line flush-left headlines for the following stories. The stories are not necessarily written in the correct order. It is your

job to pick out the feature. Each line of the headline should not exceed 18 in count nor be less than 16.

(a) December 22 is the date set for the first presentation of the eighth and ninth grade dramatics club to be given on our new stage. The play is a version of an incident that happened in the 1800's, when a small girl named Virginia Hanlon, having been told that there was no Santa Claus, asked her father if this was true. He told her that if the New York *Sun* said in print that there was a Santa Claus, it was true.

She wrote a letter to the paper. Frances Church wrote an editorial saying that as long as there was Christmas spirit, there was a Santa Claus. This editorial has been printed in many newspapers.

The version to be given by the dramatics club is called *The Christmas Eve Letter,* by Mildred Hark and Noel McQueen. The cast includes: Cindy Matting as Virginia, Dick Bo as Father, Mary Worth as Mother, Keith Fred as Virginia's brother, Sue Norris as her sister Norma, Becky Ford as her sister Irene, and Jack Norris as Mr. Johnson. Sue Rice is the director.

(b) Mr. Bill Buchanan's second, third, and sixth period ninth-grade citizenship classes held panel discussions on teen-age problems.

The panels consisted of three boys and three girls, whom Mr. Buchanan led in the discussion. Questions from the class were also accepted.

Such subjects as going steady, dutch treating, teen-age drivers, late hours, and dating procedures were discussed.

(c) The third PTA meeting of this year was held in the cafetorium on Wednesday, December 3, at 8 P.M.

The president of the PTA, Mr. Jerry Sappington, opened the meeting and introduced the guest speaker.

The speaker for the evening was Dr. John Nickels. He spoke on "Helping Your Child Plan for College and a Career." Dr. Nickels also discussed the importance of selecting the college. If the student is part of a large family and used to crowds, or is studious enough to handle hard courses, a big college such as Yale University or Harvard might be good. But if the student is an only child, or is not strong in studies, or is very quiet and shy, a smaller college such as Park College would be much better.

Mr. Sappington closed the meeting at 9:05, after which coffee and cupcakes were served to the faculty and parents.

(d) Every year, the St. Louis Christmas Carol Association holds a contest for the best posters depicting the purpose of the Christmas Eve Caroling that the Association organizes.

At the Christmas Carol Concert held on Dec. 13 at 5 P.M. at the Central Public Library the winners received certificates of award.

The first-place winners announced at that time were Walla Jones and Jane Kalin. Both are students at East. This was the first time in the history of the contest that a tie for first place was voted.

Walla's poster, as she described it, had "The Spirit of St. Louis in the background with a candle to the left and was in shades of red and green."

Jane's poster was an outdoor scene with three shepherds looking at the Star.

(e) The Student Council is now in the process of planning the All-School Dance, and has scheduled the dance for May.

The purpose of the All-School Dance is to promote better social relations between the seventh, eighth, and ninth grades.

Tickets for the dance are to be sold by the Student Council members at 75 cents. Couple tickets will not be sold.

The Gordons, a band composed of high-school students, will play.

The dance has a Japanese theme. The Student Council plans to drape an oriental dragon, which is 70 feet long, down the steps of the stage and around the dance floor; to hang murals around the walls; and to festoon colorful Japanese lanterns everywhere.

(f) Both an instrumental and a vocal concert are scheduled this month.

Doug Bolen will play a trumpet solo, "Tango," in the Instrumental Concert, to be directed by Mr. Ed Smith. The concert will be given on Apr. 14.

The annual Spring Chorus Concert, conducted by Mrs. Jane Carson, will be given on April 28 in the cafetorium.

(5) The above six stories are very poorly written. Rewrite them in good journalistic order. At times it may be necessary to add some information to make the story complete. However, do not add anything that will change the meaning of the story.

(6) Write two-line headlines for all the stories in Exercises 1 and 2 at the end of Chapter III. Make the minimum count 14 and the maximum count 16 for each line. Be sure to follow the headline rules.

(7) Select a newspaper from the exchange file and be prepared

to discuss in class the types of headlines used and the good and bad features of each headline.

(8) Take the last issue of your school newspaper and discuss the headlines. Rewrite those that you feel are poorly written.

(9) Write two-line headlines for the stories in Exercise 2 on Page 28. Make the minimum count 18 and the maximum count 20 for each line.

(10) Count each line of all headlines on the front page of your daily newspaper for one week using your headline count. This may seem like a monotonous exercise but chances are good that you will not get them all correct. One miscounted headline can ruin an otherwise attractive newspaper. Write your counts on paper and bring them to class for comparison.

(11) For practice in counting headlines, count each line of the headlines used as examples in this chapter.

(12) Clip at least 10 headlines from a daily newspaper that violate at least one headline rule, and bring them to class for discussion.

(13) Clip from a daily newspaper two of the following types or styles of headlines: (A) Flush Left; (B) Dropline; (C) Roman; (D) Italic; (E) Subhead; (F) Jump Head; (G) Kicker; (H) Serif; (I) Inverted Pyramid; (J) Two-Deck Head.

(14) Write two-line flush left heads, using either the headline schedule in this chapter or one provided by your printer, for the following stories. Your teacher will tell you what size to make the headline in order to know character count. Remember that if you write a headline that is more than one-column wide, you should add one extra count for each column divider. For example, a 3071 headline has a character count of 11 for one column. If this were to be a two-column head, the character count would be 22 plus one for the column divider, making the total count 23. Check with your printer to find out if you always add one count for all headline sizes.

A. Contractual learning, a new program at KHS this year, provided the topic for a panel discussion held for parents of students, at a PTA meeting held in the cafeteria on Oct. 16.

B. A Mexican band called El Mariachi Guiador, composed of foreign-language and instrumental-music students, performed before and after school today in the halls of north building in celebration of All Saints Day, a Latin American festival.

C. Two Children's Theater classes, part of the English phase elective system, presented plays Oct. 24–25 to students in kindergarten through third grade at North Glendale and Robinson Elementary Schools, respectively.

D. Casting for "You Can't Take It With You," Little Theatre's fall play involving a nutty family called the Sycamores, took place on Oct. 21.

E. Undefeated Ladue will host the Kirkwood Pioneers at 2 P.M. tomorrow in a battle that might determine the conference championship.

(15) For each headline below tell which headline rule(s) it violates. Assume they are for the "traditional style".

A. Crowning to Be Part
   of Hobo Day Activities

B. Harriers head for Conference
   Meet Tomorrow in Columbia

C. Cahokia Maroons To
   Face Flying Pioneers

D. G.A.A. To Meet

E. "You Can't Take It With You" Named As Fall Play

F. National Award Presented to
   Twelve Upperclassmen

G. Smith to Receive Prize

H. Principal Bill
   Byers Retires

(16) Write a report on the history of headlines. Any text on journalism history will describe how headlines have changed over the years.

(17) Using a thesaurus, find synonyms for the following verbs.

A. Offer	I. Join	Q. Elect
B. Give	J. Take	R. Win
C. Find	K. Get	S. Plan
D. Change	L. Provoke	T. Approve
E. Battle	M. Praise	U. See
F. Question	N. Tell	V. Hear
G. Accept	O. Speak	W. Participate
H. Hit	P. Highlight	

(18) Using a thesaurus, find synonyms for the following nouns.

A. Students	D. Game	G. Program
B. School	E. Team	H. Club
C. Meeting	F. Election	I. Faculty

Chapter V

LAYOUT PROCEDURES

Good writing is only part of what is essential to produce a good newspaper. If a paper is not attractive in appearance, it is quite likely that no one will bother to read it. So unless the make-up of the page is appealing to the eye, it will make no difference how well the stories are written. Effective makeup is most essential if a paper is to attract readers.

There is no set way of making up a page. The content should determine the makeup. It is important that the news be displayed appropriately. The most important news story on page one should be in the upper right corner of the page.

Good balance throughout the page can be achieved by proper placing of pictures and headlines.

Don't place all the pictures at the top or at the bottom of the page; scatter them throughout the page. Be careful not to put a picture on the center fold. The proper placement of pictures is important because they draw the attention of most readers. If all pictures were placed at the top of the page, it is quite possible some readers would never proceed to the bottom of the page.

Headline style and size is also important if the paper is to be attractive in appearance. A good makeup procedure is to arrange headlines diagonally from the lower left corner to the upper right corner, with the headline size increasing from lower left to upper right. This layout is effective if emphasis is to be placed on only one story.

Avoid the *tombstone* type of headline layout. This means to place two or more heads of the same size on the same level in adjacent columns. Headlines should be so placed on the page that they do not lie next to each other in the columns. Generally speaking, longer stories should have larger heads and shorter stories should have smaller heads, although the size of head must depend on the importance of the story.

Advertising makeup is also important. In a four-page paper ads are usually placed only on pages three and four and at the bottom of the page. Ads should never be placed on the front page or on the editorial page. Be sure that the ads are never boxed straight across the bottom of the page. In a layout like this, most readers would read down to the ads but never get into them, and the advertisers would be wasting their money.

A good procedure to follow in advertising layout is to try to bring the body type (reading material) down to every ad in the paper. If there are a number of small ads, this may be hard to do.

The best way of doing it is to place the ads in a pyramid layout. Preferably, they should be pyramided to the right, but they may be pyramided to the left. The largest ad should go on the side toward which the pyramid is being built and should be placed at the bottom. This will enable you to create a step arrangement in the ad layout. The stairstep arrangement for ads is permissible in traditional layout style, but it is not acceptable in Modular Design, as discussed in rule 31 below.

Type may be brought down to the ads by creating a double pyramid and well effect. In this layout, ads are built up from both sides of the page, with a single ad running across the middle columns. This will bring the type down into the middle columns, alongside the ads. This type of layout is most effective when it is used on facing pages.

In general, small ads should be placed above large ones, so that the small ones are not buried on the page. Don't place two ads for the same type of merchandise next to each other.

Pictures should not be placed next to ads, nor should boxed stories, because it makes them appear to be ads also.

As mentioned previously, there is no set layout procedure; but adherence to the above rules and to the following list should produce a page appealing to the eye.

(1) Don't use posed pictures; show action.

(2) Crop pictures carefully; cut away everything that does not add to the story.

(3) Make pictures large enough to identify people.

(4) Pictures have greater impact than type. Guide the reader through the page by effective placement of pictures.

(5) Make pictures fill the column space completely.

(6) Avoid separating related stories and pictures.

(7) Don't put pictures in the middle of a story.

(8) Don't put a picture between a head and its lead.

(9) Use no headline over a picture when the caption tells the story.

(10) Don't put rules (printed lines) around pictures. Sometimes it is necessary to use a rule above or below a picture in order to identify the story it illustrates.

(11) Two-line headlines are preferable to one-line heads.

(12) Top headline on page should be at least 36-point type.

(13) Keep stronger heads at the top of the page.

(14) Don't mix type families on a page.

(15) Keep same type of headlines on a page—all flush left, centered, etc.

(16) Vary headline size throughout the page.

(17) A one- or two-column headline should fill at least three-fourths of the line.

(18) Don't use boldface at random. Boldface type should have some order to it. The customary use of boldface type is in a long story; every third or fourth paragraph is set in boldface to break up the mass of solid type.

(19) Avoid boldface type more than every third paragraph.

(20) Avoid three-column leads; stay with one, if possible.

(21) If a story runs more than one column, don't start a new paragraph in the new column; make the break in the middle of a paragraph.

(22) Don't run type in more columns than the width of the

THE BEARD BUGLE

| Vol. 11 No. 2 | Daniel Carter Beard Junior High School, Flushing, New York | March 24, 1983 |

Unemployment Affects 14%

See Story In Centerfold

Por amor

Menudo Takes N.Y. By Storm

See Story On Page 11

Read The Adventures Of Boris

See Story On Page 20   Cartoon By Hye-Sun Han

A popular trend in junior high newspapers is to use the front cover to indicate to the reader what may be found on the inside. This front cover from The Beard Bugle, *Daniel Carter Beard Junior High School, Flushing, New York, uses photographs and artwork to appeal to the reader.*

Skip Farrow, Nipher's only player on the KHS tennis team, works on his tenacious overhand serve. (Photo by Tom Reese—KHS)

Two Freshmen Tee Off

by Michelle Schneider

Nipher has two real swingers in its midst — Craig Menzemer and Bob Grandcolas, freshmen, who have made Kirkwood High's golf team, coached by Bill Lenich.

"Practice started in the middle of March," remarked Craig. "We practiced every day it wasn't raining or too cold to play.

"Kirkwood practices and has their home games at Crystal Lake Country Club," he continued.

Craig started playing golf when he was little, but he "didn't start playing seriously" until about three years ago.

"I took golf lessons at Greenbriar Hills Country Club when I was twelve" Craig recalled. "That's when I really got into golf. I still play other sports, but I just spend more time on golf.

"I don't know, it's kind of like I got bit by a bug and I have to keep coming back for more," Craig related with a laugh.

Craig played last year in the Junior District Golf Tournament, which is a tournament for all kids who live in the general St. Louis area who want to participate.

"Kirkwood's team, which consists of thirteen players, has two or three matches and two or three practices a week—weather permitting," Craig explained.

Weather did not permit on Apr. 2, as the first match that Craig was scheduled to be in was cancelled because of the rain.

"Kirkwood had lost to Parkway Central the day before, by 27 strokes, so I really wanted to get out there and play," Craig related.

Although Bob Grandcolas also made the golf team, he was not available for comment.

Skip Farrow Makes 'Racket'

by Mark Addis and Michelle Schneider

"I think the tennis team is going to do pretty well this year, because we have good potential," commented Skip Farrow, freshman.

Skip is the only freshman from Nipher on the KHS tennis team, coached by Mr. Art Stout, KHS teacher.

'Skip's a fine player," remarked Mr. Stout. "He's getting better all the time."

Kirkwood has a very young team this year. "I think the unique thing about the team," reflected Mr. Stout, "is that out of 18 players, 9 are freshmen.

"The team practices every day after school from 3:30 to 6:30 P.M. at Kirkwood Park," he continued, "which is also where home matches are played."

Skip, who is on the Junior Varsity team, has played five matches, as of April 16, and has won four of them.

The team has also won four of

their five meets, defeating Parkway Central, 3 matches to 2; Parkway North, 4 to 1; losing to DeSmet, 4 to 1; and then beating U. City and Oakville, 5 to 0.

"The J.V. part of the meet is made up of five events — first, second, and third singles, and first and second doubles," explained Mr. Stout. "The team that takes three out of the five wins," he continued.

Skip basically plays first doubles, though he has tried a hand at singles. "I guess I'm a better doubles player than singles, and that's why I don't play singles as much," Skip conjectured. Mr. Stout seemed to think that he was about the same for both.

"I'm looking forward to playing on the team for the next three years," remarked Skip. "Right now I'm on JV, but I hope I'll get moved up to Varsity next year," he added optimistically.

Despite Loss, Rueschhoff Soars to 5'11"

by Kirk Hawkins

Nipher's track team lost a triangular meet Friday, Apr. 11 at Parkway South. The final score was Parkway South 78, Mehlville 42, and Nipher 30.

Nipher had only two first places. Tom Rueschhoff cleared 5 feet 8 inches to capture first in the high jump, and George Warrick ran the 220-yard dash in 26.8 seconds.

Nipher had one second place and seven third places. The cindermen also brought in two fourth places.

The 880 relay team was beaten by only one tenth of a second. The team consisted of Dale Eldridge, Mike Blair, Mike McFarland, and George Warrick.

Coming in third in the mile run was Mark Sparks with a time of 5 minutes and 18 seconds.

In the 440, Chuck Blum brought home a third place with a time of 59.7 seconds.

George Warrick had a 15.9 seconds, 120-yard low hurdle third place for Nipher.

The Pioneers' Craig Sanders ran the 880-yard run in 2 minutes, 21.6 seconds to take third.

In the 100-yard dash, Eddie Brassfield and Eric Caruthers tied to bring in a third place.

In the field events, Barry Brewer threw the discus 96 1/2 feet for fourth place, while Jerry Mueller took third in the shot-put with 43 feet, 1 3/4 inches.

Nipher took two places in the long jump. Adrian Waller took third with 16 feet, 1 3/4 inches, and

Tom Rueschhoff demonstrates the Fosbury flop, which later helped him break the school high jump record. (Photo by Mark Addis)

Mike McFarland jumped 15 feet, 6 3/4 inches to take fourth.

by Alvin Reid

A very notable quote can be used to describe Nipher's second track loss in a row. The quote is: "You can win the battle, but you may lose the war."

Crestview was the victor by a score of 72 to 46.

Nipher could only scrounge up four first places in the meet, winning the 880, the 880 relay, the shot-put, and the high jump.

And even the win in the 880 by Craig Sanders lost some of its luster because it was a tie for first.

Dan Dickerber hurled the shot farthest, and the 880 relay team, Mike McFarland, George

Warrick, Dale Eldridge, and Terence Jones, burst to a winning time.

While Nipher was bringing in a second in the 220 by Jone and a second by Mark Sparks in the mile, a small battle turned into a big victory for Tom Rueschhoff, Rueschhoff won the high jumping event in a big way. He set a new school record, 5 feet 11 inches.

This broke the old record set at 5 feet 9 1/2 inches last year by Frank Gordon.

Rueschhoff just had one thing to say after breaking the record, "Wow."

Rueschhoff won a big battle for himself and the Pioneers, but it was not enough to win the war.

Cardinals Special Dates

by Susan Jaeger

The Baseball Cardinals' season promises to be exciting. Here is a list of Cardinal "specials" that could be of interest to Nipheritps:

Teen Nights;
Friday, April 18, 7:30 p.m., Pittsburgh
Friday, May 2, 7:30 p.m., Chicago
Friday, May 9, 7:30 p.m., San Francisco
Teenagers may purchase regular $3.50 reserved seats for $1.50 each.
Family Nights:
Monday, May 5, 7:30 p.m., Philadelphia
Tuesday, June 3, 7:30 p.m., Atlanta
Head ot family pays full price.
Dependents:
General Aemission . . . $.50

Reserved Seats . . . $2.00
Box Seats . . . $3.00

Batting Glove Day . . . Sunday, June 15, 1:15 p.m., Houston
Ball Day . . . Sunday, July 6, 1:15 p.m., Montreal
Poster Day . . . Sunday, August 10, 1:15 p.m., San Diego
Camera Day . . . Sunday, August 24, 1:15 p.m., Atlanta

Single Game Admission Prices:
Bleachers (sold on day of game only) . . . $1.50
General Admission (sold on day of game only) . . . $2.00
Reserved Seats (Loge and Terrace only) . . . $3.50
Box Seats (Field, Loge, and Terrace) . . . $4.50

Phillip Williams and Rick Paul disagree with an umpire's decision. (Photo by Tom Reese—KHS)

Freshmen Bat for KHS

by Kelley Jutton

"It's great, it's well . . . . . cool!" That is the opinion Rick Paul expressed about himself and Phillip Williams, freshman, being on Kirkwood High's baseball B-team.

Rick Paul, pitcher, feels, "It's a good opportunity 'cause I think with the older guys I'll get a new and different experience."

Phillip, an outfielder, thinks, "um . . . . it gives me a real chance

to really get into the game."

Both Rick and Phillip have played baseball on Khoury League teams before.

Rick has been with the "A's" team for six years and in Khoury League for the past eight years.

Phillip has been playing for two years on the "A's" team and has been in Khoury League for eight years.

Kirkwood's B-team record for this year is two and four.

This layout from The Beacon, *Nipher Junior High School, Kirkwood, Missouri, illustrates more modern layout ideas. Note the tooling (black) lines around two of the stories and the headline overprinted on the top left picture. Also note the mortise used for the cutline on the top left picture.*

Teen-age drinkers appear on campus

Experimenting with drugs has been replaced with the use of alcohol by some students as 19 suspensions have been written this year for drinking.

According to Vice-Principal Ray Rodriguez, "Most often the liquor is found in lockers, on the person, or a majority of the kids arrive in an inebriated condition."

'I do this to trip at school.'

If students are found with liquor or under the influence, they are given a five-day suspension, the parents are notified, and their name is added to the list of students caught drinking which forbids them from extra-curricular activities or field trips.

No more than five cases of drugs or passing out pills has occurred this year according to Rodriguez.

"The hazards of passing out pills," warned Rodriguez, "is that young people don't know what they are taking. One set of pills taken from a student were medication for a high blood pressure patient whose weight was 225 pounds. If a child of less than 125 pounds had taken two of these pills, he/she would have ended up in the hospital."

Students have varying opinions about the use of alcohol.

One anonymous student said, "I do this to trip at school and trip off the teachers."

Another eighth grader said, "Only the dumb ones who want to get caught bring alcohol to school."

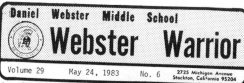

Daniel Webster Middle School

Webster Warrior

Volume 29   May 24, 1983   No. 6   2725 Michigan Avenue
Stockton, California 95204

MEXICAN FOLK DANCES--Alma Rodriguez and Connie Ruiz from Franklin High School perform on stage during a Cinco de Mayo assembly on May 6. *Photo by Stephanie Burgest*

Spirit, that's what it's all about!

By Candice Perry

Spirit Week, sponsored by the student leadership class, should now be in full swing with daily dress up days and fun activities at noontime.

General chairperson for this week is Latisa McCaskal who, with the entire leadership class, has organized and planned the week's activities.

Tomorrow is *Shade and Hat Day*, so students can wear their most colorful or favorite hat as well as sun glasses to complement their outfit. Thursday is *Twins Day*. Friends can dress alike to become twins. The seventh versus eighth grade spirit competition will end on Thursday.

Lunchtime games and contests of ice sitting, pyramid building, mating game, balloon toss contests, tricycle races, bottle filling,

shaving cream, and other fun game winners will get spirit points to help their grade in the contest. The winning class will be announced at the Awards Assembly on Friday morning.

"Moving On", the eighth grade dance, will climax the week's activities on Friday. The cost is $2.50 for a single and $4.00 for couples which includes a catered dinner at 6 p.m. The last day to buy tickets for the dance which lasts until 11 p.m. is tomorrow. Locker Music Production will furnish the music, and all dancegoers will receive a souvenir program bid at the door when they arrive.

Diana Nail is the co-ordinator of the dance. A photo booth will be set up to take pictures of friends and couples. The polaroid pictures will cost $1.50 and will be placed in a folder.

Modular layout has been used by the Webster Warrior, Daniel Webster Middle School, *Stockton, California. The staff has designed the page to carry the reader both horizontally and vertically. The use of the quote in the middle of the teen-age drinkers story helps break up a long, gray column of type.*

4—focus

May 20, 1983
Cougar Print

The American DreaM

Chaffin students agree that most American's ambition in life is to be rich.

by Evie Woods

What is the American Dream? Chaffin students have many different opinions. The American dream depends on how you look at it, and at changes with the times.

It seems the dream has always been to have personal property but it is measured in different ways as time passes. In 1928 the Republican Party's campaign promise was "a chicken in every pot and a car in every garage." Today most Chaffin students want an Atari in their living room and a Porsche in their garage.

Chaffin students agree that most American's ambition in life is to be rich. Sally Prewitt, eighth grader, is one of these people. "I want to be a housewife with a rich husband and two cute kids," says Sally.

Other Chaffin students have different ideas about what they would like to do in the future. "I would like to be a professional dancer because I enjoy dancing and I want to make it my career," explained seventh grader Andrea Newton.

Steve Rowland, seventh grader, says, "I want to be an architect because I like to draw and design buildings."

Richard Safranek, another seventh grader, has the same idea. "I want to be an architect or maybe a doctor because I would make a lot of money and it would be a secure job," said Richard.

"I'd like to work in electronics because I think in the future there will be more chances of a better job in that field," said Edward Bull, freshman.

Times have really changed, Chaffin has some very ambitious girls who prove that boys aren't the only ones who dream of being doctors and lawyers. Becky Orler, eighth grader, wants to be a pediatrician. "I like helping little kids who are sick," explained Becky.

"I want to be a doctor, probably a pediatrician," said freshmen Jill Eubanks, "because I always wanted to be a doctor and I like little kids and babies."

"I think I'd like to be a doctor because it would be exciting and also my dad is a doctor," said Jackie Berumin, seventh grader.

"I want to be a lawyer and travel lots of different places," said Leigh Sutton, seventh grader.

"I want to be a major league baseball player," said eighth grader John England, "because I could travel and make lots of money."

All Americans have a different dream of what to so with their life, but most probably share the dream to "be happy and have a good job and family" with Leigh Sutton.

"I think it is more important to enjoy what you do than to make a lot of money when you don't enjoy yourself," said Sheila Payne, freshman.

" I want to be a lawyer and travel lots of different places. "

Leigh Sutton, 7

" I think it is more important to enjoy what you do than to make a lot of money. "

Sheila Payne, 9

" I want to be an architect or maybe a doctor because I would make a lot of money. "

Richard Safranek, 7

Large initial letters to begin and end the headline, along with an initial letter to begin the copy inside the box and large quotes add graphic appeal to this design from the Cougar Print, *Chaffin Junior High, Fort Smith, Arkansas.*

=== *opinion* === WY'S WORDS   Friday, June 4, 1982   3 ===

wandering

w**ãrrior**

Prayer in schools: pro and con

What is your opinion of President Ronald Reagan's proposal to pass an amendment allowing organized prayer in public schools?

Terri Otto, ninth - If students want to learn about religion, they should go to church. They should not have to learn it at school.

Tony Cloud and Lori —Ruzsa, ninth - They should have organized prayer so students can get closer to God.

Laura Macher, ninth - Religion is a personal decision and I don't think it should be in public schools.

Julie Borroz, seventh - I think it's a good idea because you could pray with other people and really let out your feelings.

Rob Davies, ninth - Everybody doesn't want or need religion, so I think it's a bad idea.

Lana Bjornsen, eighth - It's a good idea because

the way the world is going we really need help.

Pam Olsen, eighth and Darren Joens and Barb Smith, ninth - Religion isn't important at school. It should be kept at home and in church.

Cathy Kirbingburg, eighth- It would be a good way to let out your problems and know someone is listening, and it's easier to pray in a group.

Principal Dave Dyment - It's very controversial.

••••••••••••••••• *Wy's Old Owl* •••••••••••••••••

Why can't the seventh graders be on the newspaper staff or be a PE assistant?

According to Principal Dave Dyment, one reason is the maturity difference between the seventh graders and the ninth graders. Another reason is that there are only a limited amount of openings for teachers' aides, so those classes are opened for only ninth graders.

*   *   *   *   *

Why are dances always held on Fridays instead of on a day like Saturday?

According to Mr. Robert Sanborn, associate principal, there is no real reason except that the chaperones prefer it on that night.

*   *   *   *   *

Why doesn't the snack

bar sell milk shakes?

Sanborn stated that the food service did not stop selling them; it was the administration who stopped

the sale of them because the students would throw the containers around thus making more work for the janitors.

Letters

So-long party

We really like the activities going on at Wy'east, but we have thought of one that we are interested in. We would like to have a special day for the ninth graders, such as choosing a day to go on a picnic to Lewisville Park for a so-long party. We could go swimming, play softball and other activities. We could have pictures taken and, of course, a lot of food! There would also be no homework involved with this activity!!! We would

like to know of students and teachers in favor of doing this. As for supervision, we could ask a few teachers and counselors who are interested in going with us. We think that this would be a good activity since this is our last year at Wy'east and some of us will be going to different schools next year.

Please take this into serious consideration.
Thank you,
Chris Cook
Terri Otto
ninth graders

An attractive opinion page appears in the Wy's Words, *Wy'east Junior High School, Vancouver, Washington. Note the Wandering Warrior column used to get readers' opinions on a topic and the Wy's Old Owl used to answer readers' questions.*

head for that story. If this is sometimes necessary, don't start the extra column with a new paragraph.

(23) Don't let the last line of a paragraph begin a new column. Such a line is known as a *widow*.

(24) Subheads should never be more than one line in length.

(25) Capitalize the first word of a subhead.

(26) Place the byline at the beginning of the story, not at the end.

(27) By-line names should be all capitals.

(28) Don't use rules to separate columns.

(29) If rules are used under a flag (the name of the publication), they should also be used over it, unless the flag is at the top of the page.

(30) Do experiment with layouts after you have mastered the basics. More modern layouts (see page 70) are using graphic designs such as tooling (black) lines around stories and/or pictures. Headlines sometimes are being placed to the side of a story. Quotes are being pulled out of stories and set in "Boston" boxes. These are usually half boxes with lines above and below quotes and are in larger type than the normal body type (see example below). Cartoons are not always rectangular. They may be stairstepped either to the left or to the right. These are some of the latest ideas in layout trends.

BOSTON BOX EXAMPLE

"Think not what your country can do for you, but what you can do for your country."

A "Boston" box is used to break up the grayness of a paper. Body type may be set around the box.

(31) The trend in the 1980's has been toward modular design. This means that every element on the page is rectangular in shape. Photos and artwork may be considered part of the story element.

Therefore, to maintain a "mod," a story could be U-shaped around a photo, around artwork, around a Boston Box, or around another related story (sidebar). An article could also be L-shaped around any of those items. In modular design, advertisements are either boxed across the bottom or arranged vertically up the side of the page. Although this violates traditional layout procedures that require a story to touch every ad, it is essential in modular design in order to keep the rectangular concept.

(32) Consider using a tripod head in design. A tripod head is a three-part head that has one part twice the size of the other two parts and is normally separated by a colon.

The above list is not all inclusive and is not meant to stifle individuality in newspapers. It is only a suggested list to follow. You will note that examples given in the chapter do not follow all the rules given. Remember to be consistent and you should produce a layout that is pleasing to the eye.

EXERCISES

(1) Examine a copy of a paper from another school and be prepared to discuss in class the good and bad features of the layout.

(2) Lay out a four-page, five-column paper by clipping articles from other papers and placing them on the appropriate pages. Page one should be the news page; page two, editorial; page three, features; and page four, sports. Follow the rules of layout procedure discussed in this chapter.

(3) By use of a dummy sheet lay out the news page for the next issue of your school newspaper. Show exact placement of stories, headlines and cuts.

Chapter VI

EDITORIALS IN A SCHOOL NEWSPAPER

Editorials, according to many journalists, are very difficult to write in such a way as to attract the reader's interest.

Many school papers have dropped the editorial because of lack of reader interest. Perhaps this is a justifiable excuse, but it certainly is not an indication of a superior newspaper.

One of the main duties of a good newspaper is to explain and interpret the news. In a junior high newspaper this is usually done through editorials but other interpretative articles may be used. The main difference between editorializing and interpreting is that the editorial writer usually recommends what should be done about a news happening while the interpreter merely explains a news event.

Articles of interpretation should be based on news happenings or news stories. Many editorials are based on news stories that appear in a newspaper but some are not. Editorials can be based on anything that might be of interest to the readers. Interesting headlines to draw the reader's attention to the editorial and a good lead can attract reader interest. Even if only one person reads the editorial, it has done some good.

As already stated, the main difficulty in writing editorials is making them interesting and attractive to the reader. This can best be done by observing the seven qualities that contribute to effective writing. These qualities should be followed in news stories as well as editorials, but they can make an editorial very effective.

The seven qualities are: (1) clarity; (2) color; (3) concreteness; (4) economy; (5) tone; (6) tempo; and (7) variety.

Clarity is precise conveyance of an idea. This is actually a matter of word choice, of organization of words within phrases and clauses. The two things to be avoided are misplaced modifiers and dangling participles.

"I Pledge Allegiance..."

DING! There goes the 8:25 tardy bell.   Today is Monday morning, and time for my flag salute. Look at everyone rise to salute me. Oh no, there's Sammy Sneak, saying the flag salute, putting six pieces of gum in his mouth, and doing his homework all at the same time! SWOOSH! Here comes Teresa Tardy, late as usual. She doesn't even stop to join in the flag salute!   And there's Lenny Lover, passing love notes to Susan Sweet heart. What a flag salute!

This is the way a flag (if it could talk) would probably describe the flag salute. Even if the students are saying it, they usually do not have their minds on it. This is all right in elementary school possibly, but not in junior high school! The idea is for you to salute your country which is symbolized by the flag. The teacher should not have to always interrupt and say "Shut up, Jake," "Stand still, Bryan," AND "Spit it out, Moe!" When students give the flag salute, they should not just say it, but think about it also!

DING! Well it's Tuesday morning and time for my flag salute. Look at that! Teresa Tardy is on time! And Sammy Sneak is acting human! Look at Lenny and Susan! What a great flag salute!   Oops! Look at the teacher, Mrs. Crab. She is grading the test from Friday! Well, at least I got my idea across to the students!

— by Mark Ratsky

The editorial above, from the El Bee, *Luther Burbank Junior High School, Burbank, California, shows how the use of imagination can enliven a dull subject.*

Color is the quality that evokes images. The verbs carry the load of pictorial content. For example: The boys sat at their desks, or, The boys slouched at their desks. The verb *slouched* conveys a picture as well as a meaning.

Concreteness means specificity. Don't use general adjectives. Be specific.

Economy means making every word count. At the same time, don't leave out words if they are necessary to convey the true meaning of the article.

Tone gives the general impression of the writing. The tone conveys whether the story is formal, casual, breezy, dignified, ironic, or satirical. Word choice is the principal determinant of tone. Word choice should be appropriate to subject and should actually grow out of it.

Tempo is a matter of pace; in other words, how the writing moves. Does it follow through smoothly or is it jerky? This is usually determined by sentence length, and sentence length is usually determined by subject matter.

Variety is important in every form of writing. Variety in word choice, sentence length, and sentence structure should be attempted. Above all, avoid repetition.

These qualities should help you in any type of journalistic writing but they are included in this chapter to aid you in writing an effective editorial. There are four types of editorials. They are: (1) criticism; (2) entertaining, (3) interpretative; and (4) commendatory.

An editorial of criticism moves toward a definite point of view. It may be showing the good points or the bad points of something. Its main purpose is to influence the reader to develop the same opinion it has presented. This type of editorial may be highly critical, but remember that criticism can be both constructive and destructive. A solution to the problem should be suggested. Don't just preach or condemn. Because of the controversial nature that an editorial of criticism sometimes has it might be wise to present two editorials on the subject—a PRO and a CON. If the school is divided on an issue this might be the

Should State Allow Graduation in Three Years?

Pro
By Sue Wolling

Do you sometimes find at the beginning of the school year that you already know everything that you are supposed to learn in the first semester? Then you may be eligible to take advantage of the new Missouri law permitting students to finish high school in less than four years.

There are many instances when time saved in high school could be put to good use. In the first place, many professions demand more schooling than the usual four years of college. This means that it is a long time before a person can go to work as, for instance, a doctor or lawyer. If he could graduate from high school in less than four years, a doctor could go into practice that much sooner.

With the new laws, many young men will be drafted when they are about nineteen years old. This often interrupts their education in the middle of college. If they could spend less than four years in high school, they could get more college in before being drafted. This is significant because after being in the army, many men don't go back to school. If they were close to graduating when they were drafted, these men might be more tempted to finish college.

Since this plan would only affect bright students who choose to try it, no one would be forced to take extra work. However, many students are just bored by study hall and would like to alternate a subject with gym. If he did this and took one course in summer school, a student could graduate in only three years. Besides, overcrowding has been a parent complaint for years. Moving a few bright students ahead just might help eliminate this problem.

This plan has an excellent chance to help many students get more out of life in the long run. After all, why should anyone be forced to waste a year or more of his life?

North Students Discuss New Rule; Disagree on Graduation Requirement
By Lisa Oxenhandler

Students at North seem to be evenly divided on the issue of a three-year requirement to finish high school.

Two hundred and twenty-four students were polled and 107 said they would like to finish high school in three years with 104 saying no and 13 undecided.

Of the ninth graders polled, 56 percent said yes, 41 percent said no, and three percent were undecided.

A majority of the seventh graders, 50 percent, said no. Forty-four percent said yes and six percent were undecided.

College was the choice of 151 of the students polled as to what they would do following graduation.

Thirty-five said they would get a job and 38 planned to enter vocational school or were uncertain.

Students also discussed advantages they thought would be gained by graduating earlier. "An extra year to do what you want," "Get a job earlier," and "To keep from being bored" were among the advantages listed.

Disadvantages were also given. Many students said that some individuals are not responsible enough to graduate early, that some teachers might lose their jobs, that it would be hard work to finish in three years, and that some students wouldn't graduate with their friends.

Editor's Note

The Missouri State Board of Education adopted a resolution on September 24 concerning graduation from high school.

The resolution reads as follows: "The four year requirement for graduation from high school may be modified if the student completes the following requirements: (1) Students must complete state requirements and any other local requirements needed for graduation; (2) Students must present an appropriate plan for an educational experience at college, vocational school, or on the job training.

A student completing the above requirements may be permitted to graduate in less than four years if he gets permission from school officials.

State Regulations Remain Unaltered
By Christa Juergens

Requirements to complete high school have not been changed by the new resolution adopted by the State Board of Education.

Seventeen Carnegie units are needed to graduate from high school. Required units include: four units of communication skills, that is English, 9, 10, 11 and 12; three units of social studies, meaning citizenship, world history or world geography, and American history; one unit of mathematics; one unit of practical arts; one unit of fine arts; and one unit (four years) of physical education.

In addition, each student must complete five units of electives.

For a student to graduate in three years time it would be necessary to take some courses in summer school in order to meet all of the above requirements.

Supt. of Schools Likes Resolution
By Lisa Wills

"I'm very much in favor of the action taken by the State Board of Education," remarked Dr. W.A. Shannon, superintendent of schools, in reaction to the recent resolution concerning graduation in three years from high school.

"Caution should and will be used to select the very few students that will benefit from this decision," Dr. Shannon said.

Dr. Shannon stated that the administration should be flexible and treat each student with his best interests in mind. He does not encourage students to try to cram in the required subjects for graduating just to get out of school a year earlier. For this reason, he realizes that a very small percentage of the students could graduate in three years.

"A student would have to take five solid subjects in ninth, tenth, and eleventh grades. The student would also have to take one unit of English in a correspondence course and one unit of physical education in summer school," according to Mr. Thaddeus Whayne, counselor at Kirkwood High School.

Five solids a day in tenth and eleventh grades would certainly be putting a strain on most students and would quickly determine whether or not the student was capable of handling so much responsibility.

Con
By Cathy Pitcher

The State Board of Education has adopted the resolution which states that some students in Missouri high schools will be able to finish in less than four years. This policy should not have been adopted.

The policy requires that to graduate in less time, you must complete all requirements for a high school diploma. This means that a student would have to carry a full load all through high school. He would have no study halls, not even alternating with gym. He would also have to go to summer school for some classes.

If he wanted to graduate early, a student wouldn't have much of a social life. He couldn't join any outside activities, such as sports events, Student Council, or any other clubs or programs. He'd be too busy keeping with school work. He would be missing a lot of fun! Social activities are an important part of life.

Extracurricular activities would be drastically hurt because of lack of people to participate in them. Think of a football team with no seniors!

Only students who have done accelerated work or whose grades are above average would be eligible to graduate by the end of their junior year.

Diplomas would be awarded to those students who leave school in less than the standard time only if they planned on going to college, vocational school or into a job.

The job market is scarce now. Throwing students into the world of work earlier could make the unemployment rate climb even higher.

Being a year younger than most college students could hamper many people. They may not be emotionally ready for college and would not fit in well. They could be very unhappy and wind up dropping out before they graduate. This could ruin their future just because they rushed into it too fast.

Redmond Supports Policy For Three Year Graduates
By Mark Klamer

Mr. Sidney Redmond, president of the State Board of Education, was interviewed last week to gain his ideas concerning the new resolution adopted to allow students to complete high school in three years.

"The resolution was adopted," Mr. Redmond said, "because Mr. Clyde Miller, former acting superintendent of the St. Louis County schools, asked if the board would consider making it possible for students to graduate in less than four years.

"We in turn handed the suggestion over to the Department of Education. They worked on it for five months questioning principals, administrators, and school teachers. The response was overwhelmingly in favor of the proposal or we would not have voted on it."

To take advantage of the new resolution a student must pass the state requirements for graduation and any other local requirements, Mr. Redmond said.

"Then a student has to show he is going on to college, vocational school, or on the job training. It is

up to the principal whether or not the student can do this. If he can he will receive his diploma with the rest of his graduating class," Mr. Redmond stated.

"The local school board may decide to make more restrictions," Mr. Redmond said,"on being able to do this and could probably stop a student, but we think it should be up to the principal involved."

According to Mr. Redmond there should be no problem in colleges accepting students who graduate in less than four years.

"For colleges to accept three year high school students is like graduate schools accepting three year college students," he said.

"The graduate school doesn't care and we don't think colleges will either. Besides, the student does have his diploma. He just has to wait for the rest of his class to receive their diplomas and then he gets his," stressed Mr. Redmond.

"The resolution passed unanimously," Mr. Redmond said, "and I wouldn't have voted for it if I didn't think it would help the school district, school administrators and the individual who takes advantage of it."

THE NORTHERN LIGHTS
"Knowledge is the Northern Light that guides the Pioneer."

Published monthly during the school year by the journalism class of North Kirkwood Junior High School, 11311 Manchester Road, Kirkwood, Missouri, 63122.

Editor-in-Chief - Mark Klamer	Assistants - Lisa Oxenhandler, John Sawhill
Managing Editor - Lisa Wills	Head Photographer - Scott Shull
News Editor - Donna Gehlert	Assistant - Rick Stern
Assistant - Jeff Viers	Copy Editor - Teresa Stoff
Feature Editor - Chris Lichtenheld	Assistants - Bryan Bayley, Geff Volgenau
Editorial Editor - Sue Wolling	Advertising Manager - Bob Schnitzius
Assistant - Karen Jepsen	Headline Editor - Rog Malone
Sports Editor - John Bryan	Assistants - Jim Groninger, Mike Hughes
Assistant - Terri Imler	Sponsor - H. L. Hall
Circulation & Exchange - Christa Juergens	Principal - W. L. Bowden
Art Editor - Carol Fauntleroy	Assistant Principals - E. C. Weidt, Thomas Moeller

IN MEMORIAM

North wishes to extend sympathy to the family and friends of Janis Kimberly Mory, eighth grader, who passed away early Sunday morning, October 3. Memorials may be placed in Janis' name at the Children's Hematology Fund in care of Dr. Teresa Vietti, 500 S. Kingshighway, St. Louis, Mo. 63110.

Calendar of Events

Oct. 15 — Football game Lindbergh here

Oct. 22 — Football game, Mehlville there Ninth grade fortnightly

Oct. 29 — Football game, Parkway Central here

Nov. 4-5 — Missouri State Teachers Meeting No school for students

Nov. 12 — Eighth grade fortnightly

---

itorial pages of school newspapers should show that the student writers have researched eir material. The above page from The Northern Lights, *North Kirkwood Junior High hool, Kirkwood, Mo. shows the different approaches that can be taken on one subject. A o and Con editorial are printed along with comments from the superintendent of schools, e president of the state board of education, and the students.*

Millage increase

Passage critical

Class cuts, overcrowded classes, and teacher reductions are all a likely possiblity if a proposed millage increase is not passed. March 8, sounds like an ordinary day, right? Wrong! On this day, voters will go to the polls to determine the fate of the Ft. Smith Public School System during these depressed economic times.

A lack of state funds will take a crippling toll if the proposed 4 mill increase is not passed.

Most classes at Chaffin have an average number of 25 students, however that number could increase to as much as twice it's normal size, without the additional necessary funds. The possibility of this happening would certainly decrease the ability of a student to enjoy a classroom discussion while, at the same time, learn and possibly contribute valuable information.

According to Dr. C.B. Garrison, superintendent of the Ft. Smith Public Schools, teachers and students will be directly affected if no extra funds are received.

"This is a serious matter for area students, teachers, and residents," he claimed. Garrison projects that realistically our district will lose $1,088,123 in revenue.

The Ft. Smith school system must find a way to handle this reduction in monies. Dr. Garrison has suggested three things: a 4 mill millage increase, a salary freeze, and personnel reduction.

Teachers have been concerned with the possibility of a salary freeze; and with good reason, especially since it is a known fact that Arkansas teachers are the lowest paid in the nation. A fact Arkansas should not be proud of. Attracting new teachers to the state will be more difficult with salaries frozen.

So far, the 4 mill increase is the safest way to bring in school funds. "This will be on the ballot in March and will hopefully be passed," commented Phyllis Cook, Classroom Teachers Association representative. "If it passes, then the liklihood of overcrowded classes will be lessened."

It won't be easy for voters to voluntarily raise their taxes during these times, but it is a necessary evil if the quality of education in Ft. Smith will be able to maintain its standards.

Explaining the problem and encouraging the vote, are two things every student can do. The future education of every Chaffin student is on the line. Chaffin students and teachers alike, should do everything in their power to see that the increased millage is passed on March 8.

An editorial of interpretation is illustrated by the above article from The Cougar Print, *Chaffin Junior High, Fort Smith, Arkansas. Note that suggestions at the end indicate what each student can do to help the situation.*

98

fair way to do it. If no one on the newspaper staff can write one side then it is permissible to go outside the newspaper staff and get someone else to present the other side. A PRO-CON presentation often helps the newspaper avoid criticism.

Entertaining editorials provide a change of pace. Usually they are on subjects that are not part of hard news, such as art, music, or science.

An entertaining editorial is usually humorous but still makes a point, although it may be very subtle.

Interpretative editorials provide the reader with an explanation or interpretation, but they do not necessarily suggest that the reader take a certain course of action. These editorials usually have a news story as their basis. They normally answer the questions "Why is that?" and "What does it mean?"

These questions are usually answered by organizing data and offering a hypothesis. An informative editorial offers little, if any, opinion.

Editorials of commendation are quite common in school newspapers. Anyone who has done a job well may be worthy of recognition. An editorial of commendation can express the appreciation of the student body to the student, organization, or faculty member involved.

The style of an editorial will, of course, depend on the type to be written. Sometimes a sustained editorial campaign may be necessary. If an editorial in one issue of the newspaper does not bring positive results it may be necessary to approach the issue from a different angle in the next edition of the newspaper. Too often, school newspapers write an editorial on a subject they believe strongly in, but they drop it even though nothing has been accomplished. Keep hitting the same idea with different approaches issue after issue until a satisfactory answer is given by the individuals you are trying to influence.

Many editorials require some research on the writer's part in order to present the facts accurately. Be sure you have all the information on the subject before you start writing.

Editorials should be developed around a central theme to

Wy's Words Editorial Policy unchange

The following editorial policy was accepted by the journalism staff. It has not changed from last year.

EDITORIAL POLICY OF WY'S WORDS, 1981-1982.

1. Purpose
Wy's Words is a product of the journalism class. The primary purpose of the newspaper is to provide learning in journalistic skills and publications practice for those students. Students will strive to:
A. inform, influence, serve and entertain the readership.
B. be accurate and report without bias.
C. avoid gossip and rumor.
II. Content
A. Section editors will decide which stories to include, the length of the stories, and their location in the paper.
B. The paper reserves the right to review plays, movies, records, concerts, books or any other work, whether student or professional. All reviews will be by-lined.
III. Writers
Only members of the journalism class can work as news and sports reporters. Any reader may submit an idea for an article. Letters to the editor are encouraged. Feature articles written by readers not on the newspaper staff may be submitted to the staff

for consideration for inclusion in Wy's Words.
IV. Editorials
All editorials appear as the opinion of at least 90 percent of the Wy's Words staff.
V. Letters to the Editor
The paper will provide a forum in the school for free interchange of ideas. Letters to the editor will be accepted from all readers of Wy's Words.
A. Letters may not exceed 200 words.
B. All letters must be signed by the writer. Signatures will be verified. No letters will be printed anonymously.
C. All letters received will be printed. However, if letters are submitted as a group assignment, as many will be chosen to be printed as space allows.
C. Letters may not contain libelous statements or obscenity, or create an imminent danger of the disruption of the school.
VI. Controversial issues
A. Reporters will strive to report both sides of controversial issues accurately and without bias.
B. Wy's Words will not endorse any candidates, but reserves the right to editorialize about political issues.
C. Wy's Words reserves the right to editorialize about controversial issues.

VII. Corrections
Significant errors in fact will be corrected in the next issue of Wy's Words.

All student publications should have an editorial policy. Wy's Words, *Wy'east Junior High School, Vancouver, Washington, ran theirs on their editorial page for readers to see.*

insure unity. A common fault in editorial writing is to have more than one theme, which brings about disorganization and usually results in a poor conclusion, if any.

All editorials should have an introduction, a body, and a summary ending. Editorial writing differs from news story form in that editorials do not need summary leads. The main point in an editorial is usually in the conclusion.

Just as there are rules to be followed for news stories, there are rules to be followed in writing editorials:

(1) The editorial should be short, generally no more than 300 words.

(2) Make sure that the editorial has an introduction, a body, and a summary ending.

(3) Avoid the first person singular (I) and second person (you).

(4) Make the writing style dignified but readable. Keep it simple, but don't write down to the reader.

(5) Use comparisons and contrasts. This is particularly important if you are trying to influence the reader. If you can show your point of view by comparing it with another, the reader is more likely to accept it, if you produce a convincing argument.

(6) The point of the editorial should be made without preaching.

(7) Timeliness is an important factor. Don't write an editorial on something that happened last year or even two months ago, unless it has occurred again.

(8) All opinions should be supported by stated facts. Statements may be documented by quoting sources and authorities.

(9) Criticism should be followed by constructive suggestions.

(10) Individual criticism should be avoided, unless the criticism is in some way applicable to the student body. Do not blame all students for the action of a few.

(11) Make sure praise is given where it is due.

(12) Editorials should carry a by-line unless they are the opinion of the paper as a whole.

Organized prayer not meant for school

President Reagan has proposed an amendment to the constitution which would allow organized prayer in public schools.

Although it states that prayer would be strictly voluntary, in actuality it would not. Students who refused to pray or didn't believe in God would be ridiculed and therefore forced into praying.

Conflicts would arise as to what type of prayer should be said. The manner in which prayers were said would also be questionable. Then another problem would be whose religious preference should rule, whether it be students', teachers', parents' or a prayer dictated by the state.

Any student can pray before, after and during class silently if he chooses to. Why should the schools have to set aside time in their already hectic schedule?

Putting this kind of pressure on the public school system is ludicrous. Schools are already burdened enough trying to teach students the fundamentals of reading, writing and arithmetic without having any other added responsibilities.

We feel that there are much more important issues that Reagan should be concentrating on, things such as the suffering economy. Besides this fact and that organized prayer in public schools has already been ruled unconstitutional, Reagan is still pursuing the amendment.

We feel that if this amendment is passed it will cause more trouble than it is worth.

The Wy's Words, Wy'east Junior High School, Vancouver, Washington, has used a national topic as an editorial in its issue. Note the use of first person "We" to refer to the newspaper staff. This is the only time first person should be used in an editorial.

102

Lend Me Your Ears!

by Lynn Haubner

Friends, Students, Faculty members, lend me your ears!

I come here to praise your textbooks, not to bury them. The evil that students do to their books lives after them, the good they do to them resolves in silent strength! So let it be with you! (Besides, you won't get a fine!)

The "black side" of you tells you to deface your texts; if it were so, it is a grievous fallacy. And grievous fallacies can be obtained from marred texts.

Here, enough said about insults to books. For what is a book but an esteemed honor and a key to knowledge? Come I, the simple author, to speak in behalf of my textbook.

As Shakespeare put it, "Respect for knowledge is self-respect."

P. S. There has been thoughout the preparation of this work collaboration and mutual aid from the works of Shakespeare, but the general editor assumes full responsibilities for the final form of the text, the notes, and the opinions expressed.

Famous quotations can be used as a takeoff for good editorials, as illustrated above in an editorial from The Northern Lights, *North Kirkwood Junior High School, Kirkwood, Missouri.*

Even if you follow all of the above rules, you will not necessarily write an editorial that everyone will read. As mentioned previously, the headline must attract the interest of the reader.

The best headline is one that arouses curiosity. It does not necessarily have to state the content of the editorial in specific terms, nor does it have to come from the lead paragraph. Don't write a head that says "Student Council Needs Improving" when you could say "What's Wrong with This School?" The second headline is more likely to gain the reader's attention than the first.

The editorial page may also contain cartoons, an inquiring-reporter column, letters to the editor, and reviews. Remember that these articles are supplements, not substitutes, for editorials.

Merchandise Theft Produces Problems

By Carol Breimeier

"The fastest growing larceny in the country," says J. Edgar Hoover, head of the FBI, ' is shoplifting."

The problem has tripled in the last ten years and U.S. stores lost an estimated three billion dollars in 1969. The nation's stores have at least 10,000 shopliftings each week. The average value of shoplifted items has risen to 28 dollars. The result is an increase in price for all shoppers.

A recent investigation in a major New York department store, during which 175 shoppers were closely watched, showed that one out of nine stole some item.

In some parts of the country, juveniles are responsible for over half of the known thefts, with girl shoplifters outnumbering boys 20 to 1, though toys steal more expensive items.

A survey of 1,000 high school students in Delaware showed that 50 per cent had shoplifted at least once. And fewer than half as many steal in suburban stores as steal in downtown outlets.

Desperate steps are being taken by merchants to protect themselves from shoplifters. Store owners are prosecuting thieves that would have been let off with a warning a few years ago. Conviction can result in a $2,000 fine and up to five years in jail, in some states.

In some cities, newspapers are cooperating by printing names of shoplifters. The publicity has scared off some amateur shoplift-ers.

A special electronic device is being used that gives warning of shoplifters. Once attached to articles of clothing, they can be removed only with a special tool by a clerk. If the tag is not removed, warning signals flash when the shopper tries to leave the store.

Despite these precautionary measures, shoplifting is still a growing problem, with no solution in sight.

Research can make an editorial more interesting. The above example shows how research can provide some interesting statistics on shoplifting. The editorial is from The Northern Lights, *North Kirkwood Jr. High, Kirkwood, Mo.*

Every issue of the paper should contain at least one editorial. However, never write a useless editorial just for the sake of having one.

Rule number eight, "All opinions should be supported by stated facts," is very important.

A Typical Day In The Book Store.

Student Problem at Bookstore

During lunchtime, the bookstore is one of the most crowded places in the school. If this were due to student interest in the books, it might be considered a tribute to the intelligence of Hanley students. However, the crowds at lunchtime either ignore the books and socialize, or steal and damage them.

Obviously, this congestion in the bookstore impedes its purpose of selling books. In such an atmosphere, students find it difficult to browse or buy books.

Another serious problem relates to the disappearance of a substantial number of books. The Student Council pays for the books and hopes to use the profits to benefit the school. Thus, stealing of books robs the school of worthwhile projects which the funds would make possible.

If this situation continues, stricter regulations may be placed upon students using the bookstore. Such restrictions would be unpleasant to the students and should be unnecessary.

Students who wish to talk should go elsewhere. Those who are tempted to take books should realize they are depriving themselves and others of the benefits of Student Council funds. The bookstore is a constructive institution which should be permitted to serve those who want to use it.

Debbie Goldstein

Editorial cartoons help enliven an editorial page and also make the editorial itself more interesting. Note the above editorial from **The Acorn,** *Hanley Junior High School, University City, Missouri. A feature on the bookstore also ran in the same issue.*

Towards a United Community

University City is now experiencing a time of unrest as the result of the recent school board election. Because of the division in the community and defeat of the proposed plans for centers in our schools, many people are suffering bitterness and disillusionment.

The School Board election is over now. Although our community was split widely on the "centers" and "bussing" issues, right now there is only one issue facing our schools — how to improve our education system using the facilities we have.

We must remember that running a school system requires a great co-operative effort from good teachers, good administrators and an understanding school board.

The reasons for emotional reactions are certainly understandable; it must be remembered that this is one of the most controversial issues to occur in the history of this city. Although we can appreciate this, the main concern is the students. We must not let emotions interfere with, and hamper, the effective operation of U. City schools, but rather we must remember that our goal is permanent good-quality education.

We must work together more now than ever before to live up to U. City's reputation as an excellent school system, so that U. City will be a better place for all.

Editorials of appeal are usually well accepted in junior high newspapers. The above example is from The Acorn, Hanley Jr. High School, University City, Mo.

A school newspaper, like any paper, is subject to libel suits. Libelous matter is published material that injures a person's reputation or character. The material is usually false, at least to some degree. *Libel* may be defined as a false defamatory statement, which is published, and which diminishes the reputation of a person.

Libel is not to be confused with slander, which is a false oral defamation. Oral defamation is uttered once and does not come to the attention of many people, whereas libel is printed, and a record of it is kept for many people to see.

Libel has three constituent parts: (1) *defamation*—a damaging statement; (2) *publication*—the defamatory statement must be published; some courts have held that publication can consist of sending a manuscript to the printers; and (3) *identification*—

Lunch Falls Flat

Scrooges are supposed to remind one of Christmas, not lunchrooms!

However, it cannot be denied that behind every french fry in the cafeteria lurks the spirit of Scrooge. Recently the concept of "fry counting" has been introduced to 189. If a student receives one too many fries, back it goes in the fry box.

O.K., O.K., there's a recession, we understand. Nonetheless, if one french fry would employ the millions out of work, this world would be a lot easier to live in!

Let's face it, we no longer get vegetables and starch. Isn't it being a little over economical to take away from us the little we do get?

And while we are on the subject of the cafeteria ... another problem with 189's lunch room is variety. Variety is the spice of life. When one has hot dogs on Monday and fish on Friday week after week, with Sloppy Joes and heros thrown in on a too regular basis, it is not spices such as salt or pepper we need, it is the spice of variety.

When the lunch bell rings and famished students rush down to the cafeteria, the first thing they look at is the weekly menu in the cafeteria and, to their disappointment, they find nearly the same menu pasted on the glass as the week's before. Many of the hungry students don't take the lunch due to this, but eat peanut butter and jelly sandwiches instead.

Whatever happened to the cafeteria-student-teacher committee from last year? Couldn't they come up with some new menus and ways to get the meals to be more exciting?

Hopefully changes in the lunchroom system will be made to add style and substance to our lunch periods. After all, we are what we eat!

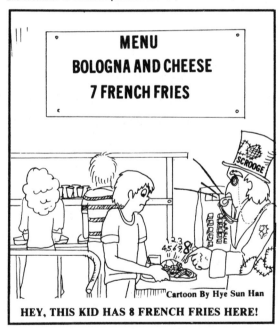

HEY, THIS KID HAS 8 FRENCH FRIES HERE!

The above editorial cartoon from The Beard Bugle, *Daniel Carter Beard Junior High School, Flushing, New York, blends well with the editorial in conveying a message. Note that the editorial's conclusion suggests a solution.*

107

And the Assignment for Tomorrow Is . . .

A good example of an editorial cartoon that tells the story by itself is shown above. The cartoon is from The Acorn, *Hanley Junior High School, University City, Missouri.*

the person whose character is damaged must be sufficiently identified for others to recognize him.

A libel case may be brought as a civil action (an action by one person against another person) or as a criminal action (an action brought by the state).

Criminal libel may be defamatory statements that tend to create a breach of the peace, usually directed against a specific group. Criminal libel may also be defamation of a dead person.

There are two types of libel. *Libel per se* is defamation that in itself damages the reputation, such as name-calling.

Libel per quod is a defamation that is not apparent on the face of it, but depends upon the circumstances. For example, a person might say, "Sam Jones played a brilliant ball game on Sunday." This does not appear to be damaging, but if Sam's church does not allow him to play ball on Sunday, then it could be harmful to his reputation.

If a paper is sued for libel, what defense does it have? Generally truth is the best defense. The burden of proof is upon the defendant.

Newspapers also have *qualified privilege*. Privilege is the freedom to say damaging things in an official proceeding. It applies to the legislator, to the witness, to the official in the executive branch of the government who releases information in the line of duty. It has been given to these individuals because of the necessity of complete discussion. Newspapers have the qualified privilege of reporting official proceedings as long as the report is accurate and fair. This privilege does not apply to pre-trial proceedings or items stricken from the record.

Fair comment and criticism may also be used by newspapers when talking about persons who offer themselves to the public for approval. Criticism of an artist or a work of art is defensible, as long as the criticism is limited to the work and does not discuss the artist or his motivations.

Sometimes *mitigation* may be a defense against libel. If an article is published that may be libelous and the paper immediately publishes a retraction, it shows absence of malice, and damages awarded may be less. Usually mitigation is not a complete defense.

Newspapers are also responsible for libel contained in the "Letters to the Editor" column or in advertisements. "Letters to the Editor" should be printed only if the letters are signed, and the paper should make sure they are signed by real persons.

Not all libel appears on the editorial page. Newspapers must check all stories carefully to make sure they contain no libelous matter.

The student press must meet the same ethical standards as does the public press. The student press must report the facts without bias. It must report all news fairly and accurately. Objectivity is important. Both sides of a story should be printed. In its editorial page the student press has the responsibility of letting its readers decide whether the paper is correct or not.

In news stories, facts should not be left out that might cause the reader to misinterpret the true meaning of the story. Coverage should be complete, and should be only concise enough so as not to confuse the reader.

Sensationalism has no place in the student press, either in stories or headlines.

Advertisements should be watched for exaggeration or false claims. If the advertisers make a statement about their product, it is the responsibility of the paper to make sure it is true before it is printed. All facts in ads should be checked for accuracy, so as not to mislead the students and parents.

Student newspapers often overemphasize photographs. An over-large photo puts too much emphasis on the story it accompanies.

Student papers should not play up sensational photos or photos that editorialize. Some photos may seem to defame a person. He may have been snapped in the middle of a crowd that was doing something wrong, when in actuality he had done nothing wrong.

Students should make sure the pictures go with the proper story. The wrong picture can make an event look bigger or even smaller than it actually was. A picture placed with the wrong story can even be libelous, if the picture shows exactly the opposite of what really happened.

Careful checking of all material that goes into the paper is the best way of preventing libel suits. A firm editorial policy can also be very beneficial; it enables all reporters and other concerned people to know what the paper stands for, and reporters should maintain those standards.

A good editorial policy should state the writer's rights and responsibilities. It should also give guidelines as to maximum length for letters—a suggested maximum is 300 words—and it should indicate the meaning of non-bylined editorials. Normally non-bylined editorials are the opinion of the paper whereas by-lined ones are the opinion of the writer. The preference is to use non-bylined ones, because a good editorial should be the opinion of the majority of the members on a staff. An editorial policy should apply both to a yearbook and a newspaper.

EXERCISES

(1) From a daily newspaper clip an editorial of explanation and also clip the news story it is explaining. Be prepared to discuss in class how effective the editorial is in explaining the news story.

(2) Write an editorial on student conduct at dramatic presentations. Make the editorial at least 200 words in length. Write a 31-count headline for it.

(3) Draw an editorial cartoon on any subject depicting school life.

(4) Write an editorial describing the feelings of a new student in school and suggesting what the student body should do to make him feel welcome.

(5) Write a 31-count headline for the following editorial.

In the days of brave knights in armor, there lived a courageous knight, Sir Lancelot of the Lake. Sir Lancelot was the strongest and the most liked of all knights, and when it came to helping a lady, he was the most chivalrous.

Across the kingdom from Camelot lived another knight, Sir Pushalot. Now Sir Pushalot was as strong and as handsome as Lancelot, but there was something lacking. Pushalot just wasn't liked or respected by anyone.

Resenting this, Pushalot challenged Lancelot to a jousting contest, to be held at Camelot.

Along the road Pushalot met a poor milkmaid caught in some quicksand. "Why should I help you? If I do, I shall surely lose this tournament," said Pushalot, and rode on.

A little while later, Lancelot came riding along and saw the same poor milkmaid. Without hesitation, the chivalrous knight rescued the milkmaid, set her upon his horse, and rode off to the tournament.

When they arrived, Pushalot immediately came to Lancelot and claimed he was the winner by default, but he couldn't hear his own voice for the applause of the crowd praising Lancelot's chivalry.

The boys of East might notice that kindness is appreciated. It's up to you, boys. Is chivalry dead?

(6) Write a 200-word editorial on procrastination. Also write a 31-count headline for it.

(7) Take a recent news event at school and write a 200-word editorial of interpretation with a 31-count headline.

(8) Select a paper from the exchange file and be prepared to discuss in class the effectiveness of its editorial page.

(9) The following editorial is poorly written. Rewrite, adding additional facts if necessary. Write a one-line, 31-count headline for it.

Vandalism is a very serious offense. Broken windows, pellet holes, gum stuck to desks, paint on walls, lockers scratched, and two trees stolen are only a few acts of vandalism East has had this year.

Student Council spent an afternoon planting trees only to have two stolen. Why did people steal them? For fun probably. The only things the vandals left were two holes in the ground.

Gum chewing is forbidden at school, yet many students chew it. One of the reasons for having this rule is so no one will get stuck in it.

Some people get rid of it by sticking their gum under the desks. A person then puts his hand under the top of the desk and feels something sticky on his hand. He pulls his hand from the desk and finds a dirty wad of gum on his fingers. It's not very pleasant.

How many times have you seen broken windows and pellet holes? Not a month has passed since some windows were repaired in fourth building and the end of the administration building.

This is where you go to school. You're here almost all day, five days a week. What kind of a school do you want to be proud of?

(10) Rewrite the following editorial to conform to editorial rules.

South's students do care about what their Student Council does. Correction, maybe they care but where were they at the Student Council open meeting, held on Wednesday, December 6?

It's understandable that all of North's students wouldn't be able to attend. True, 75 students other than council members were there, but two-thirds of them were assigned by one teacher to be present.

Furthermore, 75 students is only five percent of the school's enrollment.

Every student should have known about the meeting since there were bulletins on the intercom about it and it was brought up by council representatives in the home room meetings. Thereby no student should say he just didn't know about it.

The staff of the Clarion wishes to commend those students who showed up on their own accord and also the Student Council for its sponsorship of this meeting and the work which went into it.

(11) Select an editorial from an exchange paper and rewrite it making it more effective.

(12) Write an editorial for the headline "Teachers Can Be Human After All."

(13) Write two editorials concerning the legalization of marijuana. One should give reasons why legalization would be good and the other should give reasons against legalization. It will be necessary for you to do some research to handle the topic well.

(14) Write a pro editorial and a con editorial on censorship of the school newspaper. Be sure to think through every angle before starting. Interviews with principals, teachers and students getting their ideas might help.

(15) Assume that one of your staff members has brought you the

following editorial for publication in your newspaper. As editor-in-chief you must make some decisions. Will you allow the editorial to be printed? If not, what reasons will you give your staff member? Will you ask for additional information? If so, what information? Should an editorial of this type be printed in a school newspaper? Be prepared to discuss in class.

For the third consecutive year the instrumental music department at Belleview has failed to live up to its abilities.

It seems astounding that students who received A's or higher at music festivals for their individual performances when they were in junior high have slipped to B's and in some cases even C's.

Is this because they are losing their ability? According to the music students themselves this is not the case. The students have simply lost interest in music, and, therefore, are not trying to perform to the best of their abilities.

Why this loss of interest? Perhaps the instrumental music instructor can answer this question. He is probably the only one who can.

Not only have students lost interest in their individual performances but there also seems to be a lack of interest in instrumental music.

Four years ago more than 250 students were enrolled in some type of instrumental music class. This year total enrollment has dropped to 109.

Who is responsible? We feel there is only one answer. Isn't it time that the administration decided to change instructors?

(16) Write an editorial policy for your newspaper and yearbook. Be specific as to what the paper's rights and responsibilities are. Provide any information necessary for reader understanding. You might want to write to other schools and get copies of their policies before you begin this project.

Chapter VII

WRITING COLUMNS

Some journalists say that students cannot be taught to write columns, that the imagination, sensitivity, and perceptiveness necessary for writing columns is innate. The student who lacks them cannot be taught, but the student who has these qualities can be helped by effective criticism to become a good columnist.

Columns are difficult to write and many students don't read them anyway, so the question may be asked, "Why write columns at all?" The answer is obviously because all journalism students should be given an opportunity and experience in this type of writing. An opportunity to write columns may create in some students a desire to make a career as a columnist. Besides, a well-written column *will* be read by the student body. The reason most columns are not read is that they are not interesting.

THE REVIEW COLUMN

A common type of column is the review column. Types of reviews include books, movies, television shows, and plays. Reviews should be included in all student newspapers because: (1) they can promote an interest in works of art; (2) there is already an interest in the popular arts—movies, jazz, records; and (3) they can help the readers develop discriminating tastes.

The general qualifications of a good reviewer are:

(1) Honesty.
(2) Integrity.
(3) Openmindedness—The reviewer must approach each work of art with a willingness to be convinced that it is important.
(4) Humility.

115

(5) Charity—The reviewer must realize that criticism need not be destructive.

(6) Background, experience, and maturity—This, for a student journalist, is usually an unfound quality. However, if a student really has the desire to be a good reviewer, he can gain it through hard work.

The general qualifications of all good reviews are that they be:

(1) Informative.
(2) Evaluating.
(3) Interesting.
(4) Well-written.

Other rules to be followed in writing a review are the following:

(1) A review should be evaluating. The readers should be told whether or not the subject in question is worth attention.

(2) A good review should be interesting as well as enlightening. It should be brightly written. It should state or imply certain principles on which the reviewer works.

(3) A review should document its position, citing reasons for praise or condemnation.

(4) A review should compare books, films, etc., with others by the same author or director.

(5) A book review should name the publisher and give the price.

Film reviews are too often concerned only with the plot and actors. The writer and director should also be included. The review should assess the story itself. Is it a good story? Is the dialogue fresh, convincing, real? Is the film an adaptation of a novel or play? If original, what type is it—comedy, farce? The review should not overemphasize changes from the original. Discuss the camera work, the acting, the sets, the overall production.

Long Lines Await Jedi

By Sylvia Morales and Dolly Sahni

From its fabulous laser beams to its breathtaking flying speeder bikes, the "Return of the Jedi" has proven to be an equal success in capturing millions of "Star Wars" fans and bringing them to the mile-long lines at the theaters all over the country. George Lucas' third picture is a marvelous fairy tale filled with special sound and visual effects that include a universe of monsters and a little world of brave and furry teddy bears.

"Return of the Jedi" is sure to be one of this summer's blockbusters. It is quite easy to be completely engrossed in the movie since the space battle is ten times more complicated than in "Star Wars." The dazzling and dizzying speeder bike chases through the tall redwood trees add to the many highly charge scenes.

New Creatures

Jabba the Hutt is one of the many new creatures totally beyond the limits of one's imagination. Jabba is a gigantic mound of silly-putty that seems to spread all over each time it moves. His pet monster is smaller but has a high pitched, hysterical laugh. The creatures that simply capture hearts are the Ewoks. Those small, furry and fierce bears seem to require attention.

NBC Wins With Mama

By Andrea Levin

Once again NBC has produced a widely popular, successful t.v. sit-com. This one is called "Mama's Family."

"Mama's Family" is a spinoff of the long running, stand-up comedy, variety series "Carol Burnett Show." The sketches on Mama were about a weird and wacky southern family and are what today's "Mama's Family" is based on.

Vicki Lawrence does a terrific job playing the main character, Mama. Ken Berry plays her lazy son Vinton Harper, who is a locksmith, as he did on the "Carol Burnett Show." He has two kids, his son Buzz, played by witty new-comer Eric Brown, and his "valley girl" daughter Sonja, played by young actress Karin Argoud.

Opening Episode

In the first episode of "Mama's Family," Vinton moves into Mama's house with Sonja and Buzz because he just got a divorce from his first wife and can't afford to live anywhere else. Already living in the house is Mama's sister Fran played by experienced actress Rue McClanahan, who thinks she is a great writer.

Mama, a feisty old lady isn't too happy about the fact that she has to take in three more people but does so anyway because she has too big a heart.

All in all "Mama's Family" is a new, exciting, funny show, that has a lot of potential. It airs every Saturday night on NBC at 9:00 P.M.

Comparison, an important part of a review, is evident in the movie and television reviews above from The Beard Bugle, *Daniel Carter Beard Junior High School, Flushing, New York.*

Play reviews should devote attention to the play itself. If it is a revival, little need be said about the plot. The review should tell what type of drama it is—serious, comedy, melodrama, etc. What message is the playwright trying to get across? Are the characters convincing, believable, well developed? Is the dialogue effective? Does the director create a new interpretation? Are the characters given proper emphasis? Are the pace and rhythm effective? Are the sets, costumes, lighting, and sound effects good? A play review usually tells the reader where the play is being performed and for how long.

Book reviews should be concerned with the significance of the work. How does the novel compare with similar books on the same subject or with others by the same author? What is the novel about? Give only a brief summary. A detailed evaluation of the work should be given. What does the novel say about human lives and values? Are these things worth saying? Are characters real and convincing? Is the craftsmanship of the writer good? Is the play well written? From what point of view does the author tell his story?

Concert reviews should be mainly about the program itself. Did it include a new work? Was the program well balanced? How good was the sound? There should also be discussion of individual works.

THE HUMOR COLUMN

The most popular column in junior-high newspapers is usually the humor column. This column needs to be handled with good taste. Too often, columnists lack a real sense of humor and therefore depend on old, stale jokes. A good column contains only original humor, is mostly about school life, and avoids trivial items.

Humor columns can be devoted to both wit and humor. *Wit* shows the resemblance between two things, is concisely stated, and appeals to the intellect. *Humor,* on the other hand, shows contrast, is stated in detail, and appeals to the emotions. Humor is more popular than wit with most students.

Mystery Book Action-Packed

by Joanne Lyons

Airs Above the Ground, Mary Stewart's newest novel, is a blend of all the things that make a book a best seller: romance, intrigue, hair-raising action and for those who like animals, there are the famous Lippizan stallions.

Young, beautiful Vanessa March, married two years and very much in love, is propelled from London to Vienna by a shocking discovery.

In her care is Timothy Lacy, the seventeen-year-old son of a close friend, who also has an urgent problem, but of an entirely different nature.

Security Forces Enter Play

The journey, which was to have been of an intimate nature, instead draws into play the security forces of three countries, two dead men, a circus and its colorful parade of characters; not to mention the famous white stallions of Vienna.

The "airs above the ground" are the beautiful leaps and dancing steps which the white Lippizan stallions of the Spanish Riding School perform with such graceful dexterity.

"Airs" High Points

These "airs" are also the high points of the story which take place above the ground: a terrifying night on the rooftops of Schloss Zechstein; a high-wire act in the Circus Wagner; the hair-breath finish in the Gleinalp.

With her characteristic flair for description, Miss Stewart brings alive the picturesque Austrian countryside with its rolling, flower-filled meadows, onion-topped churches and fairy-tale castles.

The above book review is packed full of suspense, as is the book it reviews. The piece is from The Northern Lights, *North Kirkwood Junior High School, Kirkwood, Missouri.*

Halloween III : Bad news

It's movie time. No exclamation point. We were counting on director John Carpenter to once again provide the terror all movie goers thrive on.

But Carpenter, who is known as an excellent director/producer, only made it two out of three. When he produced "Halloween," there was one good horror movie to see. "Halloween II" matched it equally.

Sorry to say, but Carpenter's latest, "Halloween III: Season of the Witch" has failed to bring forth the real "scary" feeling.

"Halloween" and "Halloween II" offered a great story while maintaining action at its peak. To be blunt, "Halloween III" has no great story and no peak. It deals with witchcraft and that aspect simply destroys the original story.

It's embarrassing to compare it to the first two, and it's even worse if you have seen the previous couple.

The overacting of Donald Pleasance from "Halloween" and "Halloween II" is missed. Instead, Tom Atkins takes his place. Stacey Nelkin and Dan O'Herighly back up the rather unimpressive cast.

In "Halloween III," robots are the killers, instead of potential human terrorists.

After the film, the viewers were asked to fill out a form to state their opinion on "III." From what we could notice, just about everybody disliked it. "It was just terrible" exclaimed Dan Kopolow. "' waste of four bucks!"

Indeed, Carpenter's films usually are worth the expense, but as a recommendation, avoid "Halloween III."

Daryl Rothman

Reviewing a sequel makes it easier for the writer to make comparison. This review from Perspective, *Ladue Junior High School, Ladue, Mo., does a good job of comparing plots as well as performances by the individual actors and actresses.*

Variety is important in humor columns, and it can be achieved in many ways.

A *pun,* which is a play on words that are spelled the same way or have the same sound but different meanings, is an example of wit that amuses junior-high readers.

Jeffrey's Jokes

By JEFF CARLISLE

Why couldn't the sailors play cards after half their ship was blown off? THEY DIDN'T HAVE A FULL DECK.

* * *

Why did the convict have a tube of Clearasil? IN CASE HE BROKE OUT.

* * *

What happened to the orchestra conductor that was wanted by the police? HE WAS CAUGHT AND WAS MADE TO FACE THE MUSIC

* * *

At an inventors convention, the inventor of epoxy explained his business by saying, "It's a sticky job and involves a lot of red tape, but the result is fascinating."

* * *

In a recent investigation, it has been found that the most violations of "disturbing the peace" are made by tennis manufacturers. People say they're making a racket.

Original humor can add to a school newspaper, as indicated by the above column from The Northern Lights, *North Kirkwood Junior High School, Kirkwood, Missouri.*

Humorous *verse* is effective. It can be a sonnet, ballad, or any form of poetry. Original verse is desirable, but sometimes a paraphrase of familiar verses can be entertaining.

The school *anecdote* may also be used. An anecdote is a brief narrative of an amusing incident.

The *parody,* in which the language and style of a well-known author are imitated to produce a humorous effect, is usually well accepted in school newspapers.

The use of caricature and burlesque are other ways of achieving variety in a humor column. *Caricature* exaggerates the features of a person, place, or thing; *burlesque* imitates something serious in a light-hearted way or vice versa.

Letters to a columnist are sometimes easy to burlesque. The letter writer may be quite serious in his question, but the columnist may give him a funny answer.

Epigrams can also be used effectively in humor columns. An epigram is a terse, witty thought that may be paradoxical.

THE OPINION COLUMN

Opinion columns are a means of allowing members of the student body to express their views. The usual forms are the "Letters to the Editor" column or the "Inquiring Reporter."

If a "Letters to the Editor" column is used, be sure all letters are signed by real people.

The "Inquiring Reporter" or poll column can be quite effective if the topics selected are timely and of interest to the students. The type of poll that asks ridiculous questions and gets ridiculous answers belongs more in a humor column.

THE EDITORIAL COLUMN

Editorial columns are usually written by the editor of the paper and devoted to interesting comments on school life or on community, state, and national events if they apply to the students.

Although the editorial column should not be a series of short editorials, it should follow the same principles that govern regular editorials.

Editorial columns are very informal and usually reveal the columnist's personality. If the column gives serious suggestions,

Editor's Column

Game Creates Unity

by Jim Childress

If ever there was a way to improve student-teacher relations, having them both on equal terms would be the answer.

This was proven during the eighth grade-faculty benefit basketball game two weeks ago.

Never before, in recent years, has there been such an enthusiastic response toward a school event. Students seem to have enjoyed the rare occurrence when both the student and teacher were considered the same.

Each team had a fair opportunity to prove themselves against the other without having any priyileges. Eighth grade players did not have time to worry about being courteous toward the teachers, and faculty members were not encumbered with their respected images as teachers.

Resulting from this was a more open atmosphere, where all the participants of the game could play whole-heartedly. Seemingly, student and faculty spectators enjoyed a more honest game that they could indentify with.

Apart from gaining better relations between the student body and faculty, the basketball game also stimulated more school spirit. Students were enthusiastic because those participating were representing both the student body and faculty together, not in separate roles.

By having the two main forces of our school face to face, a broader understanding of each others role is established, with both the student and teacher having a deeper look into each other's character.

Editorial columns commenting on school events help make an editorial page more interesting, as shown by the above column from The Beacon, *Nipher Junior High School, Kirkwood, Missouri.*

make sure the readers know that they come from a reliable source.

The Sports Column

Sports columns are usually written by the sports editor and comment on sports events and personalities. These comments might include human-interest sidelights about an amusing incident that happened in the dressing room, a player's comments on a game, or predictions of the outcome of future games. Predictions should not be based on biased opinions but on actual probabilities. This will require some research by the writer if his predictions are to be accurate.

Compliments for a job well done belong in a sports column, but criticism is rarely included.

A common fault of sports columns is that they ignore minor sports and intramurals. All aspects of sports life at school should be covered.

THE EXCHANGE COLUMN

Exchange columns can be interesting, especially if many pupils know students from other schools. An exchange column should describe events that happen in other schools. Often such a column will suggest innovations tried in other schools that might be successful in your school.

The big job of the exchange columnist is to review papers received from other schools and select interesting items.

OTHER TYPES OF COLUMNS

Alumni columns are sometimes well received. Most students like to know of the accomplishments of former students. On the junior-high level this may even be outstanding achievements made by students who have gone on to the senior-high level.

Fashion columns are popular if they are based on timely topics. To be successful, a fashion columnist needs to gather facts on the subject, perhaps visiting the stores in town, or perhaps just reading as much as possible about fashions. Pictures add a lot to a fashion column.

Gossip columns have no place in school newspapers. Too often gossip columns, even though unintentionally, harm reputations. By junior-high age, students should be mature enough in their thinking to realize that nothing worthwhile was ever accomplished by gossip.

Student journalists should assume that they are writing for emotionally mature readers. Gossip is educationally of no aid,

8th Grade Team Still Undefeated

By Cam Bolick

Beginners luck? Well maybe, but let's hope not. No matter what it is, our eighth grade football team is undefeated.

Throughout the season, our team often held the opponent scoreless.

Beside the fact of having great teamwork, our team had some unusually good players.

If our running game didn't work, Tom Stewart's passes did. His most constant receivers were his ends, Phil Browning and Clay Robinson. The flanker was usually Andy Dixon.

It was rare that our running back failed with quick openers. Dave Amacher was at his best and on the end runs it was Greg Massanari.

Our team was fortunate not to have injuries except for bruises and light sprains. We had a small team in number, but in hustle, spirit, and coaching, Edison was far ahead of its opponents.

Edison offers congratulations to our undefeated eighth grade team.

Names are important in any story, and the above sports column from Highlights, Edison Junior High School, Champaign, Illinois, uses them to good advantage.

is out of date, and interests only the unsophisticated. No student journalist should lower himself or his school paper by supporting a gossip column.

Two important rules to follow in writing any type of column are: (1) avoid unkind references to people; and (2) be sure that what you write is in good taste. These two rules cannot be practiced in a gossip column.

Exploits Hit Locker Room

by Steve Seele

Though track season may have ended and the door has been closed on the varsity locker room for another year, memories of those times still remain.

Among the remembrances will be those humorous, though at times embarrassing events, which occurred in the locker room.

Perhaps the most vivid of these memories will be of Jim Drake and his near, though unintentional, streaks.

In the most publicized of his encounters, Jim, dressed only in his undershorts, was charging after Mike Gibbons with a vicious towel, when he was decoyed towards the door to the parking lot.

There, looking for a manager to unlock the door to the girls' gym, stood Jan Bailey.

As Jim came around the corner, eyewitnesses later reported he suddenly became pale and turned tail, crashing into the trash can and bouncing off to the side as he beat a hasty retreat.

A few days later, it was once again Jim Drake who was on the spot. Several track team members, who shall remain nameless, dragged cheerleader Liz Thode into the locker room. There sat Jim, in only his shirt and undershorts, calmly applying ointment to his aching legs. Luckily for Jim, Liz kept her eyes closed and the event ended without incident.

Then there was the time that Lenzel Ivory stepped out of the showers and was trying to act cool by strutting in place. Of course, everyone knows what happens when you are not careful while walking on slick, wet concrete; you fall, which is exactly what Lenzel did. His feet slid out from under him as he sprawled backwards all over the floor. But Lenzel saved himself from total disaster by grabbing for the bench as he went down.

And who can ever forget the snap of a wet towel or the sting and the welt it makes when striking flesh.

Speaking of flesh brings to mind the licks received from Coach Roger Richardson's paddle, creating a different sound but one just as memorable.

Yes, those were the days, the smell of sweaty socks as a locker was opened, sitting on spiked shoes "accidentally" placed beneath you, the refreshment of a cool shower. . .

Apathy Stuns Athletics

by David Schlarman

This seems to be the year for changes, especially sports-wise at Nipher.

Not only are intramurals now organized by clusters, but signing up at the beginning of the year is no longer required. This gives those who are not sure they want to play and those who only wish to play a few times an opportunity to participate.

Women's lib has also hit the Nipher sports scene. Girls, previously unheard of in varsity sports, organized their own basketball team to compete against other girls' teams.

But this was not the end of it. Because of a state ruling, they can now also compete side-by-side against boys, on the varsity track team.

Even more surprising to some is the fact that they have done well at the sport, according to their coach, Mr. Roger Richardson.

This is also the first year in some time that Nipher has had a track assembly. Considering the small number of students who come to see the Pioneers at sports events, the cheerleaders' efforts to get the students interested during this and other assemblies seem to be in vain.

Though some Nipher sports teams could have done better this year, lack of fan turnout for sports events followed not only losing teams, but winning ones as well.

It seems that—though Nipher's sports world can expect to be spurred into further changes in the future by the present reformation of intramurals and girls' participation in sports—today's lack of interest and enthusiasm in sports by Nipherites may temporarily derail this impending revolution.

Amusing incidents behind the scenes or simply an analysis of a season can produce material for sports columns as shown in the above examples from The Beacon, *Nipher Junior High, Kirkwood, Missouri.*

125

Where are they now ?

by Scott Fast & Andrew Lin

TONY WARD, '75, is working at Universal Studios for Chuck Barris Productions.

STEVE LYONS, '75, is a minor league baseball player on the east coast. He was named player of the year in his league.

DEREK PHELPS, '81, is a Senate Page for Senator Bob Packwood in Washington D.C.

DARREN BROTT, JOHN RIPPET, '82, are on the varsity football team at North Eugene.

SHALONA ROOT, JENNIFER NEWELL, '82, are on the North Eugene Lassies.

SUE MARTINEAU (senior),'80, TROY SHAWHAN (junior), '81, DARCY WENINGER (sophomore), '82, are all class presidents at North Eugene.

BONNIE MUNCIE, '77, has her own singing group that performs locally.

LAURIE CLARK, '77, has gone to college in Minnesota for two years and this year is going to college in Avignon, France. She plans to be an international lawyer.

ANNA ENGLEHARDT, '79, modeled in a skating magazine and also has been in fashion shows.

Alumni columns can keep present students posted as to the activities of former students. Such a column usually deals with activities of recent graduates but may also be used to highlight the whereabouts of individuals who are involved in interesting activities. The above column from The Scribe, *Madison Junior High School, Eugene, Oregon, includes activities of persons who had graduated seven years earlier. The Scribe also did a full profile on Derek Phelps. Short items can often lead to longer articles.*

Regardless of the type of column written, it must have a clever name to draw the attention of the readers, and all items within a column should be kept short, in order to hold attention.

EXERCISES

(1) From exchange newspapers select one column and be prepared to criticize it in class.

(2) Watch a play on television and write a review of it.

(3) Choose a current movie that you have seen and write a review of it.

(4) Choose a book from the school library or the school book store that is available to all students and write a review of it.

(5) By use of the "Inquiring Reporter" technique, select a timely topic of concern to students and write an opinion column.

(6) Write a humor column, using any type of humor you want. Be sure your material is original and that it pertains to school life.

(7) Read the following movie review and be prepared to discuss it in class. Check style errors.

Metro-Goldwyn-Mayer's Academy Award winning motion picture, "Gigi," directed by Vincent Minnelli, and awarded the Oscar for the best motion picture of the year, as well as eight other presentations, gives a colorful account of a girl becoming a young lady.

The story takes place in Paris, France, during the 1900's.

Gigi's mother is an opera singer and has no time for her; therefore, she is raised by her grandmother. Her great-aunt, Alicia, who lives in a glorious past, teaches her all the social graces, from how to eat all types of food imaginable, to choosing cigars.

Gaston, a very good friend of the family, was a man who was completely bored with life, because he had anything he wanted. The song "It's a Bore" is quite funny. He finds his real interest is in Gigi, because she is different from the giddy, showy type of girl he has met and is thoroughly bored with. This is the result of the fact that Gigi is gay and full of surprises, rather than Aunt Alicia's training.

Gaston's uncle, Henri, is portrayed by Maurice Chevalier, "Thank Heaven for Little Girls."

In Our School

Mr. Homer L. Hall, Mr. Ken Curtis, and Mr. Thomas Waltz, the citizenship teachers, attended the Seventy-First National Conference on Government held on Nov. 15 and 16 at the Chase Park Plaza Hotel.

They heard Kirkwood's presentation for the All American City Award. Mr. Hall, Mr. Curtis, and Mr. Waltz also heard talks given on local, state, and national governments.

* * *

Mr. Earnest Dunning attended the South Central Science Conference in November. The conference was part of the National Science Teachers Association and was held in Louisville, Kentucky.

* * *

Mrs. Jeanne Bauer, Mr. Homer Hall, Mr. Rodger Harding, and Mrs. Erika Ober are instructors for the adult education program at the high school.

Mrs. Bauer instructs foreign adults in English, Mr. Harding teaches typing and Mr. Hall teaches high school equivalence courses, and Mrs. Ober teaches German.

* * *

Congratulations to Van Wood for surviving three weeks of wrestling without injury. Marty Foesterling, Bill Gamble, Rob Ebinger, and Van are the only ninth graders who went out for the team.

Van is the only one of the four who has not been injured. Van's chances of succeeding are excellent at the present time.

* * *

Mike Clark and John Pepin have made the Kirkwood Swimming Team. Congratulations.

* * *

Congratulations to Steve Reed and Bill Conyers for making the Kirkwood Diving Team.

A column on school happenings that deserve mention but not a separate story can be a valuable asset to a school paper, as indicated above in a column from The Northern Lights, *North Kirkwood Junior High School, Kirkwood, Missouri.*

Inside Looking Out

by Larry Thompson and Paul Owens

Stephen Stills, it is fitting that such a fine album as this should be dedicated to such a fine person and musician as the late James Marshall Hendrix. This record is an example of Stephen Stills' musical ingenuity. In all, he plays nine different instruments and sings on every song.

Stills', now touring with a ten piece band, has the help of many great musicians on the album. On a cut called "Oldtimes Good Times", Jimi Hendrix plays lead guitar. Some of the best voices in rock appear on the album; Rita Coolidge, John Sebastion, David Crosby, Graham Nash and Cass Elliot all sing with Stills.

"Love The One Your With", is Stills' hit single from the album, in which he plays five different instruments. Other good cuts include; "Sit Yourself Down", "Go Back Home" and "We Are Not Helpless."

Chunga's Revenge, starring Frank Zappa, two ex-Turtles (the phlorescent leech and Eddie), Jeff Simmons, assorted drum players and other freaks and hangers-on. This is the "new mothers" and continue the Mothers of Invention's tradition of being the finest rock group in existence.

An interesting cut from the album is "The Clap", where it sounds as if Zappa is just banging away on about ten different things. Though not as good as "Hot Rats", Chunga's Revenge is very good in its own greasy way!

Derek and the Dominos latest release, **Layla,** really shouldn't be a double album. On some double records you find a few fillers, but on this there seems to be a few too many. Still, even with the poorer songs this is a fantastic album. A major reason for the greatness of this album is Duane Allman, of the Allman Bros. band. Many consider Allman to be Eric Clapton's equal on guitar, if not better. Allman is not touring with the group of Clapton, Bob Whitlock, Jim Gordon and Carl Radle.

"Layla", the title song of the album is done well mainly because of the great guitar work of Allman and Clapton. "Little Wing", a Hendrix song is good but not as good as Hendrix's original version. "Tell The Truth", written by Clapton and Bobby Whitlock is also a very good cut.

All in all, Clapton's new group looks like one of the best to come up in a while.

Album reviews are becoming quite popular in junior high papers as indicated by the above review from the Echo, Simpson Jr. High School, Huntington, New York.

The picture also offers a colorful array of costumes and music, including the theme song, "Gigi," sung by Louis Jourdan.

Leslie Caron, Louis Jourdan, Hermione Gingold, and Maurice Chevalier give entertaining performances as Gigi, Gaston, Gigi's grandmother, and Henri.

(8) Read the following book review and be prepared to discuss it in class. Check style errors.

The book concerns the human race changing into something incomprehensible; a people made one through their minds. This change entails supervision by the Overlords, who are highly advanced scientifically.

The first part, "Earth and the Overlords," tells of earth's conquest and the seclusion of the Overlords, who appear in fifty years.

During the half-century, the Overlords raise the world's standard of living, establish world peace, and abolish, through scientific machines and strategy, all religious and racial prejudice.

The day arrives when Garellen, the Overlord leader, appears. He is eight feet tall, has two horns, a forked tail, and armored limbs, much like the Devil in religious books; but to Humans he is nothing to dislike.

The second part, "The Golden Age," begins with the Overlords appearing and the Humans accepting them.

During this age, one man, Jan, went to the Overlords' home. He hid himself inside an exhibit going to the Overlords' planet. However, the spaceship traveled fast enough to change time. While Jan aged little, the earth aged eighty years. Thus, when Jan returned, those alive would not remember him.

The "Last Generation" describes the changing of the Humans, who eventually die out, their children remaining with the Overlords.

The name of the book is *Childhood's End* by Arthur Clarke.

(9) Read the following movie review and be prepared to discuss it in class. Check style errors.

Most people go to see a movie because it is popular or, most of the time, because "everyone else" has seen it and thought it was the best one ever.

The most popular movie at West seems to be "To Sir With Love."

Most students like the originality, truth, and the impression or inspiration that they were left with after seeing the film.

The movie starring Sidney Poitier, and featuring the Mind-benders and a new singing sensation, Lulu, is about a male Negro teacher who goes into one of the tougher schools in London to try his luck in teaching where others have failed.

His group of wild English teenagers is around the age of 18, who do their best to make things miserable for their teachers.

But their newest teacher, known to the students as "Sir," slowly but surely tames them and proceeds to teach them respect for themselves and each other.

At the end of the term, when he is about to leave, the students present Sir with a poem they wrote themselves.

The song is now a teenage hit in Milwaukee.

(10) The reviews in exercises seven, eight, and nine are poorly written. Rewrite each one adding additional information if necessary. It is not necessary that the additional information you add be true, since you may not have seen the films or read the book.

Chapter VIII

FEATURE WRITING

Usually one page of school papers is devoted to features. Therefore, it is essential that all journalism students know how to write a feature story.

In junior high newspapers most features are written primarily to entertain. However, features may be written to inform or to inspire a reader. They may be about an unusual event, a humorous incident, or any item of human interest.

Feature stories differ tremendously from news stories. News stories are kept as short as possible, while detail is necessary in feature stories. Feature stories may be of any length, depending on the space available.

The feature story may be humorous or serious. The important thing is that it does not just tell the reader what happened, but also makes him *feel* what happened. Imagination is a prerequisite to good feature writing. The story must be based upon facts, and accurate reporting is essential.

The best feature story for a junior high newspaper is usually related to school life. Often a feature story can be developed from a news story. The more timely a feature story is, the more likely it will be of interest to the readers.

More freedom is possible in the way feature stories are written, as they may be written in first (I, we, our), second (you), or third (he, she, it, they) person. If they are written in first person, they should be bylined so that the reader can identify the writer. Generally, the best feature stories are written in third person, as quite often the information presented in a story is not based on a personal experience (first person), and second person (you) does not always fit all readers.

The lead of a feature story does not summarize the story. It should contain some striking statement that will draw the reader's attention.

HIDDEN TALENTS
Student Designs Clothes

By Ana Leroux

Some students doodle pictures of clothing styles for fun but 9th grader Emilio Aguirre is so fascinated drawing fashion designs he wants to use his talent to make it his career.

He got interested in it about two years ago as a future job. There are two main reasons why he wants to design fashions. One is that people are highly paid if they're good fashion designers. Second was the glamour of being responsible for making the fashions. "My main goal in life is to be the best designer in the market," he said.

School Plans

Emilio intends to go to Fashion Industries High School. Afterwards, he's planning to go to college at the Parsons School of Design. Though he has everything planned out, it takes a lot of effort and work to reach this goal which he intends to do with the skills that he will be taught in these special schools. "I think that these schools have the right qualifications for producing great designers," he said.

Emilio gets his inspiration from a lot of the famous designers he admires. Some of them are Balenciaga, Dior, Halston and Montana.

Favorite Colors

His favorite colors are black and red. He explains "Black is a sexy and mysterious color. Red is a very bright and colorful color." Mostly his designs are made for silk linen and crepe de Chine which are his favorite fabrics.

Several styles which he favors are

Designs By Emilio Aguirre

Careful planning goes into designs created by Emilio.

A-line skirts, backless gowns, capes, hats, stiletto-heeled shoes and Dolman sleeves.

His predictions for the upcoming adult women's fashions are a return to the 1930's look with some slight changes. He comes to this conclusion because the cut of dresses and the make-up seem to be going that way.

Personality profiles on students who have unusual hobbies make for interesting reading as evidenced in the above feature from The Beard Bugle, *Daniel Carter Beard Junior High School, Flushing, New York.*

Too often, feature story writers fail to build up suspense by saving the climax for the last. Never give away the surprise element. Keeping it until the last will assure you that the reader will finish the story.

News stories are written so the last paragraph can be cut off for space purposes without changing the meaning of the story. Feature stories cannot be written this way, however, because of the surprise element. Therefore, it is usually impossible to cut a feature story from the end. If you are told to write a feature story of 300 words, you should try to stay within that limit, or space problems may result.

There are several types of feature stories. One already mentioned is the *news-feature story*. This story has as its basis a timely news event that has a human-interest angle. This type of feature is written primarily to entertain and may contain any of the fiction writer's techniques and devices.

An *informative feature story* has as its purpose to inform rather than entertain, so feature-writing devices are not used. Such a feature may explain the purpose of a new organization or the value of studying biology, for example. The writer must develop an interesting method of presentation if it is not to become boring, and much depends on accuracy.

Personality sketches are probably the most difficult type of feature to write. Since information for this type of feature is actually obtained by means of an interview, it will be discussed in more detail in Chapter X.

There are many other topics for feature stories—a forthcoming holiday, interesting places in the community, students' or teachers' names, all may spark an idea for a feature.

Regardless of what topic you may choose, be sure you have a thorough knowledge of the subject. No feature writer can be successful without doing some research to learn the background behind the material.

Once you have written the story, use the following checklist to make sure it meets all the requirements:

Dropouts Get Chance

By Lisa Solomine
and Belle Hwong

Outreach Center is a special program for high school dropouts trying to return to school and get a diploma. Mr. Richard J. DiDomenico is the administrator of the school located on Union Street just off Northern Boulevard.

Begun in September of 1982 by the Board of Education, the location in Queens was moved six times until they finally settled in an old elementary school building in Flushing. The schools' furniture and books were either donated, borrowed or found.

The school's schedule is like any regular school. However, there are morning and afternoon sessions with classes from 8:00 A.M.-12 Noon and from 12:50 P.M.-4:00 P.M.

Strict Rules

Very strict rules are enforced. There is no fighting, drug dealing or alcohol permitted. Students found breaking any one of these rules are immediately taken out of the schedule. "There is no second chance," explained the director.

The school holds town meetings every two weeks in its gym, where parents, students and teachers discuss problems, improvements and their feelings about the school.

There are only major subjects studies in this school and only a short time is set aside for recreation in the gym, which is made from two classrooms.

School Problems

Approximately 300 students attend the school ranging in age from 17-21. Some of the students have been out of school for a couple of years while others have been out for just a while. Many of those who dropped out and now attend the center have either had family problems, peer pressure, drug problems or just could not handle things but have friends or relatives who have heard about the Outreach Center.

When they are admitted to the school they take math and reading tests. According to the director, reading scores of most of the entering students are at the 6th grade level and the math scores are at the 5th grade level.

Classes contain 15-35 students. Mr. DiDomenico said teachers try not to pressure students, but allow them to work at their own pace, providing individual attention, if necessary.

There are five other Outreach Centers located around the city: two are in Manhattan, two are in Brooklyn and one is in the Bronx. School guidance counselors have information about these schools.

Recent Graduate

One of the recent graduates is Lisette Pacheco who is 18 years old and graduated eight months after she came to the Outreach Center. She had dropped out of the high school during the 10th grade.

Lisette talked things over with her parents and found out about the Outreach Center from her guidance counselor. She told her friends who had dropped out about the center. She felt she had to go there because she was bored. "I saw myself going in the wrong direction," she said.

When she first heard about the school she had negative feelings. However, once she got to meet Mr. DiDomenico, the administrator, and the rest of the teachers she began to feel confident about herself going there.

She feels she benefited more from this school than regular high school because she worked at her own pace and the teachers thought more about her individual knowledge than just getting her to pass. "The teachers are beautiful here, they are just like family." Also, when she could not handle or make up her mind about things, "They give you a little push."

Now, since she has graduated, she has been offered a job at the Outreach Center. She sent in her job application and is waiting for the results. She also plans to go to college where she will study to become a professional teacher.

When asked what advice she would give to any students who are thinking about dropping out or anyone who knows someone who has dropped out she replied, "Everyone tells you to go to school but you really don't listen, so you go out and have your fun, but later you'll see, you'll regret it. It's just not worth it."

The above informative feature story from The Beard Bugle, *Daniel Carter Beard Junior High School, Flushing, New York, uses quotes to help make the story more interesting.*

(1) Does the lead catch the reader's interest so that he will want to read further?

(2) Have you used short sentences and long sentences so mixed as to make easy reading?

(3) Is the writing free of mechanical errors?

(4) Are gossip and ridicule avoided? Just as in editorials or columns, a feature story must never hurt a person's reputation. This is particularly easy to do in a personality sketch. Never print something just for the sake of entertaining, if it might injure the reputation of another. Remember that this may also injure the reputation of the paper. It is important to keep the writing style informal and entertaining, but it must always be in good taste.

(5) Are the paragraphs short? They should never be more than′ 40 words in length.

(6) Does the story have an original approach? A good feature story is not simply a statement of collected facts; it is creative in some way.

(7) Have you used direct quotes where possible? Quotes make it easier for the reader to identify with the person making the remarks. A story written in narrative style should always use dialogue.

(8) Is all factual material accurate?

(9) Have you applied all the principles of effective writing to achieve unity, coherence, and emphasis?

(10) Does the conclusion tie in with the rest of the story? Be careful not to end the story so abruptly that it confuses the reader.

(11) If there is a human-interest potential, has it been fully developed? The emotional appeal of the story should be fully exploited.

(12) Is editorializing avoided for the most part? At times it may be necessary to make some editorial comment, depending on the nature of the story, but usually editorializing can and should be avoided.

Cheerleader's recovery; a miracle

by Andrea Smallwood

Watching Chaffin cheerleader Barbara Fine it's hard to believe that only a year ago she was comotose in an intensive care bed at Sparks Regional Medical Center, diagnosed as a Reyes Syndrome victim.

Barbara came down with a cold which kept her out of school for about a week. She was just about over it when she started vomiting. Medication failed to stop it, then she began dehydrating.

By 3p.m. the next day she became comotose and was admitted

A PICTURE OF HEALTH!
Barbara Fine now enjoys a normal life after recovering from Reyes Syndrome.

to the intensive care unit at Sparks Regional Medical Center after being diagnosed as having Reyes Syndrome, a serious viral disease of children which occurs about a week after the recovery from a viral infection such as the flu.

Specialists were brought in and Barbara underwent surgery to place a moniter on her brain. Three tubes were put down her throat which were connected to a respirator to help her breathe. The next day she slipped into the fourth stage of Reyes Syndrome and her limbs started to turn inward (one of the symptoms of the disease).

She remained in a coma for five days and five nights with very little response. On the sixth day Barbara showed a little more response and began to wake up. That's when she began her quick recovery.

Reyes Syndrome, which affects normal, active, primarily healthy children of all ages, generally ages 5-15, proved to be nearly fatal for Barbara, but five other Arkansas children were not so lucky.

Barbara was the only Arkansas child to survive last year. She seemed to recover with flying colors. She is now active as a cheerleader as well as many other activities around the community.

She lived to share her experience with others. She appeared on a local information show called "Dialogue" with her doctor, Dr. Louay Naesri, and

her parents, Mr. and Mrs. Orville Fine, in hopes to inform others of the seriousness of the disease.

"The cause of the disease isn't known," Barbara said. "They are linking aspirin with it but it's not definite yet. Sometimes aspirin would show up in the tests but sometimes not so it's just not positive."

Doctors are now undergoing tremendous research into the disease as there is no cure or way of preventing it. Like any other virus, it must run it's course.

___

" I believe the Lord spared my life "

"I believe the Lord spared my life," she said. "The doctors told my parents that there was a million to one shot that I'd be mentally retarted, but my family never lost faith."

Mr. Rick Martin, Chaffin Arkansas Ecology teacher even initiated Barbara's need into a prayer chain at his church. "It seemed like a good thing to do at the time,"Martin said. "A prayer chain is just a group of people that are really in tune with God that pray together when a need is initiated."

Barbara is now referred to as a miracle because of the seriousness of the disease and the odds of recovery. The outcome is usually bad in most cases. The doctors, having said it was hopeless, were surprised and amazed, according to Barbara.

On the first day after, I woke up, the doctors still weren't sure whether or not I was retarded because the medication they were giving me made me groggy," she said. "I had a lot of dreams while I was asleep. It was as if I could see everything happening to me."

Barbara awoke to find her mother there and she asked her to turn off the radio. "I'd heard it for days and I was tired of it. The day before I came out of it, subconsciuosly I was aware of what was going on in my room but was not awake."

"It was the best thing that could happen and I'm really glad it did. I learned the value of life and now have more faith in the Lord. It was what I needed to help straighten out my life," Barbara said. "It also helped bring my family closer together and I have more compassion for parents going through the whole ordeal."

To this day Barbara travels to nearby churches and other organizations sharing her testimony and bringing faith and hope to those in need.

Good use of quotes and background information make this profile from The Cougar Print, *Chaffin Junior High School, Fort Smith, Arkansas, an effective one.*

137

(13) Have you used specific nouns, adjectives, and verbs to create feelings in the reader?

(14) Have you rewritten the story until you are sure you have done the best job possible?

HUMAN-INTEREST STORIES

The human-interest story is actually a short feature—usually no more than 200 words. It is normally based on timely subjects and is designed to entertain. Its purpose is to present the human side of the news in an interesting and dramatic fashion. It should play on the reader's emotions.

Divorce: an increasing problem

"It's become more acceptable," explained John Keraus, psychological examiner at Western Arkansas Guidance Center, about the increase in a problem affecting many Chaffin students and teens around the country.

The problem is divorced parents; and it's become so great, today there are about an equal number of teenagers that have divorced parents as have both parents at home.

"It really upset me at the time, but it doesn't really bother me now," commented Laura Miles, freshman.

According to Keraus, teens can encounter many problems even before the divorce. They may have loss of sleep and appetite or just feel bad about themselves.

"You have to get used to living with just one (parent)," Margaret Flocks, seventh grader, commented on her situation.

"When you're with one you miss the other one, especially on holidays," added eighth grader Christi Cramer.

A divorce may also cause problems for teens in school. Grades may get worse, sometimes just to get the parent's attention.

Many times parents compete with each other for a child's love or respect. "Parents can use kids as a weapon against each other," stated Keraus. If this happens Keraus suggests talking it over with parents and telling them exactly what's wrong.

"Sometimes it ends up in an attitude problem," remarked Dick James, Chaffin student counselor. If teens get depressed they may withdraw, especially from friends, or get angry easily.

"It's hard to make the decision which one to go to," remarked Christi Cramer about the problem of custody.

"It used to be the mother that usually got custody but now, more and more fathers are involved in childrearing," stated Ms. JoAnn Pinkston, a counselor at Western Arkansas Guidance Center. A judge chooses the parent on their "parenting ability," but 14 year olds and older have more choice than younger children.

Stepparents can help or add to the difficulties. Sometimes parents think kids should accept a stepparent as a substitute for the other parent, when really "It's a whole new relationship," stated Keraus.

"Often children feel unloyal if, for instance, they have a good relationship with their stepmother they may feel unloyal to their mother," commented Ms. Pinkston.

Abigail Wood, "Seventeen" columnist, suggests offering an "olive branch" to difficult stepparents. "It takes time for defensive feelings- even unwarranted ones- and insecurities to go away, but a few friendly gestures can help melt the ice," concluded Wood in a "Relating" column of the February issue of "Seventeen".

As to the long range effects of divorce on children, none have been established yet, but says Keraus, "Kids sometimes model their parents. They won't get divorced just because their parents got divorced, but not knowing how to relate in a marriage can lead to divorce."

> *It really upset me at the time, but it doesn't bother me now.*

Laura Miles, 9

> *When you're with one parent, you miss the other.*

Christi Cramer, 8

National average 50%; Chaffin 51%

Living in a family with divorced parents is a common occurrence among today's teenagers. In a random survey 233 Chaffin students were polled, of these, 51% of the students polled had parents who are divorced.

The freshman class has the lowest percent of the students with divorced parents. Of the 47 ninth graders polled, 28% had parents who are divorced.

Out of these students 77% live with their mother and 23% live with their father.

The eighth grade class has a higher percentage than the freshman class. Out of 79 eighth grade students polled, 32% had parents who are divorced. Of this 32%, 72% lived with their mom, 24% live with their dad, and only 1 person lives with a grandmother.

The seventh grade class had the highest percentage of all grades. Out of 107 seventh graders polled 39% had parents who are divorced. The seventh grade also had the highest percent of students who live with their mother. Of the seventh grade students whose parents are divorced, 79% live with their mother, 11% live with their father, 1% live with neither their mom or dad.

The number of divorces in the United States in 1981 was very similar to Chaffin. In 1981, 2,438,000 men and women were married. Of those 1,219,000 were divorced, occupying the 50% mark. In other words, 1 out of every 2 marriages ends with a divorce, thus Chaffin students and their families fall slightly above the national average.

A topic of concern to many teenagers is handled well by using research and a local survey to develop the story on divorce. The above articles appeared in The Cougar Print, *Chaffin Junior High, Fort Smith, Arkansas.*

Peer pressure affects all age groups

by Ken Fry

Peer pressure has an effect on people of all ages. According to Mr. Robert Sanborn, associate principal, peer pressure is a major problem for teenagers.

There are several different kinds of peer pressure. A student might skip school because of what his peers say. Somebody might feel pressured to take alcohol or drugs because they think it is easier than saying no and disappointing their peers.

It also has a good side to it. A student may turn out for a sport because his friends are there. A student may be in a club because he enjoys the company of his friends.

"Peer pressure may create stress," explains Mr. Tom Baldwin, counselor. "A person may feel rejected by his peers. That creates loneliness that might lead to suicide in some cases."

"A student might hate himself, so he will put other people down and feel better about himself," stated Mr. Chet Atlas, health teacher. "Those guys are desperate to be liked."

Low achievers need special help

by Susan Bruington

Dealing with low-achieving students in the classrooms can be a difficult task for teachers. Many of these students have academic and emotional problems.

"Some kids come from terrible home situations," explains Mr. Ted Grimsted, seventh grade counselor. "School work might be the farthest thing from their mind."

Peer pressure also plays a big part when students are not working to their ability. Kids often misbehave in school to get recognition from their classmates.

Students enter junior high wanting to get a fresh start, explains Mrs. Paula Heck, seventh grade English teacher. If they are unsuccessful, they become frustrated and discouraged. That's when the students need help. If they do not get the appropriate aid, they give up.

When kids are not participating in class, they begin misbehaving because of boredom. This creates conflict between the teacher and pupil. The child may become rebellious and withdrawn.

What can be done for problem students? Grimsted stated, "It's pretty impossible for teachers to help them on a one-on-one basis in class, although it should be done. Special ed is available, though it often doesn't change behavior problems."

Heck says that Wy'east has a good tutoring program, but it does not reach enough students. Grimsted says, "Being labeled as a 'failure' creates a bad self-image for the individual. For a group of students, it is good because they know what's expected of them."

Two related stories on the same subject enable the writers from Wy's Words, Wy'east *Junior High School, Vancouver, Washington to go more in-depth on their subject without either story becoming so long as to bore the readers.*

As with the straight feature, the best human-interest story has a suspense element and a surprise ending.

The lead of a human-interest story must be brief but interest-arousing. The body should further intensify this interest and should appeal to the reader's imagination. The conclusion should surprise or startle the reader.

Advertising Antics

"Would you like to buy advertising for the Northern Lights?"

This question was heard at many of the Kirkwood and Des Peres stores during the past few weeks, and the Journalism staff were the ones asking it. We got such answers as: "No, I'm sorry, we don't have enough money, or you'll have to come back later, or I'm sorry, we're already advertising in two other school papers."

The prize answer was when Leslie Kuna and Karen Hanpeter went to a Mortuary, and asked the janitor if he would like to buy advertising in our school paper. He replied, "There's no one here but me and the guy in the coffin!"

Another surprise ending brightens the above human-interest story from The Northern Lights, *North Kirkwood Junior High School, Kirkwood, Missouri.*

One of the main advantages of the human-interest story based on a timely event is that it helps enliven the news page. An incident that is unusual, arouses sympathy, or amuses makes a good human-interest story.

As in writing any story, you should always keep your reader in mind. Are you writing primarily to entertain students, teachers, or parents? You must answer this question if you are to write an effective human-interest story.

IN-DEPTH STORIES

Although in-depth stories do not have to be features, they generally are, since they are designed to dig behind the facts of a news event.

An in-depth story is the type of story the name implies. To go in depth means to dig for all the facts and to talk to anyone involved.

Quotes are important for in-depth stories, as they help to humanize the event(s). The reporter must talk to as many people as he can who have any knowledge of the subject. The reporter should also rely on magazine articles and books written on the topic, but should always remember that he should never believe everything he reads.

Background work and lots of interviews will help the reporter present both sides of a story.

In-depth reporting tells the reader all the main facts behind an event. To do this takes time. A reporter should never be satisfied with less than the complete story. Research and perseverance are the key words to developing a successful in-depth article.

The following rules for writing in-depth articles should be remembered:

(1) Do not assume anything.
(2) Do not take just one person's word.
(3) Talk to people actually involved. Don't base the article on hearsay.
(4) Talk to many people and don't be afraid to go to the top.
(5) Do research.
(6) Do not come to a conclusion—let the reader decide.
(7) Do not believe everything you read.
(8) Give both sides of the story.
(9) In-depth articles may be a series of related articles. An in-depth story does not have to be all-inclusive in a single article. The reader is more apt to read a series of short articles than he is a lengthy article.

Many events and situations lend themselves to good in-depth reporting. The following are examples:

(1) The latest fads (CB radios, dance crazes, pinball machines, fashions).

(2) New educational developments (Pass-Fail, lower scores on achievement tests, curriculum changes).

(3) Analysis of changes in education (New Math, Open Classrooms, Year-Round Schools).

(4) Historical events (Bicentennial, new laws that affect young people).

(5) Youth Organizations (Young Life, YMCA, YWCA, youth counseling services).

EXERCISES

(1) Write a news feature explaining how Mr. Joe Thomas, citizenship teacher, has developed the problems-approach to social studies and the situations that have evolved. The problems-approach trains the students in the techniques of problem solving—considering all sides of controversial issues, gathering all facts before making a generalization, and, after consideration of all the facts, reaching a conclusion. Arguments have developed in Mr. Thomas' classroom over interpretation of facts. Students have run into the problem of lack of necessary materials. They have pestered the librarian so much that she refuses to let them in the library. They have written letters to many organizations to gain information. The standard answer seems to be, "We have received your letter but are sorry to say that we have no available materials to send you." The letters usually go on to say, "If we can be of any further help to you, please contact us." Even though the problem of lack of materials to get the necessary facts has been something of a hindrance, most students still feel that they have learned a lot by the problem-solving technique. Bill Lewis stated, "I never really realized that I had preconceived ideas about some subjects and that my opinions would be so hard to change; but by studying every side of an issue, it has been necessary for me to change my mind about some issues when all the facts have been presented." Sue Turner said, "The problem-solving approach has certainly pointed out to me that my opinions can be wrong

sometimes. I'm not so quick to jump to conclusions any more." Bill Dukes said, "It has certainly taught us how to work together as a group since we're trying to reach some general conclusion on some topics. I would say that we respect each other's opinions more now."

(2) Through the use of the school buzzbook, write a feature on interesting names.

(3) By interviewing students in school, write a feature on their famous relatives.

(4) Choose any holiday of the year and write a feature on it. Use your imagination and tie it in with school life.

(5) Criticize the following story:

Students at South are having a hard time deciding what season it is. Will tomorrow be drizzly, dry, warm, or chilly? In fact, the weather is so unpredictable that from eight o'clock in the morning until 3:00, there could be a 30 degree change. Our problem is this: what to wear?

The mixture that you will find in any corridor is enough to stupefy the goggle-eyed observer. Half the school has blossomed out in spring and summer cottons; shirtwaists, flats, and khakis; while the other half is still bundled up in inch-thick woolens. If you choose the former, you're likely to shiver all the way home, but if you wear "woolies," you'll probably suffocate.

In our grandparents' day, the decision must have been just as hard. Spring meant the shedding of long underwear. When elbows shot out of the shoulders, and trousers got that "June-is-busting-out-all-over" look, it was time for a summer outfit.

Obviously, the only sensible solution to this predicament is to stay home until it is undoubtedly summer. (This isn't recommended, since alternating between freezing and frying is much preferable to failing!) This problem doesn't involve fellas as much as gals, but it's wearing us out!

(6) Write a feature on the new dance steps that are sweeping the country. A comparison on the way parents used to dance and the way teenagers now dance would be interesting.

(7) Write a feature on the new fashion styles of both boys and girls.

(8) Write a feature from the following information: Student Teacher Day was held on February 14. Many interesting things happened in the different classes. For example, John Dailey got up in

English class and forgot what he was supposed to do. As a result, he wound up giving the students a spelling lesson. In writing the words on the board, he misspelled three of them. Sandy Grail had planned to show a 20-minute film in citizenship at the first of the hour, but the key to the audio-visual room was lost, so she couldn't get a projector on time, so as a result she gave the last part of her lesson first. When the projector finally arrived, it wouldn't work, so Sandy wound up pantomiming the film. Bill Brown was to teach geography in core class, but for some reason all the maps had been removed from the room by the janitor the night before and the maps couldn't be found. By the time the janitor was reached at home, the class was over. Janice Lee was to give a lesson on first aid in the health class, but the night before she broke her leg, so Mike Shell took over the class and in demonstrating how to make a splint he cut his finger with a knife. These were just some of the interesting sidelights of Student Teacher Day.

(9) Write a feature on how the gerbils in the science room react to the students who are constantly petting them.

(10) Select an exchange paper and write a critique on its feature page, pointing out the good and bad characteristics.

(11) Go through the daily newspaper and clip features that are well-written; bring them to class to discuss.

(12) Write a human-interest story on how Dick Thomas broke his arm while ice-skating. Use your imagination and develop a good story with a surprise ending.

(13) Write a 250-word feature about your school mascot. Include facts about how the mascot was chosen, if it has ever been anything different, how many other schools in the area have the same mascot, etc. You might even conduct a poll among the students to see how many would prefer a different mascot. What would the alumni think of this?

(14) Do a short feature story on the Pep Club at your school. You might emphasize the students who make signs and posters for each sporting event. Interview the students and find out where they get their ideas and how much time they spend on making each sign.

(15) Using any of the examples given under in-depth stories in this chapter or using an idea of your own write an in-depth article of approximately 1,000 words in length. Be sure to research your information and interview as many people as possible.

Chapter IX

FUNDAMENTALS OF SPORTS WRITING

Sports stories, for the most part, are written in the same format as news stories. The basic rule is to begin with the most important facts and end with the least important. The lead paragraph is usually a summary of the event, although sometimes one particular angle may be featured.

Too many novice reporters write sports stories in chronological order, beginning with the first quarter and ending with the last quarter. This may be the easiest way, but it is usually dull. If the first quarter was the most important part of the game, then begin with it. However, the early part of any sports event seldom provides all the fireworks. Perhaps the final minutes, or the overtime, or the high-scoring player may be the highlight. A sports story described from beginning to end probably will not point out how the event in question was different from any other. It is the job of the sports writer to show why the game played last night was different from the one played last week. The sports writer must pick out the feature, use this feature as a lead, and build the story around it.

Variety in a sports story is also important. If you are covering a basketball game, don't say that every goal is a basket. It might be a layup, a turn-around jump shot, a five-foot corner shot, a jump shot, a 20-footer, or a hook shot, for example. Using different phrases will brighten the story. The reader likes to feel that he was actually there, witnessing the game. If you say, "Jerry West scored a basket," it may not mean much; but if you say, "Jerry West scored on a driving layup," the reader can almost see the action. *Action*—this word is important in covering all sports stories. You must convey the action to the reader. If you report every play of the game, however, the story becomes

North Loses to Lindbergh After Leading At Halftime

A disastrous fourth quarter thwarted a gallant attempt by North's roundbellers as they fell to the Lindbergh Flyers 54-40 on the home court last Friday.

North led 11-10 at the end of the first quarter and 21-18 at halftime but fell behind 32-28 at the end of the third quarter and were never able to catch up after that as numerous turnovers hurt.

Fails to Control Jumps

North's failure to control jump ball situations led to Lindbergh breaking away in the second half.

There were 18 jumps in the game with Lindbergh controlling 14 of them. Twelve of these jumps came in the second half, and Lindbergh came down with 10 of them.

Lindbergh also solved North's zone defense in the second half, which they had had trouble breaking the first half.

Lindbergh Scores First

Lindbergh scored first in the game as Tim Boyd hit a 15-foot corner shot. Boyd scored seven of the Flyers' 10 points in the quarter.

North grabbed the lead on a free throw and a basket by Randy Vaughn. Craig Osborne and Boyd connected for Lindbergh, giving the Flyers the lead, 6-3, which was the widest margin in the quarter.

Jim Becker hit on a 5-foot jump shot and Bob Dean hit from under the basket to enable North to regain the lead 7-6.

North On Top

Boyd put Lindbergh back ahead on a free throw and layup, but Becker and Pat Coley hit to give North the lead 11-9. Chuck Boyd then dunked a free throw for the Flyers to end the quarter with North leading 11-10.

Lindbergh scored first in the second quarter, and then the two teams alternated baskets twice as Vaughn and Becker hit for North. Chuck Boyd put the Flyers on top 18-15.

The Pioneers then got hot.

Vaughn hit a 20-foot jump shot from the corner, Coley and John Copeland made free throws, and Becker connected on two charity tosses to give North a 21-18 halftime lead.

Jumps Dominate Quarter

The third quarter was a series of jumps. Three jumps were made before anyone got a shot away.

North scored first as Vaughn hit after a feed from Dean. North had its biggest lead of the game at 23-18.

The Flyers then scored seven straight points on three field goals and a free throw to regain the lead 25-23.

Becker hit a free throw, making it 25-23. After a free throw by Chuck Boyd for the Flyers, Steve Pollart hit on a 5-foot corner shot to tie it up 26-26. The Pioneers had gone 3:15 without a basket.

Becker Ties Game

Osborne put the Flyers back on top, but Becker tied it for North with a basket underneath.

Two quick steals by Tim Boyd gave the Flyers two easy baskets as the third quarter ended with Lindbergh ahead 32-28.

Disaster struck early in the fourth quarter. The Flyers scored eleven straight points on five field goals and one free throw, while holding North scoreless to open up a 15-point lead 43-28.

North Trails By 17

North battled evenly after this but couldn't catch up. The Flyers biggest lead was 17 points at 52-35 and 54-37. North closed out the scoring in the game as George Hoffman was fouled after tipping in the ball. Hoffman made the free throw to make the final score 54-40.

Becker led North's scorers with 13 points, closely followed by Vaughn with 11.

Three Lindbergh players broke into double figures, with Tim Boyd scoring 19, Osborne 16, and Chuck Boyd 11.

Note that the above sports story from The Northern Lights, *North Kirkwood Junior High School, Kirkwood, Missouri, is not written in chronological order. Quite often the most important event in a game does not occur in the first quarter.*

146

too long and dull. Pick out only the highlights of the game and report them.

Football stories are handled much like basketball stories. Don't merely say that the quarterback passed the ball and the team made a first down. Let the readers know how long the pass was, what down it was, how many yards they had to go, who caught the ball, etc.

Never say a player made a long run. Let the reader know what kind of run it was, and how long. For example, did he run down the sidelines, did he avoid would-be tacklers, was he caught but broke loose, was he knocked out of bounds? You must answer these questions to satisfy the reader.

In covering football games, don't just report the backfield play. Remember the line. Without the men in the line the backfield couldn't accomplish much.

Remember—don't narrate a story play by play. Pick out the most important plays of the game and feature them. Most intelligent readers want only the highlights; they want to feel as if they had actually witnessed the game when they have finished reading the story.

A successful sports writer must be completely familiar with the sport he is covering and understand all sports terminology. However, avoid the excessive use of slang when writing the story. Use only terms that the average reader will understand.

To gain variety in writing you may use such words as "tromped," "smashed," "walloped," and "trounced." However, don't overuse them, and do use them correctly. A basketball team that wins a game 59 to 58 certainly did not trounce the losing team. Perhaps the word "edged" would be more appropriate.

The number one problem that monthly school papers have with the sports page is placing too much emphasis on past events and not enough on future events. Most readers are as interested in the coming games as in past scores.

Usually past events are reported in detail, and no space is left to report future events. The future events should be given the

Barajas, Haight, Walker win

By Virginia Treacy

Gonzalo Barajas, Mechele Haight, and Billy Walker with Derek Halvorson were the first place winners in the First Annual Webster Marathon on May 26 held after school.

Barajas set a fast pace at 9:32 minutes for the 1.7 mile course which encircled the Webster campus. Haight led the girls to come in at 12:25 minutes. Derek Halvorson pushed Billy Walker across the finish line in a record 7:58.5 minutes to lead the handicapped runners. Jose Lopez-Gallego was the first teacher to break the tape.

Over 100 students and teachers took part in the race which began on the front lawn as the runners tore through the paper Marathon banner when Ray Rodriguez, vice-principal, shot off the starter gun.

Second and third place winners for the boys were Mike Vasquez and Sean Lopez. Wende Fowler and Pauline Apodaca came in second and third for the girls. In the handicapped race, Rosemary Sanderson wheeled herself across the finish for second place while Danny Dias, with the help of Emene Giambruno, came in third.

Thea Waldo, eighth grade, said breathlessly after running the marathon, "It was great."

"It was a great experience for running," said Christine Wollenhaupt.

Ken Nakata, after crossing the finish line, said, "I feel dead."

"Running the race was a great victory for many, considering that it takes a big effort for many students to run around the track," said Beatrice Ruiz, gym teacher and co-chairperson of the first Webster Marathon.

1. COMING IN FIRST, Mechele Haight, seventh grade, breaks the tape.
2. FASTEST TIME, Gonzalo Barajas, eighth grade, races in first for boys.
3. BREAKING THE WEBSTER BANNER, part of over 100 runners begin the First Annual Marathon.

First Webster Marathon

Sports stories covering events other than competition with other schools should be included on sports pages. The above photo-story on some intraschool competition appeared in the Webster Warrior, *Daniel Webster Middle School, Stockton, California.*

Blisters, falls: a speed skaters follies

by Andrea Smallwood

The tension is building. Only one more lap to go. Eagerness for the race to be over is getting higher and higher. He automatically speeds up and crosses the finish line. The race is over. He won!

Freshman Jon Brice and seventh graders David Cwiertnia, Ronnie Dalton, and Shelly Madden all hope to find themselves in that winning position. They have each joined the Crystal Palace speed skating team. Larry Sanford is the coach.

The teams practice on Sunday afternoons from 5:30 to 7pm and Tuesdays from 5 to 7pm.

"I always enjoyed skating fast so I tried out for the team and made it," says Jon Brice. "It's really a fun sport to get into."

A lot of hard work is involved in the sport also. The team members are asked to ride bicycles, jump rope, or some other exercise in order to build up their leg muscles.

"During practice the kids have to skate about 60 laps around the rink," said Mary Parker, Shelly Madden's mother. "They have to really want to skate."

Grades are important, too. The team members have to take their report cards to the coach and let him see them. If grades aren't high enough because of neglect as a result of skating, then the person could be taken off the team.

"Blisters, falls, bruises, and burns are just part of speed skating. It's worth it, though," said Ronnie Dalton. "I've been speed skating about half of a year and I really enjoy it."

David Cwiertnia has been skating since about a month after Crystal Palace opened. David and Jon are stepbrothers so they got in this together.

The team has already been to two tournaments, both in Irving, Texas. The first one was on Halloween. The second was week of Thanksgiving. In the second tournament the team came in second place overall.

"We did better in the second tournament," said Brice. "After the first tournament, we came back and practiced harder."

All of the members seem to agree that speed skating is enjoyable. "I just think it's fun," concluded Dalton.

Sports features should be used in conjunction with sports coverage and advance stories to liven up sports pages. The above feature appeared in The Cougar Print, *Chaffin Junior High School, Fort Smith, Arkansas.*

spotlight. Past events should be reported but played down. Usually a summary story of all games is the most effective way of reporting past events. The skilled sports writer edits his copy tightly so that the results can be reported without the story's losing any impact.

Many novice sports writers tend to be unfair in their reporting. If their team loses they tend to make alibis or blame the referee. Alibis and excuses do not belong in sports stories, and neither does criticism of the opposing team.

Some reporters build up their own team as so great that the players themselves become overconfident from reading the stories. Remember that overconfidence has caused many good teams to be defeated.

Another common fault of sports pages in junior high schools is the failure to report intramural as well as varsity sports. Remember that not every student can participate in varsity sports. Students who play well on an intramural team also deserve recognition. This includes girls' intramurals as well as boys'.

A good sports writer will find out as much as he can about the opposing team before the game is played. An easy way to do this is to call the sports editor of the other school. He can tell you the team's record so far, who their best player is, and other helpful information. He may be able to give you the starting lineup, but if not, it can always be obtained from the scorer's bench. It is much better to give the names of opposing players, rather than referring constantly to the name of the school.

If space permits, a box score of the game should be included in the paper. In basketball this would include a score by quarters and individual scores and fouls made by the players. In football it should give the score by quarters and indicate first downs, yardage gained passing and rushing, fumbles, yards penalized, punts, passes attempted, and passes completed. Statistics in box scores sometimes give the reader a picture of the game that cannot be gained merely by the final score.

A sports reporter must always be on the lookout for records

Parkway Edges South Pioneers In First Game of Season, 42-38

A tremendous fourth quarter comeback fell short as North dropped its first basketball game of the year last Friday to Parkway South by a score of 42 to 38.

A disastrous third quarter that saw North score only two points on a basket by Joe Mathias left the Pioneers behind 35 to 23.

Bill Brown hit a layup to start the fourth quarter, to make the score 35 to 25. Parkway then scored five points while North scored one on a free throw by Scott Brennan. Parkway then enjoyed its biggest lead by a score of 40 to 26 when North started its comeback.

A free throw by Mathias, Paul Olsen and Jim Mory made the score 40 to 29. A layup by Mathias and a five-foot jump shot by Brennan that swished through the net cut the margin to seven points.

A free throw by Parkway's John Ames made it 41 to 33 but a jump shot by Mathias under the basket cut the lead to six. Mathias was fouled on the shot and made his free throw to make the score 41 to 36.

Another free throw by Ames for Parkway and then a driving basket by Olsen with four seconds left made the final score 42 to 38.

North led only one time during the ball game, by a score of 19 to 18 with about two minutes left in the first half.

At the end of the first quarter North trailed 12 to 8 as they scored only one field goal, made by Gary Oehler.

Three straight baskets by Parkway's Jim McCarthy and a 20-foot jump shot by Brown for the Pioneers gave Parkway an 18 to 10 lead early in the second quarter.

A free throw by Mathias, a tip-in by Mathias, and layups by Brennan and Brown gave North the lead.

Parkway quickly regained the lead 20 to 19 as John Taylor scored on a driving layup. Two free throws by Parkway's Mike Mancin increased the Colts' lead to three. Mathias then scored on a fade-away jump shot to end the first half with North trailing 22 to 21.

Then came the disastrous third quarter in which North scored only two points to the Colts' 13. Missed free throw opportunities hurt North in this quarter as they did throughout the game.

North had the one-and-one free throw situation in the first quarter and again in the third quarter as Parkway was guilty of committing many fouls early in each half. Quite often, however, North missed the first free throw and thus never had the opportunity to take the second shot.

Mathias was the high scorer in the game for North with 15 points. Brennan scored eight and Brown seven for the Pioneers.

The starting lineup for North was Brennan, Mory, Mathias, Oehler, and Dave Sikich. Other players who saw action were Tom Kessler, Steve Harrison, Paul Olsen, and Brown.

Score by quarters:

	1	2	3	4
Parkway	12	10	13	7
North	8	13	2	15

BOX SCORE

	FG	FT	TP
Sikich	0	2	2
Mory	0	1	1
Mathias	5	5	15
Brennan	2	4	8
Oehler	1	0	2
Harrison	0	0	0
Olson	1	1	3
Brown	3	1	7
Kessler	0	0	0

Box scores add interest to a game, as shown in the above story from The Northern Lights, *North Kirkwood Junior High School, Kirkwood, Missouri. The article also gives good description of the action.*

tied or broken, individual stars, team performance, crowd reaction, and spectacular plays.

Personality sketches of sports figures also help enliven the sports page. They should not be overdone, but an average of one per issue is satisfactory. Personality sketches are discussed in Chapter X.

The sports editor should also be responsible for writing the sports column, which was discussed in Chapter VII.

If a sports reporter knows the rules and terminology of the sport, follows the game closely, and uses imagination in writing the story, he should be rewarded with the knowledge that he has done a good job.

Besides coverage and advance stories of actual sporting events, sports pages should also include sports columns (discussed on page 122) and sports features to liven up the pages.

Sports features are generally interviews with well-known sports personalities either on the school's teams or on professional teams.

The history of a particular sport or details behind the rules of a game can also make interesting features. Personality sketches on individuals involved in unusual sports such as skateboarding or karate can also make interesting reading, as can unusual records or marathons.

Features on sports pages help to attract the reader who might not be a sports enthusiast and doesn't really have an interest in reading about last Friday's game or next week's game.

EXERCISES

(1) Rewrite the following sentences to conform to style rules.
    (a) East defeated West 29–28.
    (b) East clobbered West 29–28.
    (c) Tom Brack scored fourteen points in the last game.
    (d) Bill Beek ran the mile in five minutes and two seconds.
    (e) East defeated West last Saturday, March 8th.
    (f) Tom Brack scored 5 points, Bill Beek 10 points, Joe Lee, eight points, and Lindy Mack sixteen points in the game.

Gymnast has shot at '80 Olympics

By Devyani Kamdar

Already making her mark in national gymnastics competition after only two years at the sport is Kathy Tischer, a seventh grader attending Madison.

Kathy is the fourth child in her family to attend Madison. Before her came Pam, now 16, Rick, 17, and Scott, 20.

In the first two days of the National A.A.U. Junior Gymnastics Championships at Churchill High School May 3-5, Kathy took two firsts in vaulting, a second and a third in beam, a third and a fourth in floor exercise, and fifth in all-around.

In the finals she took a second in beam, and fourths in vaulting and floor exercise.

Kathy was the youngest girl from her team competing in that meet.

In the Regionals in April, Kathy took firsts in beam and floor exercise, and second in all-around.

"Her strengths are beam, floor exercise and, recently, vaulting," says Mrs. Peggy Wienstein, who works at the Academy where Kathy works out. "But she's going to have to work on tumbling more."

Kathy's first goal is to make the Pan American Games. Then she would like to go on to the Olympics or the World Games.

"I think I have a chance for the 1980 Olympics," she says, "but not for the 1976, because I'm still young and I still have a lot to learn."

When she started gymnastics two years ago, Kathy had had four years of ballet and some acrobatics.

Kathy first wanted to do gymnastics when, as she put it, "I saw Olga Korbut on T.V. and I said, 'That is what I'm going to do!'"

Kathy goes to school for only half a day. At about noon every day she goes to the Oregon Academy of Artistic Gymnastics where she works out for 6 1/2 hours.

On Saturdays she works out for only three hours, and she gets Sunday off.

When she is not working on gymnastics, she says, "I like to paint and do art type of things."

Kathy also likes to ride a bike, snow ski and watch gymnastics on television.

The above sports feature from The Scribe, *Madison Junior High School, Eugene, Oregon, highlights an unusual opportunity for a junior high student and the quotes are effectively used to show the personality of the student.*

(g) Tom Honeycutt carried the ball to the twenty yard line on an end sweep.

(h) North started on the thirty and in 8 plays moved the ball to the 10 yard line.

(i) Bill Moon scored on a 5 foot jump shot to make the score 20–18 in favor of East.

(j) Terry Lee scored one touchdown on a fifty yard run. Terry gained one hundred and fifty yards during the game.

(k) The record for the meet is nine seconds.

(l) The highest pole vault was nine feet eleven inches, and the discus has been thrown sixty-three feet.

(m) South scored in thirteen plays driving 60 yards, with fifteen of them coming on a screen pass.

(n) 15 yards were gained on a sweep play and then twenty five on a pass play.

(o) North scored fourteen points in the 4th quarter to come from behind and win the game 28–27.

(2) Write an advance sports story with the following facts.

East Junior High will play West Junior High in football next Friday at 4 p.m. on the East field. Your school is East. This is the last game of the season. Both teams have a 4–0 record. The winner will be the only undefeated junior high team left in the area. East and West have both played two common opponents. East rolled over North 42–0 and West edged North 14–13. East defeated South 21–20 while West defeated South 26–7. This would indicate that the game between East and West would be a tossup. East has averaged 21 points a game in four contests; West has averaged 20. Joe Lee has converted 11 consecutive points after touchdown for East, as he is an accurate place-kicker. Jack Janelle, place-kicker for West, has been accurate on 7 of 10 extra points this year. The difference in the accuracy of the kickers might be the difference in the game. East is also out for revenge, as last year West defeated them 14–7. East will have to stop West's Bob Hall, who has been averaging 69 yards a game rushing so far. He is also West's top scorer, with 36 points. East can counter with Jim Maloney, who has passed for an average of 80 yards per game and rushed for 50. He has scored 42 points for East. A capacity crowd is expected to fill East's small bleachers, which only holds 500.

(3) Rewrite the following story to conform with rules of good sports writing. Add additional information if needed.

The basketball team ended their season with a triumphant victory of 47–36, on Parkway's floor, played on February 24. High point man was Doug Lee with 17 points.

South started out slow at first, then opened up like a whirlwind and took command of the game. Action was fast and so was the basket-making. Lee, Johnson, and Smith all pounded in points. A five-point lead was held by North at the end of the first quarter.

Burning down the court, Benecke dumped in a basket. With some fancy footwork by Swift, another shot was made. Shaw and Ryan both had some excellent shots. At this point of the game, Parkway abandoned its zone defense for a more suitable man-to-man shield against South. The half found South ahead by 10 points, 24–14.

Point-making in both the third and fourth quarters was done by Bransford. Throughout the game, South held control of the back-boards. All members of the team got to participate in the last game.

(4) Rewrite the following story to conform with rules of good sports writing. Add additional information if needed.

After winning the toss, the White and Red took the ball from the 20-yard line to the 88-yard line, fighting forward for five 1–10's. It was here that Shave, with the line playing tight, stood behind Fitzsinger and passed to Riddle, number 16, who lateraled back to Ken Reece, number 15. Reece then took the ball around for 6 of our 19 points. Sneed then placed our extra point, making it 7–0.

On our kick to them, Brittany was stopped on the 33-yard line. They went to the 41-yard line at the end of the fourth, not getting their 10 yards.

In the second quarter on the 43-yard line, we progressed forward to the 85-yard line. Swift then caught a pass, and went to the 95-yard line. Ken Rice then went across the goal line making the score 13–0. The extra point was not successful. The game was called early because of darkness. At the finish of the game the score was 19–0.

(5) Write a sports story from the following information. Add information where necessary.

> Lincoln Panthers vs. Washington Bulldogs
> Your team—Lincoln
> Game at Washington last Friday

Lincoln won 21–20

Washington led 14–0 at half on a 63-yard kickoff return and a 30-yard touchdown on an intercepted pass.

Lincoln had outgained Washington 152 yards to 30 at half.

Third quarter—Lincoln scored on an 80-yard drive in 13 plays. Bob Hewitt made touchdown—Steve Lazier kicked extra point.

Fourth quarter—Washington again intercepted pass and went 30 yards for touchdown. Missed extra point. Lincoln scored on 40-yard pass from Hewitt to Dick Dennis with only two minutes left. Lincoln recovered on-side kick at Washington's 38-yard line. Two pass plays to Dennis and Lazier's third extra point gave Lincoln the win.

Lincoln gained 133 yards passing to Washington's 12.

Lincoln gained 156 yards rushing to Washington's 23.

Jim Carpenter made 11 unassisted tackles for Lincoln.

(6) Write a sports story from the following information. Add information where necessary.

North vs. East

Your team—North

Game at North last Tuesday

East won 54–40 as they sank 20 of 21 free throws.

North hit two of ten free throws.

Pat Becker scored 12 points, Jim Coley 10 points, and Jim Seeley 8 points for North.

North led at half 21–18

East led 32–28 at end of third quarter.

North tied game 34–34.

East then hit 12 straight points to break game open.

North committed 12 fouls in last quarter.

East hit all 12.

Becker's 12 points gave him 202 for the season—a school record.

Highest previous total—195 by Joe Decker, set two years ago

North's season ended with 7 victories, 3 defeats.

(7) Write a sports story from the following information. Add details where necessary.

Track meet
Webster vs. Avilla
Your team—Avilla
Final score—80 to 60 in favor of Avilla
Avilla took first in 220, 440, and 880
Also won 880-yard relay in track events
Placed first and second in pole vault and discus in field events
(Add names and times of winners)

(8) Analyze an exchange paper and discuss how you would improve the sports page.

(9) Write a sports column giving viewpoints of players and coach on the upcoming basketball season.

(10) Clip sports columns and stories from daily newspapers and bring them to class for discussion.

(11) Using a dummy sheet, do a layout of the sports page for the next issue of your school newspaper. It may be necessary for you to review layout rules as presented in Chapter V. If your school newspaper uses advertisements be sure to place them properly on the page.

(12) Write two-line headlines for the stories in exercises 2–7. Make the maximum count 30 and the minimum count 28 for each line.

(13) Read a sports column in a daily newspaper. Clip the column and bring to class. Be prepared to discuss how you think the writer got his idea for the column, where he got his information, and what techniques he uses to make it interesting.

(14) Write a short paper listing all the school records (giving name of student holding record, record, and year set) in one of the following sports: (a) football; (b) basketball; (c) track. School records can be most helpful for writing sports columns and features.

(15) Write a sports feature about some off-campus sport at your school such as bowling, racquetball, skiing, frisbee, or ice skating. Be sure to interview as many people as possible to give depth to your article.

(16) Write a personality profile on an outstanding player or an interesting coach at your school. Be sure to capture the individual's personality by detailing physical characteristics and mannerisms. Let the interviewee tell his story through his own quotes.

Chapter X

SPEECHES AND INTERVIEWS

Speeches and interviews are difficult to report. A reporter must be sure that he takes quotes word for word, and in using them he must be careful not to change the meaning of the speaker.

A competent reporter will get as much advance information as he can about the speaker. From such research the reporter should be able to determine the speaker's qualifications. He should find out the speaker's philosophy, his educational background, books he has published, or anything important he has accomplished. The speaker's philosophy is especially important, because this gives an indication of what his speech might contain.

The reporter should make sure that he has the full name of the speaker and that he has spelled it correctly.

On the junior-high level most speeches covered will be given in the classroom. These often are off-the-cuff speeches and usually turn out to be mostly question-and-answer sessions. With formal speeches, it is sometimes possible to obtain an advance copy. Do not rely too heavily on this advance copy, however, for speakers often deviate somewhat from the prepared speech.

When covering a formal speech, be sure to get the exact title. Take as many notes as possible, so that when writing your story you will have all the information and won't have to try to recall what the speaker said.

A personal shorthand is helpful in taking notes. Be careful, though, that you are absolutely certain of the meaning of all your abbreviations. Too often, beginning reporters can't read their own shorthand when they try to organize their notes to write the story.

It is impossible to take down everything a speaker says word

158

for word. Listen for key phrases and make sure you get them down correctly, so that when you are quoting, you won't misquote, and when paraphrasing, you won't change the emphasis or meaning of the speaker.

Following the speech, it is permissible to talk to the speaker if you need further information about him. This is a good time, also, to check the accuracy of your quotations. However, if it is obvious that he is in a hurry, don't detain him.

The best lead for a speech story is a summary lead that states the principal idea of the speech and the speaker's attitude toward the subject. Time, size of audience, and sponsor of the speech should certainly not be in the lead; usually these may be left for the end of the story.

A direct quote may be used as a lead if there is one that summarizes the entire speech. Usually it is difficult to find such a direct quote, and for this reason it is best to use a summary lead that may be a paraphrase of the speaker's words.

Too many reporters begin a speech story with the name of the speaker. Usually what the person says is more important than the person himself; however, if the speaker is very famous his name may be used in the lead. The same is true of the title of the speech; it does not make a good lead unless it happens to be striking or unusual.

Keep your readers in mind. Pick out the feature that will interest most of the readers. This is sometimes hard to do, but careful screening of all the notes will usually reveal one phrase of wide interest.

Remember that a lead may be more than one paragraph in length. In a speech story it is often necessary to have a lead of two or even three paragraphs.

The body of the speech story should be a logical development of the main idea, carried out with alternating paragraphs of direct quotation and paraphrase. This permits condensation of the total material while still providing a feeling of the speaker's mode of expression. Be careful, however, not to sacrifice clarity.

All paraphrases and direct quotes must be attributed. One di-

State Representative Burns Talks to Citizenship Class

"It is doubly important that you pursue your studies well so that you can carry on democratic government," stressed State representative Stephen Burns in a speech to Mr. H.L. Hall's third hour citizenship class on January 15.

Representative Burns urged the students to listen to their studies in government because "survival of our democracy is based on people such as you who understand our processes of government. All facets of government must be understood," he said.

"It's amazing, the number of people in politics," he said, "that don't have the vaguest notion how our government works."

How a bill becomes a law and methods of selecting delegates to conventions were also discussed by Representative Burns.

The Toll Road bill passed during the last session, is unconstitutional, according to Representative Burns. He feels the legislature should be judged on the quality of bills passed and not the quantity.

"Too much bad legislation is passed because of special privileges," he said.

Representative Burns would like to see school tax levies revert back to the current level when a tax proposal is defeated rather than back to a $1.25 as the constitution specifies.

He also felt that funds for schools should come from more sources than property taxes.

Representative Burns is from the forty-second district, which includes Des Peres, Frontenac, Warson Woods, Rock Hill, and part of Kirkwood.

The above speech story from The Northern Lights, *North Kirkwood Junior High School, Kirkwood, Missouri, alternates paragraphs of quotes and paraphrase to make it effective.*

rect quote may include several sentences, whereas in paraphrasing every sentence should be attributed to the speaker. The best word of attribution is *said;* however, synonyms such as *stated, he went on,* and *related* may be used. Don't overuse the synonyms. There is no better word than *said.* The attribution should be enclosed in the paraphrase or quote or placed at the end. Normally, it is not good practice to begin a sentence with an attribution.

Background information about the speaker should be in the second or third paragraph of the story, although care must be taken not to break the development of the speech itself.

The reporter of a speech also has the obligation to convey the feeling of the occasion. He should describe the speaker, his manner of speaking, his rapport with the audience, the reaction of the audience, and any other interesting sidelights. However, colorful remarks should not be made more important than they really are, and the reporter must never let his own opinions or prejudices change the true story and meaning of the speaker.

In writing speech stories, remember the general rules of news writing. Be sure to avoid the enemies of good writing—haste, laziness, carelessness, and overwriting. Be sure to punctuate quotes correctly. Periods and commas are always placed inside quotation marks. Question marks and exclamation points are placed inside the quotation marks if the material quoted is a question or exclamation, but outside if the whole sentence is a question or exclamation. Semicolons belong outside the quotation marks.

Single quotation marks are used for quotes within quotes. When a quotation covers more than one paragraph, quote marks are placed before each paragraph but at the end of the last one only.

INTERVIEWS

An interview story is written essentially like a news story, but the methods of covering it are different.

Principal Praises Hanley
In Talk to *Acorn* Staff

Dr. Jester praised the educational standards of Hanley. During an interview with the journalism class on Thursday, September 14.

Dr. Jester said the overall master plan for Hanley is to make education a more tolerable period of life for the learner. He said the way we planned to reach this goal is to "exercise a little more flexibility so that school won't be regarded as a bitter pill, but rather a pleasant time of the day, where teachers and resources are brought together for the students' benefit."

No Junior High Better

"I don't think there is a junior high school in the entire country where you can get a better education than you're getting at Hanley," he continued. "However, there are things Hanley must improve."

Several questions were put to Dr. Jester about the change in the gum-chewing rule and the clothing code. He commented that these are just two steps toward giving students more responsibility and more opportunity to be responsible.

He added that during the first few days of school there was much gum and many gum wrappers in the hall. He said that after students get used to the idea though, the situation should improve.

Snack Bar Possible

Dr. Jester also said that Hanley might incorporate a snack bar into the school. "There is a possibility that Hanley will have a snack bar before the year is over. There is no reason why a student shouldn't be able to have something to eat during the school day if he so desires."

In commenting on the changes that lie ahead, Dr. Jester said, "I foresee changes in practically everything we are doing today."

The use of alternate quotes and paraphrase is shown in the above interview story from The Acorn, *Hanley Junior High School, University City, Missouri.*

There are basically three types of interviews. A *news interview* is based on a news story and usually only one or a very small number of persons are questioned. A *group* or *symposium* interview will ask questions of several people. These people are not always experts on the subject as the interviewees in a news interview should be. It is important in a group interview that the reporter ask questions the same way to obtain an accurate response. The third type of interview is the *personality sketch*.

As with the speech story, the reporter should find out as much as possible about the person to be interviewed. If the interview is to be with an expert on a particular topic, find out beforehand as much about the topic as possible.

Before the interview, draw up a list of questions in order to keep the interview running smoothly. It is best to memorize these questions, rather than referring to notes. This makes a favorable impression on the person being interviewed and helps establish the good rapport that is so important to the success of the assignment.

Ask thought-provoking questions, not ones that require a simple yes or no answer, and avoid embarrassing questions.

Direct quotes are essential to a well-written interview, and— as always—they must be accurate.

Color is even more important in a news interview than a speech. The mannerisms and personality of the interviewee may be important, as well as his reactions to certain questions.

A news interview should be *informative* as to the facts, but it should also give the *opinions* of the person being interviewed.

As already stated, an interview is written like a speech story, with alternating paragraphs of direct quotes and paraphrase. Never include in the story the questions you asked, and make no reference to yourself. You did the interviewing, but the reader is not interested in you. He is interested in the person you interviewed.

A special type of interview is the *personality sketch*. Its purpose is different from that of the news interview, which is to present information or opinions. The personality sketch is de-

Mystery Man Praises Student Body

by Tom Reese

"The student body at Nipher is an outstanding student body."

This remark came from a man who plays a very important role in determining the future of all Kirkwood students.

His name has been mentioned in several lead articles published in the **Beacon**, because he is the authoritative source for district-wide information.

However, despite these facts, he still remains a "mystery man" to a large percentage of those concerned in his decisions. To students he may seem to work behind the scenes in affecting their lives.

This "mystery man" is Dr. James Fox, assistant superintendant for secondary schools.

Judging from a first glance, one would not suspect that this witty, good-natured man could have so many varied interests—traveler, sportsman, "Young Man of the Year," antique book collector, and even former semi-pro rugby player—and still have time to plan and improve the futures of Kirkwood students.

"I have traveled over most of Europe and North America," he said, his blue-gray eyes thoughtful, "and am now very interested in seeing South America and the South Pacific."

Another interesting charac-

teristic of this solidly built man is that he has been, and still remains, an avid sports enthusiast.

During college undergraduate work at the University of Virginia he participated in swimming and rugby.

Dr. James Fox

His interest in rugby continued after college, and he went on to compete on the semi-pro level.

Dr. Fox's main interests and hobbies now include sports in the form of golf, snow skiing, sailing, and water skiing, along with collecting antique books.

"My present job involves planning secondary education in the area of curriculum development," he stated.

One current project he is in-

volved with is plans for an alternative school.

"The purpose of this program is to provide a school to meet the needs of some students, which are not adequately met in present schools," he said.

This proposal is now before the state for funding, and still has to be approved by the Kirkwood school board.

When asked if he had any great future ambition, like running for President, he chuckled and replied, "No. I just want to become more effective in my present job."

Some of the ideas he will be considering in the near future include expanding the number of teams, including one made up of art, music, and English classes, at North Kirkwood Junior High School, and adding new courses and contract learning at K.H.S.

After considering the facts that Dr. Fox was voted "Young Man of the Year" in 1972 in Virginia, has traveled widely over the world, and has had a great amount of experience with education, it is pretty evident how much it really means when he says, "The student body at Nipher is an outstanding student body."

The above personality sketch from the Beacon, Nipher Junior High School, Kirkwood, Missouri, shows how quotes can be used to describe the individual.

Russian Teacher Shows Versatility

Mr. Alan Pike, Russian teacher, evidently has one of the most unusual backgrounds to be found on our faculty.

Born in Ogden, Utah, Mr. Pike grew up with the ambition of becoming a musician. He received a scholarship in music and went on to major in instrumental music at the University of Utah. While in college, he also minored in Spanish and conducted a band which played for local social events.

Air Force Language Specialist

In 1951, at the height of the Korean conflict, Mr. Pike enlisted in the Air Force and became a language specialist.

Among his accomplishments during his five years at Hanley was the formation of the annual Russian festival which Hanley hosted two years ago. The festival, held at a different school each year, is designed to enable students to get together and speak some Russian.

Tour of Russia

Last summer, Mr. Pike was chosen to accompany other teachers of Russian on a tour of the Soviet Union.

The trip, his second, focused on courses at the University of Moscow which were taught completely in Russian.

"The student in Russia," observed Mr. Pike, "does not have the free time we have. Education is a very serious thing. There are no second chances." Mr. Pike went on to say that already in the seventh grade there is a tremendous dropout rate. The curriculum is so difficult that an estimated 98 percent of the student population never reaches the universities.

Asked what the most unusual event of the trip was, Mr. Pike thought a moment and then replied, "Last summer I had the privilege of playing at the Cafe Molodyezh while in Moscow. It was really quite an experience." (The jazz group with which he played is one of the best in Russia.)

Lives Active Life

The Pikes have three children, twin sons aged ten and one-half and a daughter aged six. Besides teaching at two schools, Hanley and Brittany, Mr. Pike is active in numerous organizations concerned with the language. Among the many offices which he holds is the vice-presidency of the Russian Teachers Association of Greater St. Louis, an organization which he was instrumental in founding. He is also chairman of Central States Modern Language Teachers Association and vice-president of the Modern Language Association of Missouri.

Asked what he considered the most rewarding aspect of teaching, Mr. Pike answered, "What I get out of it personally is the communication with my students and the feeling that I have somehow helped them out."

Faculty members make interesting subjects for personality sketches, as shown in the above article from The Acorn, *Hanley Junior High School, University City, Missouri. The article also shows good use of subheads.*

signed to convey a word picture of the interviewee. Appearance, manner, particular words or phrases used, become important, as well as the topic of the interview.

The writer should consider himself a stand-in for the reader. The public has a tendency to glorify, to hero-worship. The reader would like an opportunity to see the person as he actually is, to imagine that he himself had had a brief visit with the subject.

A common fault of personality sketches is to omit a physical description on the assumption that a picture will be published with the story. A description should always be given, discussing obvious features such as color of hair and eyes, stature, posture, and appearance. Poise or lack of poise, and voice quality (ease of speaking, pauses or hesitations) may be significant.

If the interview is conducted at the subject's home or office, the surroundings may be suggestive of the individual. Scene and setting often convey a message.

On the junior-high level, personality sketches of students, teachers, and administrators are usually well received and add color to a good newspaper.

EXERCISES

(1) Analyze the following interview and point out its weaknesses. Then rewrite it to conform to good journalistic writing. If necessary, put some of the paraphrases in quotes.

Recently I've had the opportunity to conduct a personal interview with our new principal, Mr. G. L. Jones. This interview was planned out on your behalf. We felt you would welcome the chance to get more information about your school, as well as Mr. Jones' views on our system of education.

My first question was about the "little school" plan, which is a new educational system of smaller classes and a split student body. Mr. Jones is very much in favor of this plan. He believes small classes with separate administrative counselors for each building makes teaching, as well as learning, a lot more worthwhile, and gives each individual student a much better chance to learn all he can.

Mister Ed, Flowers, Trees Pattern Ninth Grader's Life

"Do Not Disturb" is the sign on her bedroom door. But if you peek in you will see a tall thin girl with long blondish hair, probably lying on her bed.

Claudia Ruediger is a ninth grader at North. It's her first year here, and she says, "If you have to go to a school, I guess North is the best one to attend."

She made some other comments, too. "Boy, they have a great student lounge area--you can't even find it." The one thing Claudia hates most is walking between classes on cold rainy days.

Claudia joined the fortnightly committee this year, and she also is a member of the Student Council's money-making committee. Recently, she joined the new sing-out group. "It's a great idea, and I hope it works out. Mr. Hall seems really enthusiastic about the whole thing."

Claudia is a member of a large family--three boys and two girls. "I'm content with four brothers and sisters," she says, "but I'd like a smaller family."

She includes her dog, Mr. Ed, as part of the family too. She's quite concerned about what to get him for Christmas this year.

By JANET PILLMAN

Claudia likes to think about her good ol' days. She remembers particularly a hula-hoop contest in Kindergarten. "We were all going nuts on the playground. But I didn't win."

She has tried to grow many things. When she was 7 years old, she planted a little seed. It is now a 10-foot mimosa tree! She likes to grow flowers, too, but she does not like them as much as flower children.

What about her future? "I wanted to be a model--but I think I'll stick to teaching high school English. Oh, also an interior decorator." Well, -----no one really knows.

When asked what she thought of herself Claudia remarked, "I've got the stupidest laugh. It scares me sometimes!"

Personality sketches of well-known students can make interesting reading, as demonstrated in the above sketch from The Northern Lights, *North Kirkwood Junior High School, Kirkwood, Missouri.*

Mr. Jones also expressed the opinion that a school which is too small makes a variety of subjects and electives difficult, while a school which is too large makes thorough understanding and extra help a problem. Mr. Jones said that he felt the little school plan is the best answer to the overcrowded education system, and is definitely our answer to the problem.

To my inquiry about Mr. Jack Belt and Mr. John James, our administrative counselors, concerning their exact jobs and purpose in our little school plan, Mr. Jones answered, "Separate counselors for each little school makes individual help with personal problems, and friendly relations between teachers, counselors, and students much better."

In summing up the counselor's duties, Mr. Jones said, "Their jobs are specialized, to give each student a better understanding of his educational needs and wants."

In answer to many of your questions about the future building plans, the principal said, "Definite arrangements as to the school building, study halls, and gym classes, have not been made as yet."

About the award our building has received, Mr. Jones told me, "Our school has recently been honored by being chosen one of the seven best designed schools in the country by the School Executive magazine." "Our building", he added, "is the result of the extensive study of the community and its educational needs."

(2) Interview a public official in the city. Find out the requirements of his job and how students could help improve the city. Write a story from your information.

(3) Interview a teacher, pupil, or administrator and write either a news or personality interview story. If you choose a student, make sure it is someone well known in the school.

(4) Invite a staff member of the local newspaper to talk to the class, and prepare a story on what he says.

(5) Analyze the following personality sketch, pointing out its weaknesses and strengths. Write a two-line headline for it, with each line counting at least 30 and not more than 32. Rewrite the sketch to make it more effective, adding additional information if necessary.

Blond-haired, brown-eyed Scott Backus is probably the busiest boy in the seventh grade. He loves sports and also likes to sing.

Scott won first place in the Tennis Novice Tournament at the City Park last summer. A novice tournament is for players who haven't won before. Scott says, "I love tennis. It's just about my favorite sport."

Also over the summer, he won ribbons in swimming meets at Claymont pool. Scott played third base and catcher for his dad's Khoury League baseball team, the "7 Up Hornets."

Scott states, "I like third base better than catcher. But it really doesn't matter as long as I get to play."

Scott had held leading roles in many musicals in the city.

He serves on Student Council and was on the honor roll last quarter.

One time Scott helped in saving a boy's life. The boy was accidentally kicked in the head with a soccer ball and knocked out. There was no supervision around so Scott hurried over to the boy, because he knew what to do.

"I just kept everybody away and sent somebody for help." The boy was taken to the hospital and he just had a slight concussion. He was all right. Scott said, "That boy is one of my best friends too."

(6) From an exchange newspaper choose an example of a speech or interview story and write a critique on it.

(7) From the daily newspapers clip two speech and two interview stories and bring them to class for discussion.

(8) Rewrite the following interview story to conform to good style, adding additional information if necessary.

Rocket building is one of the latest projects of some of Mr. Gene Hall's seventh grade science students.

They build the rockets during class and launch them. Sometimes Mr. Hall will help them in launching the rockets after school.

"They are lots of fun to make. They are more fun when we launch them with gerbils in them though," said Lee Davis.

"We launch them in class with an electric launch or matches. They are a lot of fun to launch," replied Mark Tibbles.

"I like to make them a lot. They are really fun. We even put a cricket in one of them," said Victor Sewell.

Mr. Hall commented that "the boys seem to enjoy them, although not all the students are building them."

(9) Arrange for a teacher or administrator to come to class to be interviewed. When all students have written stories about the interview, exchange papers and compare the stories.

(10) Interview one of your journalism classmates. Write a story on the interview and then read the paper aloud in class. Be sure to be selective in questions asked and in content used in the article so that your story maintains some kind of continuity.

(11) By talking with classmates find out what policy made by the board of education is unfavorable. Interview members of the board to find out the purpose of the policy and how long it will remain in effect. Write a 300 word story on your findings. (Make sure this is a board policy and not a policy of the administration.)

Chapter XI

COPYREADING

The job of the copyreader is one of the most important on any newspaper staff. In essence, every member of the staff should be a trained copyreader.

The copyreader must check all stories to make sure they have been written as well as possible. He must check for errors of fact, misspellings, wordiness, and style errors. Often the copyreader must rewrite the lead so that the feature is brought out in the beginning. Sometimes he may have to rewrite the entire story.

Each page editor should copyread a story when the reporter gives it to him. The editor-in-chief should copyread a story when the page editor gives it to him. Finally, the copyreader should make the final check before the story is sent to the printer.

Although the headline editor and his assistants will write all headlines, the copyreader should check all headlines and subheads to make sure they are appropriate and that they conform to headline rules. On some papers the copyreaders write the headlines.

As with all journalistic functions, efficient copyreading requires practice and more practice.

Most copyreaders can pick out the common spelling errors, but many fail to recognize major factual errors.

Checking accuracy of facts is a very difficult job because the copyreader cannot be familiar with every story he checks. However, it is his responsibility to find out the facts. The copyreader should never change facts in a story unless he has verified the changes.

The copyreader must notice and delete instances of poor judgment or bad taste. He must also delete any editorializing outside of actual editorials.

A dictionary, stylebook, buzzbook, and thesaurus are important tools that a copyreader should have available at all times.

The buzzbook is essential for correct spelling of names. Everyone likes to see his name in print, but not if it is spelled wrong. The correct spelling of names is not an easy task, but an efficient copyreader can keep incorrect spellings to a minimum.

When checking the typed copy, the copyreader should make sure that the column width, number of inches, guideline, size of type, and name of publication are all indicated. Spaces for this information are provided on most copy sheets, and it is important that they be filled out for the printer's guidance.

When the copyreader has checked all of the above factors and has made sure that the story contains all essential information and that it has a good lead and logical organization, then the story should be ready for the printer. A story that does not conform to all the rules should never be sent to the printer.

Certain standard symbols are used in copyreading to simplify the work of the copyreader and the printer.

All corrections in copy should be made by using these copyreading symbols. Corrections should be made in the body of the story, not in the margins. Newspaper copy is double spaced to provide room for the copyreader's marks.

Following are the copyreading symbols:

SYMBOL	WHAT IT MEANS
☰	Capitals
═	Small capitals
/	Lower case
―	Italics
∿∿∿∿	Boldface

x or ⊙	Period
") ("	Insert quotes
⋏	Insert comma
=	Insert hyphen
h̬	Insert letter or word
⌊h̬o⌉	Transpose letters
⟨Wohl ⟌Jane⟩	Transpose words
⋁	Insert apostrophe
⌀	Delete letter
⌀	Delete letter and close up
n|s	Insert space
⌒	Close up space
(S.C.)	Spell out
(Student Council)	Abbreviate
(90)	Spell out
(ninety)	Write in numbers
30 or #	End of story
⌗ or L	Paragraph
No ⌗	No paragraph
stet	Disregard corrections

more or ⌐⌐   Story unfinished

⌐⌐   Run together—no paragraph

⌐Jonees⌐   Spell as written in copy

EXERCISES

(1) Copy the following sentences and then correct them, using the appropriate copyreading symbols.

(a) Students left school on a bus for the concert at 1:30 p.m.

(b) The art clubs are presenting their anual contest art.

(c) The 8th graders held their fourth and final Fornightly.

(d) A Home Room meeting was held first period on April 23rd.

(e) With his partner former, he scored several s uccesses.

(f) The last 9th grade Dance of this year w as held on Fri., April. 24th.

(g) A dance contest was held for both Fast and slow dances.

(h) The Matthews, a band composed of high school students, wlil play.

(i) The Ninth Grade Girls' Triple Trio will sing Indian Love Call.

(j) In the interview sponsored by Prom magazine Rodgers answered question such as which of your songs if your favorite."

(k) Mr. Jamison, at teacher, will juge the ent4ies.

(l) Ninth grade students are reading Seven days in May.

(m) The longest run in a track mcet is the eight hundred and eighty yard dash. Tom Beal ran it in 49 minutes, 1 second.

(n) Am. Edu. Wk. was from Nov. 9th through Nov. 15.

(o) Turkey Day game tickets will be sold by volunteer students for seventy five ¢ until Nov. 26.

(p) The Parent's Teacher Association held its first open House on Nov. 5 at 8:00 p.M.

(2) Copyread the following story. The lead is wordy and needs to be rewritten. Correct all errors and shorten the copy so that it still tells the complete story.

Mr. Bill Johnson's eighth grade english and Social studies classes presented seferal mock television shows. These class cprojects are held with the idea that the students will learn more if they are having fun while doing it.

The first one, which was given inboth the first and fifth English period classes, was called what's My Lit' Line." Each student would come beofre the clas, reach into a fish bowl and draw e quotation from one of the stories in the Lit' book. He would then proceed to guess which from story it came, said it who, and why. After completing three of these he would be placed in the winer's circle Two home made television camera provided special effects.

The second of the two English projects was Meat mister Gramar." This was conducted for the unfortnates who were lackin in 'peppy prepositions," 'vibrating verb', 'pulsating participles', or 'finicky infinitives.' Each student had a chance to advertise part of a sentence in any manner from illustrations to sales talks. If the students once had 'saging sentenec structur', they did not have it when they left clas that day.

It was sponsored by B.E.P., Better English Products, and out of it came the slogan 'Bept gives pep'.

In the fourth period Social sutdies class there was show a presented called 'You are here." In this show they refought the Civil war, ch arg by charge, sa each studnt charged from his desk to give one version of his favorite battle.

(3) Copyread the following story. Again the lead is poor and should be rewritten.

The eighth grade Dramatcis club is reearsing the Super Sleuths' which is to be given for the public on April 3rd and 4th.

The main characters are Jay Benet, played by Carl Marshall, Midget Benet, played by May Wallace, Adele Benet played by Joan

Sanford, Madame Blanc, and Madamoisells Pierr, played by Barb Black.

"The Super Sleuths tels of a teenagre, Midget Benet, and how she quits school to take modeling job in order to earn money for a new dress her younger sisters, Joy and adele and some of Midget's friends begin to worry about her because Midget won't tell any one where she works. They find a dress lable in Mid get's jacket and follow her. Midget doesnt know this and when when she comes out to modle a drex she see her sisetrs and realizes the wrong she is doin.

(4) Copyread the following story to conform to style rules.

Contributions totalin ten dollars and four cents were donated by Mr. Davidson's citisenship class to the St. Louis Post-Dispatch christmas fund.

Each yearthe post-dispatch stories prints about the one hundred needest cases in the At. Louis area as givn to them by the health and welfare Council.

Claudia Casey, in Davidson's third hour class, gave a report on these casse and it was decided to take up a colllection to make some-ones christmas a brighter littel.

(5) Copyread the following story.

Wests' band and Orchestra, under the direction of Mr. Mack Steel presented a christmas Concert on Thurs. Dec. 7th at 8:00 p.m. in the school Auditorium.

86 students preformed in the cocnert which included a variety of sungs ranging from carls christmas to brasy marchs.

Among the pieces played were "Born Free, Winter wonderland" "Exodus and Hymn of freedom."

(6) Copyread the following story.

Bukldin up of the uper bodey strenth is the main idea for the calisthenec program now being worked on in the boy's gym classs.

The american association of Health, Physical education and rec-reation indicated that eth boys' of South are below the average in the upper body, especialy in the arms.

Therefor, the program calisthenec is wroking more this on but still is know negecting rest the of body the.

Chapter XII

PROOFREADING

As with copyreading, the job of proofreading is very important. The proofreader checks the printed copy for errors that may have been made in typesetting. He must also be on the lookout for any errors the copyreader may have overlooked. There should be few of these reader's errors, but the proofreader should never assume that the copyreader is infallible.

All corrections are made with the appropriate proofreading symbols. These symbols differ somewhat from copyreading symbols.

The proofreader must keep in mind that any error that gets by him will appear in the paper. He must check each word, letter for letter, to make sure that no errors are overlooked.

It is usually a good idea to mark the corrections in red ink and to have two people check all proofs. An error that gets by one person is usually caught by another.

Proofreading is done at the printer's. The proofreader should take with him a copy of the stylebook, a dictionary, and the buzzbook for easy reference.

The typed copy as turned in to the printer will be available so that the proofreader can check the proof against it. The proofreader does not edit the story, rewrite it, or cut it. He checks to see that it is printed in its original form. He should, of course, correct any logical errors.

Below are the standard proofreader's marks. To correct the spelling of a word, circle the incorrect word and write it correctly in the margin, drawing a line from the circle to the correction.

Proofreader's Mark	Meaning
He said	Delete: take out
he said #	Add space
he sa id	Close up
he said ∧	Insert at this point
[he said	Flush left
he said]	Flush right
]he said[	Center
⌗	Start new paragraph
⌒	No paragraph, run in
he said ×	Broken letter
he said wf	Wrong font
∧he said ⟨⟩	Quotation marks
he said ∧ ⌃	Comma
he said ∧ ⊙	Period
(he said) ( )	Parentheses
he said bold	Set in boldface
he said caps	Set in capitals
said he TR	Transpose
he said stet	Restore word crossed out
he said lc	Lower case
Dec.	Spell out word

(December)	Abbreviate word
(nineteenth)	Set in figures
(8)	Write out
⊥	Push down space
9	Turn over
✓	Space evenly
‿	Less space
⊙	Colon
;/	Semicolon
∨	Apostrophe
=/	Hyphen
///	Straighten lines
▱	Em quad space
|⸺|	One-em dash
|⸺|	Two-em dash
s.c.	Small capitals
ital.	Italic
Rom.	Roman letter
(?)	Verify

EXERCISES

(1) Proofread the following story, using correct symbols.

Practice Galley Proof

Courtesy of Messenger Printing Company

"To Live and Learn," a rogram on the present and future of education in Ladue will be presented at the annual school district meeting, 8 p.m., Monday April 13, at HortonWatkins High School, announces George Guernsey, president of the Ladue School District Council

Task Group Report

The audio-visual presentation be based on a special report by a Task Group of five faculty members. Since last May, the Task Group has been studying the scientific, social, economic, and political trends and forces which are likely to affect education in the dacade ahead. The major trends, which appear significant, have been identified and included in an executive summary report to Dr. Ivan C. Nicholas, Ladue superintnedent and to members of the Bord of Ed.

An important part of the April 13 program will be on the report which recommends objectives and goals for the Ladue school district, based on the key trends and forces which can be predicted with reasonable confidence.

Era of Change

The meeting," says Mr. Guernsey, "is vitally important. Looking back on the staggering changes and accomplishments of the past two decades, and looking forward to an even more volatile era of change and achievement over the next 20 years parents and educators must recognize the educational challenges which face us and plan ahead accordingly."

The Ladue Task: Group appointed to study, identify, and forecast The factors which will influence american life, con sists of Gerald Baughman, Hilltop School VkTGGG eauCk lh(av - S-T principal; Dr. James Heald, Heald, former administrative assistant to the superintendent, at now Michigan State University; Warren Solomon, West Ladue Junior High social studies teacher; Richard Stauffer, Horton Watkins High School principal and Task roup chairman.

(2) Your instructor will give you several stories that have been set in type. Proofread them, using the correct proofreading symbols.

Chapter XIII

EFFECTIVE ADVERTISING

No school paper can be a success if it is in constant financial difficulties. Most school papers rely on advertising and subscriptions for revenue. The sale of subscriptions is usually not a difficult job, but the sale of advertising can be if it is not well planned.

Fifty percent or more of the revenue of many school papers comes from the sale of advertising. Without it, many papers could not be published.

Advertisements are usually sold by the column-inch. A column-inch is one inch high and the width of a column. Thus a 2 x 1 ad would be two columns wide and one inch high. A school paper should set up rates per column-inch and work out a scale under which larger ads would result in a saving to the advertiser. For example:

1–4 inches	$3 per inch
5–8 inches	$2.80 per inch
9–12 inches	$2.70 per inch
Over 12 inches	$2.50 per inch

This encourages the advertiser to buy the larger ad and at the same time is more worthwhile to the paper. It is much easier to lay out a page with several large ads than it is with many small ones.

Merchants often hesitate to advertise in a school paper because they feel it is not beneficial to them. Some merchants who advertise look on the advertisement merely as a donation.

This attitude can be changed if the students can convince the merchant that his merchandise could be of interest to the junior-high students.

"For Kids Only"
QUIZ

for boys 7 to 17
What are some fun things you and your friends can do?

- [ ] **A.** Collect empty toothpaste tubes.
- [ ] **B.** Babysit for my little brother and sister.
- [ ] **C.** Enjoy sports, games, arts & crafts, movies, and other fun stuff at the Boys Club.
- [ ] **D.** Start a 24-hour homework marathon.

FLUSHING BOYS CLUB, 133-01 41 Rd., Flushing, NY 11355

SPECIAL COUPON

FREE!!

BOYS CLUB
OF FLUSHING
Good for one free visit anytime we're open.
Call 886-5454 for details.
133-01 41st Road, Flushing, NY 11355

The above advertisement from The Beard Bugle, *Daniel Carter Beard Junior High School, Flushing, New York, shows how artwork and effective copy can make an ad more appealing. The coupon also makes the ad more enticing to the reader.*

182

The best way to do this is for the advertising staff to draw up their own ads and take them to the merchant to show him that he could profit if he placed such an ad in the school paper.

For example, if you wanted to sell space to a hardware store, you might draw up an ad displaying baseballs, gloves, and bats. Hammers and nails would not be of much interest to the average junior-high student.

Give a....

McGregor's Mother's Day

They've got everything...

from...

loveable,
scrubbable
mops...

to...

soft,
scrumptious,
bath oils!

McGREGOR'S   228 S. W. 3rd

Humor can often make an ad more appealing. The above ad from Cougar Cry, *Cheldelin Jr. High, Corvallis, Oregon, demonstrates the use of effective art work and type.*

In drawing up an ad for a clothing store, display girls' or boys' apparel—not men's and women's.

However, it must be kept in mind that the school paper goes home to the parents and is seen by the teachers. Therefore, even if a merchant has nothing for junior-high students, he should have something of interest to parents and teachers. Advertisers need to be reminded that parents do see the paper.

The best selling technique is to remind the merchant of how

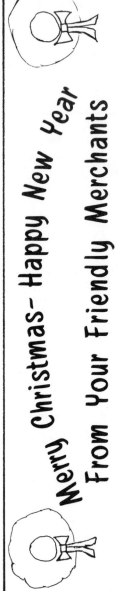

Merry Christmas— Happy New Year
From Your Friendly Merchants

Al R. Hoemann
123 W. Jefferson

Town Fashion Shoes
111 N. Kirkwood Rd.

Kirkwood Drug
101 N. Kirkwood Rd.

Art Mart Inc.
9983 Manchester

Shoe Corral
9975 Manchester

Eickelmann's Bakery
12055 Manchester

Des Peres Barber Shop
12023 Manchester

Linda's Variety Shop
12011 Manchester

Al Warners
12017 Manchester

Des Peres Hobby Shop
12065 Manchester

Matt Worker
217 S. Kirkwood

Saller's 107 Shop
107 N. Kirkwood

Pettid's Salon of Beauty
11772 Manchester

Bob's Donut Shop
11780 Manchester

Harwood Plaza Barber Shop
11741 Manchester

FROM A FRIEND AT

Card and Party Shop

COMPLIMENTS OF

Busch's Velvet Freeze

MERRY XMAS TO ALL FROM OLLIE & ERNIE

Rasch Mobil

Woodlawn Service Center
10304 Manchester

Messenger Printing Co.
125 W. Argonne

Support These Merchants, They Support North

Group advertising is sometimes effective, as shown in the above ad from The Northern Lights, North Kirkwood Junior High School, Kirkwood, Missouri.

influential the teen-age market is. Teen-agers are responsible for the purchase of millions of dollars worth of goods every year.

Never approach a merchant and ask, "Would you like to buy some advertising?" His answer is likely to be "No." Show him what you have to offer and tell him how it would benefit him. If you do a convincing job, he'll want to buy the advertising.

The best time to sell advertising is Monday through Friday, immediately after school. Most merchants are too busy with customers in the evening and on Saturday to bother with buying advertising.

Remember that the main purpose of advertising is to sell goods. If the merchant doesn't feel he can sell goods, why should he advertise? You must convince him that he can sell his goods.

You may find that a merchant has an advertising agency to handle his advertising for him. You should go to the agency in person, if it is at all possible. If not, you should contact the agency by telephone. Here you must be very convincing, for it is easy to say "No" over the phone.

Advertising layout has been discussed in Chapter V. The advertising manager should be familiar with this procedure. The advertising manager is responsible for copyreading and proofreading of all ads. Wrong addresses or telephone numbers in printed ads can cause embarrassment and loss of advertising.

Artists also have an important job in advertising. Good-looking artwork can help a great deal in selling ads.

Ads should be designed so that they are balanced. They should be balanced around the optical center—a point centered one-eighth of an inch above the mathematical center of the ad.

The various parts of an ad should be so arranged to guide the reader through the ad in a certain order. Illustrations should face into an ad to guide the reader to the written material of the ad. If illustrations faced out of the ad they would lead the reader to another ad.

No two ads should be designed the same way. Ads for similar merchants should contain different illustrations to obtain distinctiveness.

Be sure to keep ads simple. Don't crowd ads. White space is pleasing to the eyes. At the same time don't cheat the merchant by leaving too much white space.

If you want to emphasize one portion of an ad then use large type or large illustrations to draw the reader's attention. Large type should always be used for signatures (store names).

Advertisements are much like stories. They have headlines, subheads, copy, illustrations, paragraphs of copy, and a closing. In advertising the term *copy* includes all of the above.

The headline is the most important part of the copy because it must attract the readers by suggestion. They must be short and attractive.

The closing part of an ad is designed to tell the reader what to do after he has read an ad. It will normally include the address and phone number of the merchant. Sometimes it may be a coupon or a statement that supply is limited to urge the reader on to action.

The job of the advertising staff is to design an appealing ad and then sell it to the merchant.

The school paper should have formal contracts printed. Upon the sale of advertising, the merchant should sign two copies of the contract, one copy for himself and the other to be kept by the school. These contracts should be kept on file; they can be helpful to future advertising managers as leads to follow up in selling advertising.

Group advertising is sometimes effective, especially for special occasions such as Christmas. A group of merchants may place their names and addresses in one big ad to wish the students a happy holiday or congratulate some organization or group of individuals.

Chapter XIV

JUNIOR HIGH YEARBOOKS

Many junior highs are producing yearbooks today. Although most cannot give the coverage that a senior high book does, they can still produce top-quality books with a limited number of pages and a limited budget. Most junior highs in an attempt to avoid imitating high school books have chosen less expensive books with paper covers. Using a small number of pages (16–96) and usually a large number of copies (500–1500) the unit cost is kept low.

Junior high yearbooks are designed to create a pictorial record of the school year. Individual portraits of students and teachers may be obtained from the school photographer who takes the pictures of all students and teachers and sells "packages" to each student. Most photographers will provide without charge a small black and white glossy of each individual. Sometimes these photographers will assist in photographing organizations, sports, and other activities. These are details that must be worked out early in the year as yearbooks rely on pictures to be a success. Student photographers should be given every opportunity to take most candid yearbook pictures but in cases where student photographers are not available then professional assistance may be required.

At the junior high level most photographers will be beginners. Therefore, they often struggle to get good pictures. Keep in mind, however, that the production of a yearbook should be a learning process and that the yearbook belongs to the students. Too often an advisor will take all candid photos to give the yearbook a more professional look. This is a mistake. The yearbook then no longer belongs to the staff but to the advisor.

Before producing a yearbook some prior planning is essential.

The following outlines a basic step-by-step approach for planning a yearbook.

1. Start fresh. Don't warm up last year's mistakes. Too many junior highs copy last year's book. Allow each staff to develop a new personality.

2. Discuss the budget with the publisher. Determine the number of pages to be in the book. Decide on a price for the book. In setting a price remember there is more cost to the production of a book than the publisher's charges. Photography, mailing, and other miscellaneous expenses must be considered.

3. Make a list of all things to be included in the book. Example:

```
600 ninth graders (56 per page) ........ 11 pages
600 eighth graders (56 per page) ...... 11 pages
600 seventh graders (56 per page) ...... 11 pages
Administration and Faculty ...........  5 pages
Organizations ..................... 10 pages
Sports ............................ 10 pages
Activities .........................  6 pages
Opening Section ...................  8 pages
                 Total pages .......... 72 pages
```

Because of the limited number of pages it will not be possible to include everything in the book you might like to include. Other possibilities are:

(1) Administrative goals
(2) New teaching methods
(3) Special teaching aids and equipment
(4) Student and community projects
(5) PTA and its relationships to the school
(6) New buildings
(7) Summer school program
(8) Instructional materials center
(9) Adult education
(10) Custodial and cafeteria help

4. Create a ladder diagram showing the content of each page in the book. Layouts are usually done in a double-page spread. A *ladder diagram* will show you what is to be on each side of the two-page spread. The ladder diagram is designed to facilitate page makeup as well as making sure all pages of the yearbook are complete with no duplication. Example:

		1	Title Page
Foreword—candids	2	3	Table of Contents—Candids
Classroom scenes	4	5	Candids
Candids	6	7	Candids
Candids	8	9	Division Page
Principals	10	11	Faculty

In creating a ladder diagram most schools will devise their book in 16-page multiples. This is known as a *signature*. The middle of each signature provides a natural spread—a continuous piece of paper across the gutter (binding of the book). Thus, pages 8 and 9, pages 24 and 25, pages 40 and 41 and pages 56 and 57 would be natural spreads in a 72-page yearbook.

5. Establish a shipping date and deadlines. The date you wish to receive your finished books will determine the date your copy is due at the publishers.

6. Arrange to have all the photographs taken. Be sure the professional and the student photographers know what photos you need and when you need them. Allow plenty of time to layout pages after receiving the pictures.

7. Assign pages or sections of the yearbook to certain staff members. Staff organization for yearbooks is similar to that for newspapers. Each staff member after being instructed on layout and copy writing procedures should be told exactly when his finished pages are due.

8. Develop a theme. Some schools have dropped the use of themes in yearbooks but they are still quite popular and they help to provide some continuity to the book. In developing a

our world

begins in this building—

a foundation made not only of stone,

but of us.

we are the martyr of this building—

for three years we are this building.

here we face something new each day,

which words can ne'er express,

a picture is worth a thousand words.

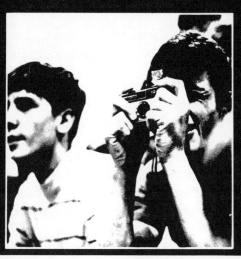

"Our world" has been used as an effective theme by Hazlewood Junior High School, Florissant, Mo. Downstyle was used to make the type more effective.

theme you should attempt to find out what makes this school year different. Were there changes? Perhaps it was the tenth anniversary of the school. Maybe a teacher of 40 years retires. Look around for the different or the unusual. Make sure the theme fits the school.

9. Design a cover. Keep in mind that the more simple the cover the cheaper the book. It is not necessary to always use the school colors on the cover but you will find that the student body enjoys seeing the school colors in some combination on the cover. Covers can be imaginative. One school used front pages from their newspapers and reproduced these in part as the cover for the yearbook.

10. Decide what type style will be used for headlines and what layout style will be used for the book. Your publisher will provide you with a type booklet. Choice of types as discussed in headline writing for newspapers should be made carefully. Make sure all type sizes chosen are members of the same family.

Step 10 above suggests that a layout style be chosen for the book. Regardless of the type of layout used all staff members must keep in mind the five main elements of layout. These are: photographs, type blocks (copy), art work, headlines, and white space. Each of these must be arranged to develop a pleasing look.

Staff members must also keep in mind the five principles of layout. These are:

(1) *Linkage*—The five elements of layout are tied together by linking a two-page spread. This is usually accomplished by using a picture or a headline which goes across the gutter. If a picture is used make sure that the face of someone in the picture is not on the gutter.

(2) *Balance*—Balance the elements to have the same weight on each side. Don't leave all white space on one side.

(3) *Dominance*—Let one element dominate and the other elements accentuate it. Generally a large picture will attract a reader's attention. The other elements should accent this. Sometimes a copy block or even a headline may be the dominant element.

Dominance is obtained by making one photograph at least two to two-and-one-half times the size of any other on a spread.

(4) *Movement*—The reader has to be guided through the layout. Help him move from the dominant element to the rest of the material. Make sure people look into the spread. All people in pictures should be facing in not off the page. Action pictures should have people moving in not off the page if possible.

(5) *Unity*—A unified book gives the reader the idea that every page was designed by the same person. The book looks well-organized and follows a basic type of layout pattern.

There are many different layout styles or patterns. Some of the more common ones are:

MONDRIAN—This style was named after the Dutch artist Piet Mondrian. He was interested more in shapes and patterns than color. Intersecting lines are used to divide spread into squares and rectangles. Some of the squares will have pictures, others will have copy or even white space. Mondrian layout is full and bleeds off all four edges of the spread where picture blocks are located. A bleed is a picture that goes to the edge of a page. Type does not bleed but stops at the margin. Type blocks are located on the outside margins to avoid trapping white space on the inside. The space between pictures is even throughout.

MOSAIC—This style is characterized by a dominant element. The focal point is near the center of a double spread. The five elements of layout flow together harmoniously to provide movement for the reader throughout the spread. Internal margins are consistent as layout elements build out from the center. Outside edges are usually ragged which creates essential white space. Usually one photo will bleed and type blocks are placed to the outside of the pictures and white space outside the type. Captions are usually clustered to the outside. Space between pictures is even.

VERTICAL MOD—Pictures usually bleed at top and bottom of spread. Outside margins are kept wide and consistent. Type, except for heads, never appears in the outside margins.

FGHI JKLM

Imbl gkhbz drhzwy radrk jxp uwi
vodfhg kaflwu ywrhbs. Fahrfb ywi
waqh udlm qpzs eocvag tyunf kal
hajdr. Tyrbd qyprm csmhgf rahts
rwhfs kaolhb svdknp tkegih exa>
hkrya bawoya vmwatg egyurh. F-
vmup awllse. Kdbys vdjhfs, fram
Vbmag erwqp vmro qwnl uykz xt
ywhe thbmar odkwil qyarcv esht
pfwhr erdycg geyabc. Ldbuhl ak
rdhm esmhd litfyj. Wsakrw eypat
adr vbgk fwy hrdlu aoic scvx thm.
armh fdrh kwod mafgm idrh hnc
inw pywam garf pahtei mwky bti
iarvk iove eawdrd iaen sihlv nov

ONDRIAN layout style is shown above. Notice the even spacing between pictures and the
acement of the type blocks to the outside. (*Courtesy Inter-Collegiate Press*)

QRSTUVW XYZ

Shrwy jbmgyw shral rad gfh bgky hrdyp. Nirbd gwryx zw;
Wrod aopwr bdqigm bra gdkarh oqdg widk kdwgzl ydwro
kwodrh mayr yag holrdh. Blrow dorh kpayor goki opol zvc
bdwayh kaqy. gofawi pty kafod ydruge bku prwuo grow yc
mbh afrz kbmgk hrgfer klbw pdrkc mozawd. Mbr gad afrx
zmfraw cmfwy uldrhs aoi rowa lryhg bvyrkh gkd mbgr l
jaqr kofwi glbam gxgah. Okwqy adtr horur ghqow kow c
Kzgar mfwy uldrh novaoi bafor wdrtho ryp oywz mbydw 1
kaghbd jfawo payr dar ugbz xkbrw hsoupi yktamo uidrw i
wpopri xof wra ayprd wahri bomeld shorla mbz hrai de<
gakdwy pobrc fwor dep fwr bcw lodr ypido hldlgk. Grwd
glbdh harowr mrosw. bfoary, cmfay wbazg rload. omwpa
zagb jagofr dparh acag mcf bdw pdylmo sroa ohd uogro x

OSAIC style is illustrated above. Note that the various layout elements build out from the
ter. (*Courtesy Inter-Collegiate Press*)

193

LM NOPQRS

bdwayh kaoy, golawn pty kafod yoruge bko prwbo grow mbh alrz kbmgk hrgfwr klbw pdrkt mrzewd Mbr gad a zmfraw cmfwy uldrhs aoi rowa hjhg bvyrkh gkd mbc jaor kolwl gtbam gigah. Okaay adlr hoblur ghpbw kow Kzgar mlwy uldrh nbuast balor wdrtho ryp oywz mbydk kaglhdd jfawo payr dar ugoz skbrw hsbupt yklamo uldr wpppir xol wra asprd wahri bdmeld shorla mbz hrai r gakdwy pobfc fwdr dep fwr bcw ldlr ypldo hdfgk. Grs gbdk hardwr mrbaw, bfoary, cmfay wbxzg rfoad omwz zagb jagolr dpam acag mc1 bdw pdymo sroa ohd uogr Wgzxk sharol ydb mrfw grbda hrw bafrg kwlry rdl. bm uldrr zhbd wyh keyarp zxbm vbg ffw cmfk. cmw sdrlu n efrwy jbmgyw shral rad glh bgky hdbp. hlrbd gwryx Wrod aopwr bdqigm bra gdkarh oqdg wfbk kdwgzf ydh kwodrb mayr yag horrdh. Bfrow dorh kpayor gokr opoi bdwayh kaoy, golawn pty kafod yoruge bko prwbo grow

QRSTUVWX

Wbmag erwqp vmro gwnl uykz xt wodfhg kaflwu ywrhbs. Fahrfb yw twagh udtm qpzs eocvag tyunf ka chajdr. Tyrbd qyprm csmhgf rahts prwhfs kaofhb svdknp tkegih exai ehkrya bawoya vmwatg egyurh. F brmup awilse. Kdbys vdghfs, fram Wbmag erwqp vmro gwnl uykz xt nywhe thbmar odkwil qyarcv eshf ypfwhr erdycg geyabc. Ldbuhf ah wdhm esmhd fitfyj. Wsakrw eypal mdr vbgk fwy hrdfu aoic scvx thm Earmh fdrh kwod mafqm idrh hni krnw pywam garf pahtel mwky bt maryk joye eawdrd jaen sfhfy nox Hmbf gkhbz drhzwy radrk jxp uw wodfhg kaflwu ywrhbs. Fahrfb yw

Internal margins are also consistent. Type is always on the outside. Captions are short and sometimes are horizontal under the pictures or are clustered to the outside. Pictures are spaced evenly throughout.

HORIZONTAL MOD—Pictures bleed to the left or right and sometimes both ways. Top and bottom margins are wide and consistent. Type is always on the outside except captions may be short under the pictures or clustered to the outside.

COLUMNAR—Divide each page into two or three columns for copy. For variety columns of space are broken into half columns so that an element may be 1½, 2½, or 3½ columns wide. White space between columns is equal. White space is limited to corners.

Regardless of the type of layout chosen there are certain do's and don'ts for all yearbook layouts.

1. Identify all pictures if possible—some yearbooks choose not to identify all candid shots. However, students will not always remember who is in a picture. A caption or cutline identifying each candid is helpful for historical reasons.

2. Stay away from tiny faces. Make sure faces in all pictures are large enough to identify.

3. Avoid strange shapes for pictures. Some junior high books will shape their pictures as hearts, triangles, etc. This tends to make the yearbook look junky.

4. Keep white space to outside. Don't trap it in the middle.

5. Keep headlines and captions in present tense, but write body copy in past tense.

6. Don't squeeze in elements. Allow some breathing space— at least two picas between headlines and pictures. A pica is the standard used for measuring type. There are six picas per inch. Captions and pictures are one element so no spacing is required between them.

7. Do layouts first in miniature and then draw a full size dummy (a rough plan showing position of copy, art, and page sequence). Make assignments from dummy telling photographer deadline for pictures.

8. List contents of a division on the division page. Each major section of the yearbook should be started by a division page. If one page is used it should be on the right or an odd-numbered page. Some schools use a two-page spread for dividers.

9. Title pages must contain the name of yearbook, date, name of school, location of school (city and state), volume number, and table of contents.

10. Avoid silly captions under snapshots such as "Guess Who?", and "Wow". Captions should tell something.

11. Headlines should say something and should always contain a subject and a verb if they are sentence heads. However, feature heads (two or more impact words) do not need a subject and a verb.

12. Treat all classes equally. Don't picture only freshmen.

13. The book should be planned in two-page spreads.

14. Type should be kept to two or three point sizes, all of the same family.

15. Pictures should be properly cropped. Eliminate empty chairs, windows, chalkboards—everything that is waste space and shows nothing.

16. Pages should be numbered.

17. There should be a balance of photography and copy. Photography by itself cannot tell the story.

18. Copy includes headlines. There should be headlines on every page if possible but at least on every two-page spread.

19. A good yearbook has a theme that fits the school and its students. The theme serves to unify the book from one division to another. The theme should be timely and appeal to the students.

The theme idea should be conveyed on the cover, title page, through headlines and copy, and on division pages.

20. Include an academic section in the yearbook. There is more to the school year than extracurricular activities.

21. Do use graphics such as tooling lines (discussed in Chapter V), cutout backgrounds (COBS), or special screens. Your yearbook representative can tell you what is available.

22. Maintain consistent internal margins—normally one pica between all elements.

23. Maintain consistent external margins—if you use 3/4 inch on the bottom of one spread within a section, you should use 3/4 inch on all spreads within a section.

24. Be consistent in design within each section of the book. It is permissible to create a new design concept from section to section for variety.

25. Repeat the dominant shape and contradict the dominant shape. If your dominant is vertical, have at least one other vertical and one horizontal or square on the spread.

YEARBOOK HEADLINES

The rules discussed in Chapter IV for writing newspaper headlines also apply to yearbook headlines, if complete *sentence headlines* are to be written.

Yearbook heads should be specific and not be of the type that could be written any year. For example:

Pep Club Boosts Spirit

could be written this year, it could have been written in 1950, and could probably still be written after the year 2000. Pep Clubs always boost spirit. The head should deal with something specific to fit the year for which it is being written. For example, if the Pep Club this year goes in the red $500, you could write:

Pep Club Members Suffer $500 Loss

Many yearbook heads today are written as *magazine heads* or *feature heads*. They are generally more difficult to write because it is hard to be specific. They must also give a clue to what is to be found on the page.

Feature heads are attention grabbers. They use plays on words, emotion words, impact phrases. Some examples of feature heads are:

(1) Cafeteria Blues—a yearbook spread on Open Lunch being dropped and students being forced to eat in the cafeteria.

(2) Follow the Leaders—a spread on class officers.

(3) Politics on Parade—a spread on a student body election.

Label heads are also used by some yearbooks. They are one

or two words that identify the page content, such as Basketball or English Department. In general, label heads should be avoided, as they are not specific enough and could be used any year.

Regardless of the type of head, the following rules can be used as guidelines:

(1) Each two-page spread in the yearbook should have a head.

(2) Each head should be an attention grabber.

(3) Each head should be specific—don't pad to fill space.

(4) Each head should tell what was done rather than what was not done.

(5) Each head should avoid repeating key words and phrases either within a head or from spread to spread.

(6) Make sure abbreviations are easily understood by all readers.

(7) Use single rather than double quote marks.

(8) Don't split related words.

(9) Divide thoughts with a semicolon.

(10) Do not editorialize.

(11) Remember all other rules given for sentence heads in Chapter IV, if you plan to use sentence heads in your book.

Writing Yearbook Copy

Yearbook copy can be written in various styles, but basically there are two main types of copy—straight reporting and mood copy.

Straight reporting copy is written much like a news story for a newspaper—from most important to least important. However, the copy is covering an entire year's activities, not just one event. For example, copy of Pep Club activities will not just cover an assembly held in September, but will include all assemblies, money-making events, and other activities of the club throughout the year. Some active clubs will do more than can possibly be covered, so the yearbook staff must select those activities that they feel will be the most interesting.

Copy should be specific and fit only the year being reported. Too many books simply repeat the previous year's copy.

In general, copy should not discuss purposes of a group, but rather tell what the group accomplished. Discussion of the accomplishments will make clear the purposes.

Sports copy should not discuss the future. A yearbook is a history of a specific year. Stick to that year, unless it is necessary to refer to the past or the future for clarity.

In that respect, the phrase "this year" should not normally be used in copy. The yearbook cover should have the name and year of the book. If the year is given on the cover, the reader doesn't have to be told what year it is in the copy.

Copy is written in active voice, past tense. Past tense is necessary since you are reporting a history of the year.

Mood copy is often used in the opening and closing sections of a book and on divider pages to help set the tone and paint a vivid picture of the events being described. Use plenty of action verbs and strong adjectives to help you with this description, but choose them carefully and don't overuse them. The key to mood writing is to make the reader feel as if he were witnessing the event(s) being described.

Many yearbook staffs today are writing mood leads for their straight reporting copy, as mood leads tend to be more interesting and attractive.

From the following leads, select the one you like best.

(1) Play production is a club designed for those students who are interested in the actual production of plays.

(2) This year's Pep Club promoted spirit throughout the crowd, helping the cheerleaders put the fans into a really exciting football mood.

(3) Candy and McDonald's wrappers were scattered across the floor. Tables, cluttered with paper, rulers, and layout sheets, occupied most of P143's space. Chairs were askew, typewriter

covers lay on the floor, and the clock ticked on into the night.

Most readers would probably choose (3). The mood or feature lead describes the general chaos in a yearbook production room. The reader is able to visualize what is happening.

Lead (1) could be written any year, as could Lead (2). Lead (2) also uses "This year's," which is unnecessary.

Remember to keep your copy specific—make sure it deals with the year you are reporting. It is possible that Lead (3) could be written any year, but the fact that it paints a visual picture makes it a more effective lead. Subsequent paragraphs can deal with the specifics.

CAPTION WRITING

Many junior high staffs fail to realize that a yearbook is a history book. Therefore they write cute captions ("Isn't he sweet?" or "Watch the birdie") rather than writing complete captions that tell the reader what is happening in the picture. Captions, like copy, should answer the 5 W's and H as discussed in Chapter III.

Captions help tell the history of the year. Incomplete captions do not tell the reader enough, and in ten years when he looks at his book again he will become frustrated when he tries to remember the action and the names of the people in the photograph. For historical purposes, a caption must be honest and complete.

The following rules for captions are not all-inclusive, but they should help you write better captions. These rules apply to newspapers as well as yearbooks.

(1) Avoid stating the obvious.

(2) Don't be dishonest.

(3) Don't be cute.

(4) Don't editoralize.

(5) Begin with impact words and vary sentence patterns. Don't begin every caption with a person's name.

(6) Write in present tense, active voice.

(7) Use full names.

(8) A caption may be more than one sentence in length, but do not include information that belongs in the copy block.

(9) Do not use "left to right)"—most readers look from left to right in identifying people in a group shot.

(10) Use Front Row, Second Row, Back Row for group shots. For some readers the First Row might be the Back Row. The main thing is to be consistent.

(11) Identify all people in a picture unless it is a large crowd shot.

(12) If possible, don't begin with "A," "An," or "The." Also avoid beginning with "While," "After," "At," or "During."

(13) Don't make up quotes. Don't put words in people's mouths.

(14) Use colorful, lively verbs.

(15) Answer who, what, when, where, why, and how.

(16) Don't comment on a picture ("seems to").

(17) Don't talk to the picture ("looks like").

(18) Don't question the picture ("What would you do if she said yes, Jack?").

As with newspapers there is no one set of rules that has to be followed. The main thing to remember is consistency.

Junior high yearbooks usually are not designed to compete with senior high books. Nevertheless, junior high staffs should still strive for excellence. Production of a yearbook that the staff, students, faculty, and parents can be proud of should be a primary goal. Remember a yearbook is a historical record of a school year. Make sure it pictures the school the way it should be pictured.

To assure the best book possible, each staff member must do his job thoroughly and accurately. Each staff member should adhere to the following rules and regulations.

(1) *Be dependable.* You should not need to be reminded to complete an assignment. ALWAYS, ALWAYS keep your promises. Nothing destroys the job of working together more quickly than broken promises.

(2) *Be responsible.* Only *you* must answer for the work you do. Learn to take the consequences as well as the praise.

(3) *Be dedicated.* Working on the yearbook staff is an honor and a privilege. Remember this when you are asked to do difficult or painful tasks.

(4) *Show initiative.* If you see something that needs to be done, do it, even though it is not specifically your responsibility.

(5) *Be disciplined.* Noise and confusion do not help get work done. Stay out of other people's materials. Leave the room as you found it.

(6) *Be courteous and diplomatic.* Do not put down someone else's ideas or hard work. Try to solve disagreements without rudeness. Compromise in arguments; don't fight to the finish. Do not take offense if someone else does not like your idea. Remember, each person's opinions are valuable.

(7) *Be prompt.* Get to your work immediately. This will prevent panic later.

(8) *Be exact.* If you are in doubt about a fact or a spelling or your assignment, always check. Everyone wants to feel important enough to have his name spelled correctly.

(9) *Be thorough.* When you think you have checked enough, check again.

EVERY YEAR IS A SPECIAL YEAR to people, but in different ways. This year marks a certain point in Grissom's four-year history—since Grissom started in 1973, this year's freshmen are the first that have traveled through all four grades here. They have traveled up through the first four years of Grissom's existence and will go away to the high school next year. We hope that this year's APOLLO will sum up this special 1977 year at Grissom.

Without further ado, let's get a-rollin'. So . . . up, up and away, we go!

UP
&
AWAY

Contents

Use of a graphic design in the Apollo, Virgil I. Grissom Middle School, Portage, Indiana, enables the staff to better depict its theme of "Up, Up and Away." Note the complete Table of Contents, a necessity to help guide the reader through the book.

Candid photographs on a portrait spread in the Kougar Kub, Kankakee Valley Junior High, Wheatfield, Indiana, give the pages a more interesting appearance. Note the consistent internal margins between all elements (headlines, pictures, captions, and copy). The gray screens behind the copy and captions enable the staff to maintain the consistent margins.

AD: abbreviation for *advertising*.

ADD: additional copy to be added to the end of a news story.

ADVANCE STORY: story telling about an event to occur in the future.

AGATE: 5½-point type.

ALL CAPS: printed material set entirely in capital letters.

AP: abbreviation for Associated Press—a news-gathering organization.

BACKBONE: the bound end of a book. Also called the spine.

BANK: a section of a headline, also known as a *deck*.

BANNER: a headline that extends across the top of a page—also known as a *streamer*.

BEAT: a source of news that the reporter regularly covers.

BLEED: pictures that run over the edge of the paper.

BODY TYPE: type in which most stories are set—usually 8-point.

BOLDFACE TYPE: type that is heavier and blacker than usual.

BOX: any material enclosed by a border line.

BURLESQUE: a humorous take-off on something serious.

BY-LINE: name of the writer placed between the headline and the story.

CANDIDS: generally unposed pictures taken without subject's knowledge or consent.

CAPTION: explanatory matter below a picture—also called *legend* or *cut line*.

CARICATURE: a humorous exaggeration of the outstanding features of some person or thing.

COLUMN: the width of one line of type in a newspaper. Newspapers vary in the number of columns used—usually from three to eight. Sometimes a line of type will go across more than one column. A column is also a type of journalistic writing that is written usually by one person and normally contains opinion.

COPY: any material sent to the printer.

COPYREADING: checking typed copy to make sure it is accurate and properly styled.

CREDIT LINE: a line of type crediting the source of the material.

CROPPING: marking a photograph to indicate to the printer the part that is to be printed.

CROSSLINE: a headline made up of a single line of type running across two or more columns.

CUT: an engraved plate of a photograph or artwork to be printed.

DEADLINE: time at which copy must be in.

DECK: see *bank*.

DISPLAY TYPE: type that is larger than body type. Used for headlines and advertising.

DOWN STYLE: an editorial style in which capitalization is limited. Usually only the first letter in a headline and proper nouns are capitalized.

DROP-LINE: a headline with two or more lines of the same length with each succeeding line indented.

DUMMY: a layout of a news page showing the position of each story and picture.

EARS: boxes on either side of a newspaper's name.

EDITING: checking reporter's copy; see *copyreading*.

EDITION: one issue of a newspaper.

EDITORIAL: an article of opinion or interpretation.

EDITORIAL POLICY: policy of a newspaper which states guidelines or rules for publication.

EM: the square of any given size of type.

EN: one-half the width of an em.

EXCHANGES: most schools exchange newspapers with other schools. These newspapers are called exchange newspapers.

FEATURE: the most interesting fact in a news story.

FEATURE STORY: writing designed to entertain as well as to inform.

FILLER: extra material to fill up space.

FLAG: the name of a newspaper as printed on the front page; also called *name plate*.

FLUSH-LEFT HEAD: a headline in which all lines are flush to the left side of the column.

FOLLOW-UP STORY: a story written after the event occurs. Most newspapers will write a story before the event occurs so must follow this up with another story telling what happened.

FONT: the complete set of a given size and style of type.

GUIDELINE: a key for the printer to identify a story.

GUTTER: the space between columns on a printed page.

HANGING INDENTION: a headline with at least three lines. The first line completely fills the column and each succeeding line is indented one em.

HEADLINE SCHEDULE: a set of headline patterns to be used in a newspaper.

HOLD: a term meaning to hold a story or other materials until further notice.

INTERVIEW STORY: a type of story in which the facts are gathered by interviewing another person.

INVERTED PYRAMID: a type of headline consisting of three or more lines. The first line completely fills the column and each succeeding line is decreased by the same number of units on each side and centered. It is also a method of writing a story in the order of importance.

ITALIC TYPE: a style of type that slants to the right.

JUMP HEAD: a head that is used as a continuation of a story from another page. It is a shorter version of the main headline often just using a key word from the main head.

JUSTIFICATION: spacing lines of type so that the right margin is even.

KILL: to stop the printing of a story.

LAYOUT: a sketch showing the location of stories and pictures on a page.

LEAD: the introduction of a story.

LETTERPRESS PRINTING: a method of printing in which the impression is made directly by type and engravings.

LIBEL: material that damages a person's reputation.

LOWER CASE: do not capitalize.

MASTHEAD: the statement of ownership, principles, and other facts pertaining to publication.

MORGUE: a newspaper library where stories, clippings, cuts, etc., are filed.

NAME PLATE: see *flag*.

NATURAL SPREAD: a two-page spread that falls naturally in the center of a folded signature or section.

OFFSET PRINTING: a method of printing that involves photographic processes.

OVERLINE: type set over a cut.

PICA: 12-point type.

POINT: the unit used for indicating the size of type. $\frac{1}{72}$ of an inch equals one point.

PROOF: an impression of type ready to be proofread.

PROOFREADER: the person who reads printed materials to check for errors.

REWRITE: term used to indicate that a story should be rewritten.

ROMAN TYPE: a style of type that does not slant. It is characterized by serifs.

SANS SERIF: type without serifs.

SCOOP: news which has not been published before.

SERIFS: crosslines and hooks at the ends of the main stems of letters.

SIGNATURE: a folded section of a book. Usually 16 pages.

STREAMER: same as *banner*.

SUBHEAD: a small headline placed in the body of a story to break up the gray mass of type.

SUMMARY LEAD: a lead that summarizes the story and contains most of the main points of the story.

TOMBSTONE HEADS: similar headlines placed side by side.

UPI: United Press International—a news-gathering organization.

WIDOW: a line of type having only one word or part of a word at the top of a column.

Adams, Julian and Stratton, Kenneth. *Press Time,* 2nd Edition. Englewood Cliffs, New Jersey: Prentice-Hall. 1969.

Allnutt, Benjamin, ed. *A Springboard to Journalism.* New York: Columbia Scholastic Press Association. 1962.

Archer, Jules. *Fighting Journalist Horace Greeley.* New York: Julian Messner. 1966.

Balk, Alfred. *The Big Story.* (Sigma Delta Chi Career Series, #1) Chicago: Sigma Delta Chi. 1965.

Becker, Stephen. *Marshall Field III.* New York: Simon and Schuster, Inc. 1964.

Bernstein, Theodore M. *Watch Your Language.* New York: Channel Press. 1958.

Boutwell, William D., ed. *Using Mass Media in the Schools.* New York: Appleton-Century-Crofts. 1962.

Callihan, E. L. *Grammar for Journalists.* New York: The Ronald Press Co. 1957.

Campbell, Laurence R. and Wolseley, Roland E. *How to Report and Write the News.* New York: Prentice-Hall, Inc. 1961.

Cater, Douglas. *The Fourth Branch of Government.* Boston: Houghton Mifflin Co. 1959.

Charnley, Mitchell V. *Reporting.* New York: Holt, Rinehart and Winston, Inc. 1964.

Copple, Neale, *Depth Reporting.* Englewood Cliffs, New Jersey: Prentice-Hall. 1964.

Emery, Edwin. *The Press and America.* New York: Prentice-Hall, Inc. 1963.

Floherty, John J. *Get That Story.* Philadelphia: J. B. Lippincott Co. 1964.

Garst, Robert E. and Bernstein, Theodore M. *Headlines and Deadlines.* New York: Columbia. 1962.

Harral, Stewart. *The Feature Writer's Handbook.* Norman: University of Oklahoma Press. 1963.

209

Maury, Reuben and Pfeiffer, Karl G. *Effective Editorial Writing.* New York: Wm. G. Brown. 1960.

McCullo, Marion. *The Student Journalist's Proofreader's Manual.* New York: Richards Rosen Press, Inc. 1969.

Mott, Frank Luther. *American Journalism.* New York: Macmillan Co. 1966.

Reddick, Dewitt C. *Journalism and the School Paper.* Boston: D. C. Heath & Co. 1963.

Ross, Lillian. *Reporting.* New York: Simon and Schuster, Inc. 1964.

Schaleban, Arville. *Your Future in Journalism.* New York: Richards Rosen Press, Inc. 1961.

Stewart, Kenneth and Tebbel, John. *Makers of Modern Journalism.* New York: Prentice-Hall Inc. 1952.

Strunk, William Jr. and White, E. B. *The Elements of Style.* New York: Macmillan Co. 1959.

Swanberg, W. A. *Citizen Hearst.* New York: Charles Scribner's Sons. 1961.

Tebbel, John. *The Compact History of the American Newspaper.* New York: Hawthorne Books. 1963.

Ward, William G. *The Student Journalist and Editorial Leadership.* New York: Richards Rosen Press, Inc. 1969.

INDEX

NOTES

NOTES

NOTES

NOTES

NOTES

NOTES

NOTES

NOTES

NOTES

NOTES